COSMOPOLITAN JUSTICE

COSMOPOLITAN
JUSTICE

DARREL MOELLENDORF

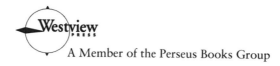

A Member of the Perseus Books Group

Westview Press books are available at special discounts for bulk purchases in the United States by corporations, institutions, and other organizations. For more information, please contact the Special Markets Department at The Perseus Books Group, 11 Cambridge Center, Cambridge, MA 02142, or call (617) 252-5298.

Published in 2002 in the United States of America by Westview Press, 5500 Central Avenue, Boulder, Colorado 80301-2877, and in the United Kingdom by Westview Press, 12 Hid's Copse Road, Cumnor Hill, Oxford OX2 9JJ

Find us on the World Wide Web at www.westviewpress.com

Library of Congress Cataloging-in-Publication Data
Moellendorf, Darrel.
   Cosmopolitan justice / Darrel Moellendorf.
     p. cm.
   Includes bibliographical references and index.
   ISBN 0-8133-6556-2 (pbk.) — ISBN 0-8133-6578-3
   1. Justice. 2. Internationalism. 3. Nationalism. I. Title.

JC578 .M64   2002
327.1'7'01—dc21

2001046870

The paper used in this publication meets the requirements of the American National Standard for Permanence of Paper for Printed Library Materials Z39.48-1984.

10   9   8   7   6   5   4   3   2   1

To Bonnie and Marino

CONTENTS

PREFACE

I began thinking about the ideas related to this book in 1990 as the United States was preparing for the Gulf War. During the time that I was a graduate student in the 1980s, I had also spent a great deal of time organizing opposition to U.S. foreign policy in Central America and southern Africa. The Gulf War was unlike most other U.S.- orchestrated military campaigns during the decade that preceded it, insofar as it was ostensibly directed toward an unambiguously wicked ruler. Hence, it was not easy for some of us to account for our opposition to the war in a way that was convincing to others and ourselves. In an effort to do just that, and to begin an account of the principles of socialist internationalism, I wrote a paper called "Marxism, Internationalism, and the Justice of War," which was published in *Science and Society* (58:3, fall 1994). Although I then thought that classical Marxism was more or less an adequate political philosophy, in writing this piece I came to believe that the determination of the justice of a war required an account of social justice. This, of course, I would not find in classical Marxism.

In the summer of 1994, I had the good fortune of attending a National Endowment of the Humanities (NEH) summer seminar on the foundations of political self-determination, hosted by Allen Buchanan at the University of Wisconsin, Madison. I would like to thank the NEH for the support that pointed me in the direction of this book. Through participation in that seminar and discussions with Harry Brighouse, I came to a greater respect for egalitarian liberal accounts of justice. Work that summer produced two papers that would be the basis of the present book. Chapter 2 of this book is a reworking of "Constructing the Law of Peoples," originally published in *Pacific Philosophical Quarterly* (77:2, June 1996). The focus of that paper was John Rawls's Oxford Amnesty Lecture, "The Law of Peoples." Chapter 2 contains substantial revisions of that earlier article, in part to take into account Rawls's book, *The Law of Peoples* (Cambridge: Harvard University Press, 1999). Chapter 6 is a revised version of "Liberalism, Nationalism, and the Right to Secede," originally published in *Philosophical Forum* (XXVII:1–2, fall/winter 1996–1997). Chapter 5 incorporates material from my entry "Imperialism" in the *Encyclopedia of Applied Ethics* (San Diego: Academic Press, 1998). People on both the political left and right will find various conclusions of this book disagreeable. Although I have tried to follow the arguments wherever they have taken me, I remain confident that this book sets out the principles of internationalism that the left should be committed to.

Moving from the United States to South Africa made me aware of certain issues that I had previously not considered and gave me the opportunity to hear new perspectives on old problems. It also presented me with a new group of interesting and supportive colleagues. I am grateful to Michael Pendelbury for using his administrative acumen to arrange to give me the time to finish this book and to Brian Penrose for generously agreeing to rearrange his teaching schedule to make it happen. I would also like to thank University of the Witwatersrand for granting me a sabbatical and supporting me with an Anderson-Kappelie grant.

Over the past five years, papers that would become parts of chapters of this book were read in many different forums, including the Radical Philosophy Association in conjunction with the Pacific Division meeting of the American Philosophical Association (APA), 1995; the Society for the Prevention of Nuclear Omnicide in conjunction with the Eastern Division meeting of the APA, 1995; the International Network of Philosophers of Education meeting, Rand Afrikaans University, 1996; the Philosophical Society of Southern Africa meetings in 1996, 1998, 2000, and 2001; the Spring Colloquium hosted by the Department of Philosophy, University of Natal, Pietermaritzburg, 1997; the Hoernlé Research Seminar of the Department of Philosophy, University of the Witwatersrand, 1997; the Department of Philosophy, University of Wisconsin, Madison, 1999; the Eastern Division meeting of the APA, 1999; the Department of Philosophy, Rand Afrikaans University, 2000; the African Studies Seminar, University of the Witwatersrand, 2000 and 2001; and the Pacific Division meeting of the APA, 2001. I would like to thank the organizers of these events for providing me with a forum to present my ideas, and the many participants— the majority of whom I do not know—for the discussions that have helped me improve my work.

I am grateful to Kate Hofmeyer and Michael Mandlebaum for their research assistance as I was completing the manuscript along with trying to teach them something about Aristotle and Kant. Over the years, many people have generously read parts of this book or discussed various ideas contained therein with me. To all of them, thank you. In particular I would like to thank Patrick Bond, Harry Brighouse, Allen Buchanan, Steve Clarke, Omar Dahbour, Parker English, Patrick Hayden, Jason Hill, Andy Kuper,

Sharon Lloyd, Hennie Lötter, Jon Mandel, Rodney Peffer, Brian Penrose, David Schmidtz, Ted Stolze, John Stremlau, Mary Tjiattas, and Paul Voice. I would also like to thank the following people who commented on the proposal or the penultimate draft of this book for Westview: David Crocker, Thomas Pogge, James Sterba, and Jeremy Waldron. Three people were particularly generous with their time and thoughts, reading all or most of the manuscript. I owe a special debt of gratitude to Bonnie Friedmann, Thad Metz, and Michael Pendlebury. No doubt there are many ways in which this could have been a better book, perhaps especially if I had listened more carefully to those who discussed its ideas with me. But I shudder to think of what it might have been without their help.

Finally, additional thanks are due to Bonnie Friedmann for living with my distraction and supporting me through it, especially during an exciting final nine months.

Darrel Moellendorf

A Tale of Two Tendencies in International Law

All human beings are born free and equal in dignity and rights. They are endowed with reason and conscience and should act towards one another in a spirit of brotherhood.

—Universal Declaration of Human Rights[1]

JUSTICE IN PHILOSOPHY AND LAW

This book focuses on matters of social justice. Social justice concerns the moral nature of the institutions that mediate interactions among persons. Although so-conceived social justice may be narrower in scope than justice per se, for the sake of simplicity I shall use the term *justice* as equivalent to *social justice*. At base our moral duties of justice are directed to other persons, but these duties are usually discharged through conduct directed toward institutions, such as obeying existing institutional rules, defying them, or advocating and aiding in the construction of new institutions that will promote just interactions. For example, although a duty of justice to others involves protecting them from criminal wrongdoing and apprehending the wrongdoer, this duty is discharged by paying taxes to support the police and judicial system and by cooperating with police and judicial investigations. It does not typically require that citizens police the streets. Duties of justice are a part of morality, but not by any means the whole of it. Not all moral duties to others are institutionally mediated. For example, a duty to tell the truth may be, and usually is, satisfied without any reference to institutional rules at all.

1

This book is particularly focused on matters of international justice concerning the justification, content, and practical requirements of duties of justice to noncompatriots. Arguments about these matters fall within the province of political and moral philosophy. Justice is, however, a legal concept as well as a philosophical one. Some writers on international justice are concerned with making legal arguments about the existence, interpretation, and consequences of rules that govern existing institutions and patterns of international interaction. Although any distinction between moral and legal approaches to justice may be controversial, one way to think about it is that the former abstracts from existing institutional requirements and develops an account of the duties that persons owe to each other by considering the nature of justice itself; whereas the latter seeks a proper grasp of existing practices and institutions, endeavoring to understand what the rules that govern them imply about a person's obligation.[2]

As a philosophical approach to the matter of international justice, this book attempts to answer questions such as, What is the justification for human rights? What duties of justice do we have to persons in other countries? What is the justification and limit of state sovereignty? When, if ever, are wars justified?

The relationship between the philosophical conclusions to these questions and the legal treatment of similar issues is important. One position in contemporary jurisprudence, known as legal positivism, holds that the law can be known without an assessment of whether it is just.[3] Ronald Dworkin rejects this position, in part, by maintaining that certain moral principles are part of the law even before they are expressed in legal holdings or statutes.[4] A philosophical approach to justice may complement legal positivism by providing an account of what the law should be. It may also complement the Dworkinian approach by providing a justification of the principles that putatively are part of the basis of law. Either as an account of what the law should be or as a justification of what it is, there is a practical payoff to the philosophical account of justice. Therefore, it may prove useful as an introduction to subsequent chapters to consider some issues concerning the nature of international law.

STATISM AND COSMOPOLITANISM
IN CONTEMPORARY INTERNATIONAL LAW

Treaties, including United Nations (UN) legal documents, are one important source of international law. This body of law includes the UN Charter, which governs relations among all member states, as well as various covenants that govern relations among the signatory states. Within these documents there exists significant tension about the proper and ultimate concern of international law. One conception of the basis of international law takes it to be based upon the principle of self-determination and respect for the sovereign equality of all states. This view holds that the UN seeks above all to protect the interests of states as corporate bodies and seeks in particular to prevent them from unwanted interference by other states. I call this view statist.

The following two paragraphs of Article 2 of the UN Charter appear to be expressions of statism:

> 2(4): All members shall refrain in their international relations from the threat or use of force against the territorial integrity or political independence of any state, or in any manner inconsistent with the Purposes of the United Nations.[5]
> 2(7): Nothing contained in the present Charter shall authorize the United Nations to intervene in matters which are essentially within the domestic jurisdiction of any state or shall require the Members to submit such matters to settlement under the present Charter; but this principle shall not prejudice the application of enforcement measures under Chapter VII.[6]

Paragraph 2(4) identifies territorial integrity and political independence as the two main interests of states. These are not expressed as indirect interests of persons, but as interests of states, which the Charter in this paragraph seeks to defend from unilateral usurpation by other states. Paragraph 2(7) seeks to shield certain matters "essentially within the domestic jurisdiction" against collective UN interference. Again, it would appear that it is states' interests that are being protected.[7]

The application of paragraph 2(4) has protected states from interference by others and thereby given them broad license to pursue domestic policy goals in the manner seen fit by their leaders. One consequence of this is that persons seeking to change the internal order of their state may not receive help from other states, whereas the state resisting the change may get help if it so wishes. Thus, the paragraph has been the basis for condemnation of what are considered to be indirect threats or uses of force by other states, such as actively assisting or encouraging civil strife or armed bands in other countries. On November 27, 1948, the General Assembly condemned Albania, Bulgaria, and Yugoslavia for aiding Greek communist guerrillas.[8]

Although third parties may not aid revolutionary movements within other countries, those countries, being sovereign, may legitimately use force to suppress such movements.[9] This is the significance of the language "in their international relations." The use of force internally is not questioned; there would be then no symmetrical condemnation of third parties who actively assisted or encouraged states in their internal struggles. The Soviet Union sought to justify its intervention into Hungary in 1956 with the claim that it was intervening at the invitation of the Hungarian government. The United

States defended its intervention into the Dominican Republic on April 28, 1965, by claiming a "threat to the lives of its citizens, and a request for assistance from those Dominican authorities still struggling to maintain order."[10] The net effect is a bias in favor of existing state arrangements. Thus, statist international legal principles have conservative implications.

Paragraph 2(4) does not impose an absolute bar against unilateral intervention. It would seem to permit unilateral intervention that does not violate territorial integrity and political independence of a state and that is consistent with the purposes of the UN. Hence, it may not be entirely conservative in its effect. It is a matter of some controversy among international lawyers, however, whether unilateral interventions to promote justice would be permitted by paragraph 2(4).[11]

Paragraph 2(7) seems to permit collective interventions that either do not affect matters essentially within the domestic jurisdiction of a state or that are required by Chapter VII. In light of the reference to Chapter VII, paragraph 2(7) is arguably more permissive of interventions than is 2(4). The most relevant section in Chapter VII is Article 39, which permits the Security Council to authorize measures in the event of "any threat to the peace, breach of peace, or act of aggression" in order to "maintain or restore international peace and security."[12] The debate about the legality of unilateral intervention under paragraph 2(4) is paralleled by a debate about the extent to which collective intervention to promote justice is licensed by paragraph 2(7). This paragraph does not directly license interventions to promote justice.[13] However, what are authorized are collective efforts to restore international peace and security that have the effect of promoting justice, such as Security Council Resolution 940 on Haiti in 1994.[14] In any case, it does seem as if paragraph 2(7) would not warrant an intervention to promote justice if international peace and security were not at risk.[15]

The Declaration of Principles of International Law Concerning Friendly Relations and Co-operation among States in Accordance with the Charter of the United Nations was adopted in 1970 as an elaboration of the principles of the charter. In contrast to paragraphs 2(4) and 2(7), the declaration does lay down an absolute bar against intervention: "No State or group of States has the right to intervene, directly or indirectly, for any reason whatever, in the internal or external affairs of other States." This is an unambiguous expression of statism.

The United Nations came into existence at the end of the Second World War when the conscience of the world was horrified by the genocidal practices of the Nazi regime. Any consistent commitment to unqualified statism would have rendered the UN impotent against similar injustices in the future. Indeed, the post-war period also witnessed the blossoming of a very different conception of the basis of international law, as a variety of statements affirming a commitment to international human rights were issued.

According to these statements, the claims of individual persons constitute the basis of international legal obligations. This view is sometimes called "cosmopolitanism."

The UN Charter expresses the cosmopolitan perspective at several points. The preamble reaffirms "faith in fundamental human rights, in the dignity and worth of the human person, in equal rights of men and women."[16] Article 55 commits the UN to the promotion of "universal respect for, and observance of, human rights and fundamental freedoms for all without distinction to race, sex, language, or religion."[17] Article 56 expresses a pledge "to take joint and separate action. . . for the achievement of the purposes set forth in Article 55."[18] However, the content of this cosmopolitan commitment to human rights in the charter is left unspecified. The Universal Declaration of Human Rights adopted by the UN General Assembly fills out this content considerably, proclaiming rights to life, liberty, security of person, recognition as a person before the law, ownership of property, freedom of expression, assembly, and association, and freedom from slavery and torture.[19] The status of the declaration, however, is less than a law of treaty,[20] though there is some debate about whether it rises to the level of customary international law after more than fifty years of existence.[21]

The International Covenant on Economic, Social, and Cultural Rights and the International Covenant of Civil and Political Rights offer interpretations of the charter's commitment to human rights that do have the force of treaty law among their signatories. Protected by the first covenant are the rights to work under favorable conditions, to join trade unions, to the enjoyment of the highest attainable standards of physical and mental health, and to free compulsory primary education.[22] The second covenant protects the rights to life, liberty, security of person, recognition as a person before the law, ownership of property, freedom of expression, assembly, and association, and freedom from slavery and torture.[23]

As indicated earlier in connection with the controversy surrounding the implications of paragraphs 2(4) and 2(7), there is considerable legal debate about how to reconcile the statist proclamations on sovereignty with the cosmopolitan ones on human rights, both of which exist in contemporary international law. This book does not take sides on the legal questions, but seeks instead a philosophical defense and extension of the cosmopolitan conception of justice. For the reasons noted above, the successful defense of this perspective will complement the efforts of international lawyers seeking to defend legal cosmopolitanism by providing a moral justification for their legal orientation. Similarly it will complement empirical work in political science and international relations by providing the basis for a moral assessment of the events and trends that they study. Finally, for those in policy studies, there are important implications of this account of what ought to be done to fulfill duties of justice to noncompatriots.

THE ROAD AHEAD

Chapter 2 takes up foundational issues in the justification of cosmopolitan justice. I defend a version of cosmopolitanism that draws heavily on the political constructivism of John Rawls. Rawls himself, however, is no cosmopolitan. So, I find myself in the unenviable position of having to argue for Rawls against Rawls. Chapter 3 attempts to arrive at a general account of the relationship between the duties of justice owed to compatriots and those owed to noncompatriots. It takes up matters of immigration limits and economic protectionism to show the application of the perspective defended. Chapter 4 presents an account of the duties of egalitarian global distributive justice and applies the account to an analysis of imperialism, and to issues such as international debt cancellation and the assignment of the costs of global warming. Chapter 5 defends a cosmopolitan account of sovereignty and justified intervention and looks at the example of the embargo against Iraq. Chapter 6 argues that cosmopolitans can accept a qualified right to national self-determination and even secession. Chapter 7 defends the cosmopolitan account of just war against a statist rival account, as well as political realist and pacifist challenges, and applies the account to the Gulf War and the Kosovo War. Finally, Chapter 8 concludes with some brief speculations about the institutional requirements of an egalitarian world order and offers reason to hope for such an order.

TWO

Rawlsian Constructivism and Cosmopolitan Justice

Political philosophers now must either work within Rawls' theory or explain why not.

—Robert Nozick[1]

One of the fundamental tenets of the cosmopolitanism that I seek to defend is that duties of justice have global scope. John Rawls has developed a theory of justice for domestic society that I find convincing in general terms. This theory is characterized by two principles of justice that require both respecting civil and democratic rights and limiting inequalities in the distribution of resources. Respect for civil and democratic rights requires a political regime of constitutional democracy. The implication of the limits on socioeconomic inequalities is a matter of debate among followers of Rawls. Rawls himself claims that the political regime must not be "directed by the interests of large concentrations of private economic and corporate power veiled from public knowledge and almost entirely free from accountability."[2] Achieving this and other desiderata of equality, he believes, would require either a regime that permits property rights in productive holdings but limits their transfer—especially in inheritance transfers—or a market socialist regime.[3]

The cosmopolitan view that I defend holds that the content of the above mentioned principles should apply globally. Rawls disagrees. He defends a theory of international justice that requires respect for a minimal set of human rights but requires neither constitutional democracy nor limits on socioeconomic equality. In this chapter I shall argue that the justification of the principles of international justice—the law of peoples—that Rawls employs in *The Law of Peoples* leaves human rights on an uncertain basis and that his reasons for excluding requirements of constitutional democracy and limitations on socioeconomic inequalities are unconvincing. I shall defend an alternative justification that extends the requirements of justice globally to include requirements of constitutional democracy and limitations on socioeconomic inequality.

I shall explain Rawls's construction of the law of peoples and show the inadequacy of his refusal to include democratic and egalitarian principles. I shall also identify alternative principles that are among the elements of the cosmopolitan conception of justice. I shall defend an alternative construction procedure, which is based upon respect for persons and establishes the alternative principles previously identified. I will follow that with a defense of the universality of the democratic conception of persons and the principles that are derived from them. Finally I will argue that the account of this chapter, and not Rawls's, is consistent with the value of toleration. The result, I hope, will establish the cosmopolitan conception of justice as superior to Rawls's law of peoples.

RAWLS'S CONSTRUCTIVISM

Rawls terms his justification of principles of justice *political constructivism*. In *Political Liberalism* he develops a constructivist procedure for domestic society, which involves modeling a conception of persons according to values that are supposed to be inherent in the democratic tradition.[4] This conception is used in a procedure, called the original position, that places persons behind a veil of ignorance so that they know nothing about their abilities, race, ethnicity, sex, or gender; their conceptions of the good; or their position within society.[5] By setting aside knowledge that could serve as the basis for bias in decisionmaking, the original position is designed to model our convictions about fairness: What ideal types of persons in this ideal setting would settle on as the principles of justice amounts to a reliable indication of what justice requires of us in the here and now.[6] The principles of justice derived by this procedure are meant to be political or freestanding—that is, not derived exclusively from any one of the many comprehensive moral, philosophical, and theological doctrines that citizens of liberal democracies hold.[7] Rawls prefers a political conception of justice because it affords the opportunity of wider assent to the principles of justice, resulting in greater stability for the order based upon them.

It is useful to compare the construction of *The Law of Peoples* with the one in *Political Liberalism*. In *Political Liberalism* the original position is said to model fair conditions among free and equal citizens because their representatives are situated symmetrically and equally. Citizens are modeled as rational by virtue of their representatives' full pursuit of their interests. Meanwhile the veil of ignorance models reasonableness by preventing decisions based upon known advantages over others. The original position in *The Law of Peoples* is set up in an analogous manner, except that seated behind the veil of ignorance are representatives of peoples, not persons.[8] By *peoples* Rawls apparently means states motivated by a conception of justice with a citizenry in possession of common sympathies.[9] Rawls's use of *peoples* is best understood as part of his ideal theory of international justice. He is, in other words, assuming that states comply with the principles of justice, and in order to signify that assumption he uses the term *peoples*. This explains why when discussing states that do not comply he reverts to terms such as *outlaw states*.[10]

The veil of ignorance prevents the representatives of peoples from knowing the size or population of their territory, their level of economic development, or the extent of their natural resources. They may assume that reasonably favorable conditions for democracy exist[11] and that peoples have an interest in preserving their territory as well as the safety and security of their population.[12] However, their fundamental interest is in their conception of justice.[13]

Rawls's Justification of Human Rights

The first stage of Rawls's construction of the law of peoples is the construction of an ideal theory in which universal compliance is assumed. The construction proceeds in two steps: The first is a construction that applies, with a significant caveat (see the section on Egalitarianism in this chapter), to relations among liberal peoples; the second expands relations to include certain well-ordered nonliberal, or what Rawls calls decent hierarchical, peoples. The eight principles that Rawls suggests that representatives of liberal peoples would agree upon in the first stage of the original position are:

(1) Peoples are free and independent, and their freedom and independence is to be respected by other peoples.
(2) Peoples are to observe treaties and undertakings.
(3) Peoples are equal and are parties to the agreements that bind them.
(4) Peoples observe the duty of nonintervention.
(5) Peoples have the right to self-defense but not to instigate war for reasons other than self-defense.
(6) Peoples are to honor human rights.
(7) Peoples are to observe certain specified restrictions on the conduct of war.

(8) Peoples have a duty to assist other peoples living under unfavorable conditions that prevent their having a just or decent political and social regime.[14]

Rawls notes that a complete law of peoples may have to include certain principles that are not included in this list and that certain qualifications apply to these principles. Perhaps most important among these, principles (1) and (4) as claims of sovereignty do not apply to states that do not honor principle (6).[15] The argument for this list is somewhat sketchy, but is based upon the assumption of the equality of peoples.[16] On this basis, classical or average utilitarianism is ruled out because it would sanction benefits for some peoples at the expense of others. This assumption may underwrite the justification of principles (1) through (5), but it is less helpful in understanding why principles (6) through (8) are included. The justification of (6) is of particular importance, given the role that it plays in limiting sovereignty.

Let's consider a possible justification of (6). In the original position, representatives of peoples are pursuing the rational interests of the peoples they represent under the constraints of the veil of ignorance, which precludes them from knowing the particular details of these peoples. Why would such representatives include a requirement that human rights be respected? Human rights would not be secured by the assumption of the equality of peoples, since the former protects the interests of persons and the latter concerns the status of peoples. The equality of peoples is violated only if there is unequal respect for corporate bodies, not for persons. Peoples may be respected as equals despite the fact that some are violators of the rights of persons. However, the fundamental interest that representatives of peoples would like to secure in the original position is the conception of justice of their peoples. Since respect for human rights is a commitment of the political institutions of liberal peoples, all representatives of liberal peoples could agree that (6) is in the interest of their peoples. The cogency of this line of reasoning is dependent upon the sense of distinguishing peoples from states since, according to Rawls, states lack an interest in justice.[17]

Democracy

A notable absence among these eight principles is one requiring constitutional democracy. If the above Rawlsian defense of human rights makes sense, namely, that liberal peoples have an interest in including their moral political commitments in the principles of international justice, then presumably they would include the following principle as well:

(9) Political arrangements are to honor the institutions of constitutional democracy.

In order to avoid the limitations of Rawls's use of the term *peoples*, I substitute here the term *political arrangements,* which may include regional and global institutions as well as state institutions. Hence, (9) does not stipulate whether global justice permits, requires, or proscribes political organization in the form of states. Representatives of liberal peoples would include (9) for the same (presumed) reason they include (6): It is part of the conception of justice of the peoples represented by the parties because these are liberal peoples; and this conception of justice is the fundamental interest of peoples that the parties seek to defend. Thus, peoples need not modify their conduct in any way by including (6) or (9). Furthermore, since the shell of sovereignty protecting the internal affairs of the state has already been pierced by (6), invoking sovereignty as reason for not including (9) is unlikely to be convincing. It is noteworthy that including (9) would bring the law of peoples more into agreement with what is, in Thomas Franck's interpretation, the general direction of current international law. "It is no longer arguable that the United Nations cannot exert pressure against governments that oppress their own peoples by egregious racism, denials of self-determination and suppression of freedom of expression. That litany is being augmented by new sins: refusals to permit demonstrably free elections or to implement their results."[18]

In defense of Rawls's omission, one might respond that since he makes much of the notion of a democratic peace,[19] he must be including democratic rights among the human rights honored in (6). He admits that a democratic peace requires that peoples observe principles of constitutional democracy (as well as certain requirements of distributive justice).[20]

The problem with this view is that Rawls claims that decent hierarchical peoples will also honor (6). Although decent hierarchical peoples have a basic structure termed a *consultation hierarchy,*[21] they are not committed to democratic rights. Moreover, the human rights that they are committed to are minimal: the rights to life, liberty (e.g., freedom from slavery and freedom of conscience), and formal equality (i.e., that similar cases be treated similarly).[22] So, there is no reason to read a commitment to democratic rights into (6). This, incidentally, suggests that Rawls is confronted with a dilemma. Either he must distinguish between the international order required by the law of peoples and that required for democratic peace, or he must require more of (6) and thereby exclude decent historical societies from the agreement. For if (6) does not include democratic rights, there is no reason to suppose that a democratic peace is possible between liberal states and decent hierarchical ones. If (6) does include democratic rights, then decent hierarchical societies will not honor it. Presumably Rawls would wish to resolve this dilemma in favor of maintaining a minimal interpretation of (6), but this then calls into question ability of the law of peoples to sustain a peaceful international order.

Egalitarianism

A second absence from Rawls's list raises other difficulties. The eight principles include no commitment to substantial socioeconomic equality. Principle (8) establishes a minimum requirement that a people be assisted up to the economic level required in order to realize the law of peoples—in particular up to being able to institute regimes that respect human rights.[23] It does not, however, require a commitment beyond this minimum as is contained in justice as fairness—Rawls's theory of justice for domestic society. Why wouldn't reasoning analogous to that which seems to be behind the inclusion of (6) require a more thoroughgoing commitment to egalitarianism?

I noted earlier that the parties in the original position represent liberal peoples, but with a significant caveat. The caveat is that, even in the first step, Rawls does not require that the liberal peoples represented have a commitment to the strong egalitarianism contained in justice as fairness. In order to be represented in the first step of the construction, a people must be committed to (a) basic constitutional rights and liberties, (b) the priority of these rights over claims of the general good and perfectionist values, and (c) a distribution of primary goods (including wealth and income) sufficient for persons to make intelligent and effective use of their rights and liberties.[24] Rawls takes the egalitarian implications of the latter commitment to be more substantial than many liberal democracies currently require. He takes it to require fair equality of opportunity in education, a decent distribution of income, society to be the employer of last resort, basic health care for all citizens, and public financing of elections.[25] A people need not be committed, however, to the most substantial egalitarian principle contained in justice as fairness: the difference principle, that socioeconomic inequalities be to the greatest benefit to the least advantaged members of society.[26]

This suggests the following two questions. Why does Rawls require among liberal peoples only a weaker commitment egalitarianism rather than the difference principle? Why does the law of peoples not contain a requirement of egalitarian distributive justice stronger than (8), which would be consistent with the egalitarianism (although weaker than the difference principle) that Rawls thinks liberalism requires?

Satisfying answers to these questions are not proffered by Rawls. The first question is significant because Rawls seems to show disregard for what many readers have thought to be among the most important accomplishments of justice as fairness, namely, an account that weds commitments to individual liberty and substantial equality (in the form of the difference principle). The closest he comes to an explanation in *The Law of Peoples* is breathtakingly brief: "Each of these liberalisms endorses the underlying ideas of citizens as free and equal persons and of society as a fair system of cooperation over time. Yet since the ideas can be interpreted in various ways, we get different formulations of the principles of justice and different contents of public reason."[27] The argument of *Political Liberalism*, however, is precisely to sort out "deeply contested ideas about how the values of liberty and equality are best expressed in the basic rights and liberties of citizens so as to answer the claims of both liberty and equality."[28] He holds that principles that include fair equality of opportunity and the difference principle are "more appropriate than other familiar principles of justice to the idea of democratic citizens viewed as free and equal persons."[29] In *A Theory of Justice*, Rawls refers to the conception of equality that includes these two principles as "democratic equality."[30] Presumably this is because just as the conception of democratic citizenship abstracts from a person's social and natural advantages for the purpose of establishing political entitlements, so the principles of democratic equality abstract from these advantages for the purpose of establishing socioeconomic entitlements.

In "The Law of Peoples," the 1993 lecture that preceded the book by the same name, Rawls offers a different reason for not requiring liberal peoples to observe the difference principle. "These features are not needed for the construction of a reasonable law of peoples, and by not assuming them our account has greater generality."[31] This reason is given without any sort of justification for why generality should trump distributive justice. It is worth considering how plausible such reasoning would be at the domestic level. Suppose Rawls argued that the principles of justice for states should require respect for individual liberty, but include only minimal commitments to socioeconomic equality because such principles would have greater generality and would meet with wider acceptance than those requiring a stronger commitment to equality. I take it that the following response would be appropriate: A theory of justice is supposed to include an account of what people are entitled to, not what many people believe people are entitled to. It is simply beside the point when considering the plausibility of an account of justice to ask how many people are likely to accept it. If this is a plausible response at the domestic level, I see no reason to believe that it is not also so at the global level.

The second question raised above asked why the law of peoples does not contain a requirement of egalitarian distributive justice stronger than (8) that would be consistent with the egalitarianism (although weaker than the difference principle) that Rawls thinks liberalism requires. Rawls seems not to notice that the reason that representatives of liberal peoples would include a stronger requirement is the same as the (presumed) reason that they include (6) and should include (9)—namely, such a requirement is part of the conception of justice that liberal peoples are assumed to be most interested in protecting.

Although a complete discussion of this matter will not be had until Chapter 4, the above considerations suggest that (8) should be replaced with the following:

(8*) Political arrangements are to honor principles of substantial egalitarian distributive justice.

Including both (8*) and (9) accords well with the presumption that in order for state coercion to be employed in accordance with justice, states must adhere to background principles that treat individuals as free and equal persons. As with the formulation of (9), the formulation of (8*) does not prejudge the question of whether the political arrangements must be global or can merely be state institutions.

Justice or Expediency

Because Rawls represents peoples and not all the persons of the world in the original position, his justification of principles requiring respect for persons is strained. To make only peoples, and not persons, the direct object of international justice obscures the fact that within regimes there may exist relations of unjust coercion. Rawls contends, "No people has the right to self-determination, or a right to secession, at the expense of subjugating another *people*."[32] He cites as an example the abrogation of the American South's right to secede because it perpetuated institutions of slavery.[33] What one would have expected Rawls to say was that the right to self-determination may not be exercised at the expense of subjugating *persons*. Presumably, he would not want to allow self-determination that was based upon the subjugation of a group of persons that did not rise to the status of peoples. However, because his principles of international justice, even at the first step, focus on corporate bodies—that is, peoples—and not persons, he has difficulty capturing respect for persons.

The omission of (8*) and (9) brings up a concern about unjust state coercion. Why, then, does he not include them? His explanation in "The Law of Peoples," cited above, for including representatives of peoples who do not honor the difference principle is telling. He is concerned that the principles following from an original position that included only representatives of egalitarian liberal peoples would exclude from possible agreement many peoples who are neither egalitarian nor liberal. In other words, he tailors the first step to produce a result that would be acceptable at the second step.

At the second step of the ideal theory, Rawls attempts to extend the law of peoples to include decent hierarchical peoples. These are peoples who respect neither egalitarian distributive justice nor a full set of civil and democratic rights. The following characteristics delineate the class of decent hierarchical peoples: They are nonaggressive; they accept a minimal set of human rights which includes only the rights to life, liberty, and the same treatment as others in the same condition; they impose duties on their citizens to pursue a common good, but these are not perceived as oppressive; and, finally, their judges and other representatives sincerely believe that the law preserves the common good.[34]

Representatives of decent hierarchical peoples would agree to principles (1) through (8) for the same reasons that representatives of liberal democratic societies do. Principles (1) through (5) follow the assumption of the equality of peoples; and principles (6) through (8) conform to the moral political commitments of decent hierarchical peoples. Principles (8*) and (9), of course, would not be agreeable to representatives of decent hierarchical peoples. This seems to explain why Rawls does not include them in the first step of the original position. He wants the principles of liberal peoples to be agreeable to decent hierarchical peoples. In other words, he sacrifices full justice for wider agreement. In so doing, he neglects Kant's injunction not to advance a political morality that is tailored to the concerns of the statesman. "[I] can indeed imagine a *moral politician*, i.e. someone who conceives of the principles of political expediency in such a way that they can coexist with morality; but I cannot imagine a *political moralist*, i.e. one who fashions his morality to suit his own advantage as statesman."[35] The goal of political morality should not be to establish principles that leaders of unjust regimes are likely to accept, but ones they ought to accept—that is, ones to which citizens might hold them accountable.[36]

There are good reasons to believe that the existence of decent hierarchical peoples is impossible. For one, there is a conceptual problem. Consider the claim that a characteristic of such peoples is that they are not aggressive. If Rawls is right that a democratic peace requires liberal, egalitarian, and democratic peoples,[37] it is impossible that decent hierarchical peoples could be a party to a democratic peace. There is also a practical problem. The claim that a society can be undemocratic and can legally enforce a conception of the good without a section of the population finding it oppressive is unrealistic. Bruce Ackerman characterizes the problem quite well:

> The fact is that none of Rawls's "well-ordered" hierarchies will be free of natives who are themselves inspired by liberal ideas of liberty and equality. There is no Islamic nation without a woman who insists on equal rights; no Confucian society without a man who denies the need for deference. Sometimes these liberals will be in a minority in their native lands; but given the way Rawls defines a "well-ordered" hierarchy, it is even possible that native liberals might be a majority.[38]

If decent hierarchical peoples are impossible, then it is all the more troublesome that Rawls tailors the outcome of the first step to match the outcome of the second.

COSMOPOLITAN CONSTRUCTIVISM

Rawls asserts that the constructivist procedure is alterable according to the subject matter it is treating. The structure of the procedure is a function of the structure of the social framework about which the procedure is deciding.

> I add that in developing a conception of justice for the basic structure for the law of peoples, or indeed for any subject, constructivism does not view the variation in numbers of people alone as accounting for the appropriateness of different principles in different cases. . . . Rather, it is the distinct structure of the social framework, and the purpose and role of its various parts and how they fit together, that explains there being different principles for different kinds of subjects.[39]

Rawls gives passing consideration to a cosmopolitan construction of the law of peoples, a construction that would include in the original position not representatives of peoples, but representatives of all persons of the world.[40] Such a construction would allow the interests of persons to be directly represented and would, therefore, secure respect for persons among its resulting principles. Rawls rejects this procedure for the following reasons:

> On this account, the foreign policy of a liberal people—which it is our concern to elaborate—will be to act gradually to shape all not yet liberal societies in a liberal direction, until eventually (in the ideal case) all societies are liberal. But this foreign policy simply assumes that only liberal democratic society can be acceptable. Without trying to work out a reasonable liberal Law of Peoples, we cannot know that nonliberal societies cannot be acceptable. The possibility of a global original position does not show that, and we can't merely assume it.[41]

This rejection is unconvincing. The cosmopolitan procedure is not based upon the assumption that societies must respect civil and democratic rights and principles of egalitarian distributive justice, any more than the construction of justice as fairness is based upon this. If there is a commitment to these principles, it is because they are derived from the procedure. There is, however, a fundamental difference between Rawls's *Law of Peoples* original position and the cosmopolitan original position. While Rawls's is based on the assumption of respect for peoples,[42] the cosmopolitan one is based on the assumption of respect for persons. If it is the implications of respect for persons that we are wanting to work out, the straightest route to this is a procedure that directly takes into account the interests of persons.

Consider further, then, the cosmopolitan construction that places representatives of persons in a global original position. Rawls supposes that realism requires a construction that does not completely call into question the international state system.[43] Nothing is lost by granting him that supposition. Take then persons represented as citizens of states without making any further assumptions about either the conditions of state sovereignty or the desirability of other political institutions. Indeed, rather than having a second original position for international justice that follows the one for domestic justice, the single construction under consideration may serve both purposes.[44] The representatives in the present construction would be ignorant of which state the represented citizens inhabit, as well as the state's character, territory, and population size. They would also be ignorant of the various natural and social characteristics of the persons they represent. The cosmopolitan construction reverses the priority of Rawls's construction; the interests of persons are represented directly and the interests of corporate bodies are represented indirectly, just insofar as they serve the interests of their citizens.

It might be objected that such a construction seems to allow too much knowledge behind the veil. In particular that persons are known to be citizens of states might be thought to be unjustified. If this were the case, then our choice might be between Rawls's construction and a construction that represents all the persons of the world, in which case cosmopolitanism would opt for the latter. However, if the original positions of *A Theory of Justice* and *Political Liberalism*—which employ representatives of citizens of a state—are justified, then this construction that utilizes the same representatives must be as well.

In the cosmopolitan construction, the original position situates free and equal representatives of persons thought to be reasonable and rational. Such representatives would be far less concerned with the interests of peoples and far more concerned with the freedom and ability of persons to pursue their own conceptions of the good life within a fair system of cooperation. They would desire that the global order, which may include state and other political institutions, reflect this concern.

Representatives with the above mentioned concerns would not be likely to limit state sovereignty only for violations of human rights. If the only way that rational persons could be prevented from living according to their reasonable conceptions of the good life were through the violation of their human rights, then rationality and reason would dictate forgoing the power of intervention once human rights had been assured. Clearly undemocratic and nonegalitarian social orders can also prevent persons from living according to their reasonable conceptions of the good life. A prohibition against intervention into a state's affairs would be an irrational choice in the absence of assurances of the kind that principles (8*) and (9) provide. In the absence of any knowledge of which state's citizens she represents, and of the state's social and political arrangements, the representative of persons would want assurances that individuals can freely pursue their reasonable conceptions of the good life or that individuals may struggle against social circumstances that make that pursuit impossible—and that in such a struggle they may, with justice, request and reasonably expect aid. Thus, respect for human rights, democratic governance, and the principles of egalitarian distributive justice are individually necessary conditions for prohibiting all forms of intervention. Taken together they may not constitute a sufficient condition for prohibiting intervention, as the foreign effects of other domestic policies may also be a concern. This matter will be discussed more thoroughly in Chapter 5.

The present construction would justify principles (6), (8*), and (9). What is more, principle (6) would be expanded to included far more than the minimal human rights that Rawls lists. For example, behind the veil of ignorance, representatives of persons would choose prohibitions against torture, arbitrary arrest, detention, exile, and discrimination. In addition to these, basic security rights and basic subsistence rights would also be chosen.[45] For the sake of clarity, I shall distinguish Rawls's (6) from (6*), which requires that political arrangements honor an expanded set of human rights as delineated, for example, in the Universal Declaration of Human Rights.

UNIVERSALITY AND POLITICAL CONSTRUCTIVISM

For an account of justice to be cosmopolitan it must be based upon conceptions that are universal in scope. The constructivist procedure that I defended in the previous section involves modeling a conception of persons drawn from the tradition of democratic citizenship. Rawls argues that this conception of persons is political in part because it is based upon a conception of citizenship implicit in the democratic tradition rather than upon metaphysical doctrines.[46] On the basis of this, Rawls concludes, "Justice as fairness is substantive. . . in the sense that it springs from and belongs to the tradition of liberal thought and the larger community of political culture of democratic societies. It fails then to be properly formal and truly universal."[47] If the conception of persons employed by cosmopolitan constructivism is merely a political-cultural artifact of the democratic tradition, then the account of justice based upon them is not genuinely global.

I believe that Rawls's appraisal of the lack of generality of the principle of justice derived by a political constructivist procedure that models conceptions of persons drawn from the democratic tradition is unwarranted. Rawls employs the democratic conception of persons in his constructivism in order that the principles of justice derived from them will be acceptable in democratic societies, thereby rendering these societies more stable. If one distinguishes between two properties of the principles of justice derived by political constructivism—namely, their acceptability to those who share certain conceptions that are part of the democratic tradition and their justification—then there is the basis for avoiding Rawls's unwarranted conclusion.[48]

The Democratic Conception and the Self-conception of Persons

The cosmopolitan construction might be objectionable because the democratic conception of persons may not correspond with a person's self-conception—many traditional moral, political, and religious views hold that people are not all free and equal.

One problem with this objection is that appeals to conventional empirical conceptions of personhood and citizenship do not decide the suitability of employing a given moral conception of persons. The democratic conception of persons is a moral ideal that is used to come to a clearer understanding of what justice requires of us. It involves a moral psychology that explains why persons are thought by democrats to be free and equal. Generally speaking, moral ideals are not invalidated if people do not explicitly subscribe to them. For example, simply because someone believes special treatment from me is undeserved does not imply that I am under no obligation to offer that treatment. This example, I hope, is suggestive of something that is important to bear in mind in discussions of the "imposition" of democratic conceptions of persons. To treat someone as democratic equality requires is often to treat that person as worthy of greater respect than the traditional hierarchical culture allows.

In *Political Liberalism* Rawls distinguishes among three points of view:[49] that of the parties in the original position, of the citizens in a well-ordered society, and of us. The first is an artificial psychology that serves as a device for constructing justice. The second is an ideal that might be (but is not yet) realized in the world. The third is the perspective (our perspective) from which the results of the construction are to be assessed. The point of Rawlsian modeling is not to represent individuals' actual self-conceptions or the metaphysical conception of the self that is affirmed by the tradition to which they belong, but to model the values that are implicit in the functioning of democracies.[50]

An exposition of a political conception of justice has two stages. The first sets out the principles of justice as freestanding by basing them on political and not comprehensive conceptions of persons. The second develops an account of the conception's stability, which account involves appealing to an overlapping consensus.[51] A concern appropriate to the second stage is that not all of us—that is, not all of the people of the world—will positively assess the result of the construction because it is the result of modeling values that we do not all share. That not everyone will positively assess the principles of justice does not impugn the appropriateness of the construction at the first stage. The stability that is generated by overlapping consensus requires a political conception of justice that coheres with political conceptions of citizenship and society under ideal conditions, not necessarily conceptions currently held.

In *Political Liberalism* Rawls recognizes that not every citizen of a state in the liberal democratic tradition will accept the two principles of justice that are constructed from the original position. Many people will not do so because they are unreasonable. Such citizens desire to impose their own comprehensive doctrines on others, or the comprehensive doctrine that these citizens follow is unreasonable and does not overlap enough with the principles of justice to allow them to affirm both. In any case, parties to the original position of *Political Liberalism* would be all the more concerned with securing such features of the two principles of justice as the full scheme of liberties, if they knew that in the real world there were unreasonable people who might try to subvert individual liberties.[52] Therefore, concerns appropriate to stage two about the self-conception of persons and the resulting likelihood of acceptance need not forestall the construction at stage one.

Justifying the Democratic Conception of Persons

Rawls's political constructivism employs a conception of persons as possessing two highest order moral interests. One is the interest in developing and exercising the power rationally to form, revise, and pursue a conception of the good.[53] The second is the interest in developing and exercising the power to apply and to act upon publicly acknowledged fair terms of cooperation.[54] Persons are equal insofar as they have the two moral powers to a requisite minimum degree to be fully cooperating members of society.[55] Defense of the democratic conception of persons involves, among other things, a defense of the two highest order moral interests.

Consider first the claim that persons have a highest order moral interest in developing the capacities for rational formation, revision, and pursuit of a conception of the good. All persons necessarily value their conception of the good since this conception is the basis for establishing what is of value in life.[56] Anyone who has a conception of the good has an interest in the capacity to have it, since the capacity is a necessary condition of the conception. We necessarily value the capacity that allows us to have a conception of what is valuable. Indeed, the interest in the capacity to have a conception of the good is more fundamental than the interest in the particular conception that we have, since the former makes the latter possible. According to this argument, the interest is an objective one. A person has an interest in the capacity to have a conception of the good even if she does not (as presumably she often does not) think about the capacity and recognize her interest in it.

In valuing our conception of the good, we take it to be correct or true. We would not value it if we believed it to be fundamentally mistaken. Since we are fallible and may be wrong about what is truly of value, we also have an interest in the ability to revise rationally our conception of the good. Because this ability is directed toward rooting out error, in our conception of what is most valuable in life, our interest in this capacity is of the highest value. We would not value our conception of the good if we did not believe it to be right, but the ability to revise rationally our conception of the good—given our fallibility—is of greater value than the particular conception of the good we have at any given time, because this ability alone gives us any assurance that our particular conception of the good is correct. Again, this is an objective interest. Its value derives from the value that a person places on the conception of the good, but does not depend on its recognition.

There are, of course, many people who are so committed to their conception of the good that they believe error is impossible. These people are wrong, not necessarily in what they believe to be good, but in their belief that they are infallible. Anyone who has an objective account of the good, an account that distinguishes between what is good and what is believed to be good, should be open to the possibility of error in belief. Anyone who has a subjective conception of the good ought to accept that subjectivism may be wrong. Since all persons are fallible and value having the correct conception of the good, all persons have a highest order interest in the capacity to revise rationally their conception.

Consider next the claim that persons have a highest order interest in the capacity to apply and act upon publicly acknowledged fair terms of cooperation. Generally comprehensive conceptions of the good contain some conception of the social good, social responsibility, or justice. Such a conception of justice provides one with a moral interest in living under a just social and political arrangement, since one has interest in what is good and the social good is a part of the overall good. Most conceptions of justice do not include an interest in the capacity to apply and act upon publicly acknowledged fair terms of cooperation, but the fact that they establish a basis for an interest in justice is enough for this particular interest under contingent conditions that currently exist globally.

These contingent conditions may be characterized as follows:[57]

1. There exists moderate scarcity of resources.
2. There exists a reasonable pluralism of comprehensive moral conceptions.

3. One may be justified in holding moral beliefs that one cannot rationally convince other reasonable and rational persons of, and vice versa.

The first establishes a need for a distributive principle since there are insufficient resources to satisfy everyone's wants. The second indicates that
there is likely to be disagreement about what the principle should be if
those discussing it proceed on the basis of the conception of the social good
contained within their comprehensive conceptions of the good. The third
establishes that the disagreement mentioned in the second may not be rationally resolvable despite the fact that there may be a truth of the matter. Although the third speaks of moral beliefs, in fact the condition is not peculiar to moral theorizing but is perhaps more pronounced there. For
example, two scientists looking at the same ambiguous piece of evidence
may each be justified in drawing different factual conclusions, depending
on how they weigh different factors. This does not mean that there is no
fact of the matter. It means only that rational people may disagree on what
the facts are. Similarly, people may disagree about the facts upon which
value judgments are based. In addition, people may disagree about the relative weight to give to two different values—for example, the relative weight
of the values of honesty and loyalty in friendship.

If one has a conception of justice, then one has a highest order interest in
the capacity to apply and act on publicly acknowledged fair terms of cooperation, given the above three contingent conditions. Any given person has
an interest in the social good, or justice, in virtue of moderate scarcity and
of having an interest in one's broader conception of the good of which justice is a part. This interest is frustrated by living in unjust circumstances. In
light of condition 2, any conception of justice derived solely from the comprehensive conception of another will potentially be at odds with one's own
conception. Should this be the case, recalling condition 3, it might not be
rationally justifiable from within one's comprehensive conception. Since
each person is threatened by what appears to be the imposition of unjust
principles, each has an interest in establishing principles that she can accept. If a set of principles is publicly acknowledged, this entails that there is
broad public agreement that satisfies the interests of each person to live under just arrangements. The interest in such principles is of the highest order
in the sense that it trumps an interest one might have in pursuing a sectarian conception of justice under conditions in which others do the same,
since these conditions pose the credible threat that one may end up living
under what one takes to be unjust arrangements.

This interest exists even if one does not recognize it. For example, one
may wrongly reject condition 3, in which case one may believe that one's
interest in justice is in a sectarian conception of justice that is not justifiable
to others who hold reasonable comprehensive conceptions of the good. In

this case, one is mistaken about one's interest in justice because one is mistaken about condition 3. In other words, one's interest in a publicly acknowledged conception of justice is objective under the three contingent conditions noted.

There is a second defense of an interest in publicly acknowledged fair terms of cooperation. Given human fallibility, any account of justice might be wrong. So, it is important that the principles of justice be of the kind that can be widely scrutinized in order to ensure their truth, since to force people to comply with false (that is, morally wrong) principles is odious. Such scrutiny must be public, because if it is limited to, say, a council of those with a particular comprehensive conception, it may make assumptions that are false.[58]

If one has an objective interest in a publicly acknowledged conception of justice, then one has an objective interest in the capacity to apply and act upon it. A conception of justice is not merely a theoretical idea, it is inherently action guiding. Hence, under the three contingent conditions noted earlier, which I assume characterize our global condition, one has an objective interest in applying and acting upon fair terms of cooperation.

Characterizing the Nature of the Justification

The upshot of the preceding arguments in defense of the two highest order moral interests can be put in at least two ways. One might conclude that it is true that persons have highest order moral interests in the capacities rationally to form, revise, and pursue a conception of the good and to apply and act upon publicly acknowledged fair terms of cooperation. Alternatively, one might conclude that it is rational to develop and maintain these capacities. Although these two conclusions may appeal differentially to those with different meta-ethical convictions, I do not see a significant difference between them. Indeed these claims seem to be mutually entailing. If one has such an interest, then *ceritus paribus* it is rational to pursue it; and what it is rational to pursue is in one's interest, as long as one accepts the possibility of moral interests in addition to prudential ones.

If the preceding arguments in defense of the two highest order moral interests are sound, then the conception of persons used in political constructivism is, at least in part, true. If the conception of persons is true, then its use cannot be objected to as being parochial and of limited applicability. If it is true that persons have these interests, then the fact that the conception of persons originates in the democratic tradition cannot count as reason not to apply it elsewhere.

Nonetheless, the conception of persons may remain political in three senses important to Rawls: It accords with the conception of citizenship implicit in democratic constitutionalism; it does not require denying any reasonable comprehensive conception of the good; and, it is employed only to make a point about political morality.[59] If Rawls is correct in making these three claims in *Political Liberalism* regarding the conception of persons, there is no reason to think that any of the three political properties of the conception have altered as a result of the justification that I have provided for the conception.[60] The first and the third would remain true so long as the conception originates in the democratic tradition and is applied only to matters of justice. The second remains true so long as the conception of persons may be affirmed from within any reasonable comprehensive conception of the good. I see no reason to think that because an argument has now been given to justify the conception, it can no longer be affirmed from within the same comprehensive conceptions that had previously provided affirmation for it. So, in supporting the universality of the conception of persons that serves as the basis for the principles of cosmopolitan justice, we do not sacrifice the suitability of the principles of justice to be the object of an overlapping consensus.

The Truth of the Principles of Justice

I have been arguing that cosmopolitan constructivism could be defended against the charge of parochialism by giving an account of how the conception of persons that it employs may be thought of as true and thus universally applicable. A corollary of that argument would seem to be that the principles of justice themselves are true. For it would seem strange to say that the principles of justice appropriately derived from a true conception of persons are themselves not true because they are not subject to truth-value. Rawls, however, maintains that the principles of justice as fairness are reasonable but not true.[61] He seems to think that political harm would be done by asserting that the principles of justice are true, rather than reasonable. Presumably this is because such a truth claim may conflict with some reasonable comprehensive conception. If he is right about this, it would provide the basis for a challenge to the position that I argued for in the previous sections insofar as it would indicate deleterious political consequences of the position.

One place where Rawls states his worry about affirming the truth of the principles of justice is the following passage:

> The advantage of staying within the reasonable is that there can be but one true comprehensive doctrine, though as we have seen many reasonable ones. Once we accept the fact that reasonable pluralism is a permanent condition of public culture under free institutions, the idea of the reasonable is more suit-

able as part of the basis of public justification for a constitutional regime than the idea of moral truth. Holding a political conception as true, and for that reason alone the one suitable basis of public reason, is exclusive, even sectarian, and so likely to foster political division.[62]

The reasoning in this passage is, however, fallacious. It slides from holding a political conception of justice as true to holding a particular comprehensive conception as true. If a particular comprehensive conception were acknowledged as true, then other conflicting conceptions by implication would be taken to be false. However, the truth of the principles of justice does not entail the truth of any comprehensive conception in which it has been affirmed.

Consider three possible ways that a comprehensive conception might provide a basis for affirming a political conception of justice. First, certain of the comprehensive conception's principles may entail the principles of justice. Second, the principles of a comprehensive conception may simply be consistent with the principles of justice. Third, certain of the principles of the comprehensive conception may appear to contradict the principles of justice, but the conception has the resources for allowing the principles of justice to outweigh the application of its own principles that seem to be in conflict. For example, the principle of utility may be in conflict with taking rights seriously, but a utilitarian might argue that the best happiness maximizing strategy under the appropriate circumstances requires following apparently nonutilitarian principles. The utilitarian may accept the great political virtue of the principles of justice in uniquely making possible the conditions of fair social cooperation on the basis of mutual respect, and this may receive a utilitarian justification.[63]

In each of these three cases, the truth of the principles of justice does not entail the truth of the comprehensive conception within which it has been affirmed. Take the case in which the comprehensive conception entails the principles of justice: If the latter are true, it does not follow that the former is. To claim otherwise is to commit the fallacy of affirming the consequent. Nor would the truth of the principles of justice entail the truth of the comprehensive conception that affirms them in the case where the principles of justice are merely consistent with, or even appear to be in contradiction with, some of the principles of the comprehensive conception.

Rawls may have a different worry about the third case. If the principles of justice are thought of as true, this perhaps falsifies those comprehensive conceptions that they appear to contradict. This depends upon the way in which the principles are affirmed within the comprehensive conception. I assume that even if the principles of justice are taken as reasonable, rather than true, they cannot be affirmed from within an unmodified comprehensive conception with which they stand in a relation of contradiction. For this would involve the holders of the comprehensive doctrines in believing what—according to their comprehensive conceptions—they take to be false. Rather, any contradiction between the principles of justice and the comprehensive conception must be resolvable in some manner. Utilitarians may follow Sidgwick's example concerning the morality of common sense and take the two principles of justice as middle axioms of utilitarian theory.[64] Rawls believes that it is possible for someone to affirm the principles of justice taken as reasonable, even if they stand in contradiction to certain commitments of that person's reasonable comprehensive conception of the good.[65] It is not obvious why it should be any harder to find the resources within a comprehensive conception to accept principles of justice as true rather than reasonable, in those cases in which the principles stand in apparent contradiction to certain commitments of the comprehensive conceptions. For even to find the principles of justice reasonable, one must nevertheless somehow render them consistent with one's comprehensive conception. In other words, if Rawls is right that it is possible to reconcile such comprehensive conceptions with principles regarded as reasonable, it must also be possible to reconcile them with ones regarded as true.

Taking the two principles of justice to be true need not commit one to a particular meta-ethical theory of moral truth, although some constructivists have developed such theories.[66] Rawls's constructivism is not meta-ethical, and he rightly wants the principles of justice to be compatible with many meta-ethical theories. To say that the principles of justice are true is to say nothing more than that they are appropriately derived from true conceptions of persons. In other words, asserting that they are true is not different than simply asserting them.[67] Perhaps Rawls's concern is that taking the principles to be true contradicts those meta-ethical theories that reject moral truth. If it is skepticism, nihilism, or subjectivism that Rawls wishes to appease, he never says so. Given his arguments that the moral principles established by political constructivism are objective, although not true, it's doubtful that the followers of such views will go along with political constructivism, even if it denies the truth of its product.

Whether or not the principles of justice are true does not change their political character in the three senses important to Rawls. They accord with the conception of citizenship implicit in democratic constitutionalism, they do not require denying any reasonable comprehensive conception of the good, and they are employed only to make a point about political morality.

TOLERATION

A theory of international justice founded on respect for persons ought to incorporate the value of toleration. Rawls seems to believe that a requirement that regimes be committed to principles (6*), (8*), and (9) would violate the principle of toleration.[68] This seems to me to be a misunderstanding of what tolerance requires. In any case, it stands in contradiction to the account of tolerance that is developed in *Political Liberalism*. Rawls's claim about the demands of tolerance in *The Law of Peoples* is wrong, but explicable by the construction that he employs.

In *Political Liberalism* tolerance requires a freestanding political conception of justice that is not justified solely by reference to any particular comprehensive conception of the good. This is required because there are a variety of reasonable comprehensive conceptions of the good. "Thus, it is not in general unreasonable to affirm any one of a number of reasonable comprehensive doctrines. We recognize that our own doctrine has, and can have, for people generally, no special claims on them beyond their own view of its merits."[69] It would be unreasonable for the state to endorse any one particular comprehensive conception of the good life, since this would suggest that all of the others were false and since there are no final noncontroversial grounds upon which to base such truth claims. If the state were to endorse any particular comprehensive doctrine, it could not maintain this without being oppressive— that is, without placing unreasonable demands on those who adhere to other comprehensive doctrines.[70] Reason, then, demands state tolerance—lack of endorsement—of any particular comprehensive doctrine. What is required is a set of principles of justice that do not require for their justification any one comprehensive philosophical conception of the good exclusively and that can be affirmed from within any reasonable comprehensive doctrine.[71] However, reason does not demand equal treatment for unreasonable comprehensive doctrines. In cases where such doctrines lead to injustices, the doctrines themselves may have to be denied.[72] With respect to individual actions, justice defines the limits of tolerance.

A line of reasoning analogous to this is developed by Will Kymlicka in a discussion of the value of culture. He argues that liberals should value cultural membership more highly than they often have because culture provides the context in which choices between a variety of conceptions of the good life take on meaning.[73] Kymlicka argues that cultural membership is important to liberals insofar as that culture contributes to that individual's capacity for freely choosing and pursuing a conception of the good life. Protecting cultural membership does not, however, entail respect for those activities, practices, or institutions of a culture that restrict this capacity of individuals.[74] By analogy there are many activities, practices, and institutions that liberals should not tolerate, specifically those that violate the principles of justice. The point is that the limits of tolerance with regard to activities, practices, and institutions are set by the principles of justice.

In *The Law of Peoples* Rawls seeks to establish that the limits of tolerance extend to decent hierarchical societies.[75] So the principles of international justice must be such that they can include decent hierarchical societies in addition to liberal ones. This he takes as important because he believes that judging such peoples by liberal values will be damaging to their self-respect (where "self" refers to the people).[76] As I have already noted, there are good reasons to believe that decent hierarchical societies are impossible. So it is by no means obvious that the principle of tolerance developed in *The Law of Peoples* in practice broadens the basis of agreement about principles of international justice.

From the perspective of cosmopolitan justice there is a more significant problem with Rawls's extension of the limits of tolerance to regimes that are organized around comprehensive conceptions of the good and lacking an endorsement of democratic institutions. Such regimes are internally unreasonable, intolerant, and oppressive by the standards of *Political Liberalism*. To be "tolerant" of such regimes is akin to being "tolerant" of unjust actions or oppressive cultural practices. In short, there are no good reasons for being so. In fact, just as institutionalizing an arrangement that permitted individuals to be unjust could be seen as being complicit in the injustice, so institutionalizing principles of international conduct that licensed oppression could be seen as being complicit in the oppression.

Rawls finds his way into this problem because he represents the interests of peoples in his construction. This allows him to assert that just as there are many reasonable individual comprehensive moral doctrines that should be tolerated, so there are many state ideologies that should be tolerated.[77] This statism subordinates the interests of persons to those of peoples, and that is prima facie incompatible with respect for persons.

CONCLUSION

In sum, Rawls's statist account of the law of peoples appears ill founded. Not only are Rawls's eight principles insufficiently sensitive to the situation of individuals within a state, but his omission of principles ensuring democratic governance and egalitarian distributive justice is ad hoc. This, however, does not impugn the political constructivist project either in general or with regard to this particular subject matter. An alternative construction procedure is viable. This procedure derives three important principles of the cosmopolitan conception of justice.

The implication of this argument is significant for a theory of international justice. The cosmopolitan construction can justify human rights but will also require democracy and egalitarianism. Principles (6*), (8*), and (9) are part of the cosmopolitan theory that I have been defending and will continue to defend in subsequent chapters. If a concern for human rights is admitted as limiting what can be done in the name of sovereignty, then democratic and egalitarian concerns about the treatment of persons should count as limiting sovereignty as well. Where any one of these three principles is not observed, there would appear to be a prima facie case for other states not complying with the principle of nonintervention. This alone does not license intervention in such cases. Other necessary conditions for justified intervention apply as well. Those conditions will be defended in Chapter 5. For now, further concerns remain about whether justice to noncompatriots is consistent with justice to compatriots. This and other matters are discussed in Chapter 3.

THREE

The Borders of Justice

The problem of establishing a perfect civil constitution is subordinate to the problem of a law-governed external relationship with other states, and cannot be solved unless the latter is also solved.

—Immanuel Kant[1]

In Chapter 2 I argued that a broadly Rawlsian political constructivism entails three important principles of cosmopolitan justice: commitments to human rights, democracy, and socioeconomic equality. I also argued that the conception of persons that Rawlsian political constructivism employs is true, regardless of the fact that it is also consistent with the underlying conception of citizenship in constitutional democracies. The cosmopolitanism I am defending might be challenged on the following grounds: The present account has derived principles of justice where justice simply is not an issue because duties of justice are not global. Alternatively, even if there are global duties of justice, these are necessarily trumped by the morally prior duties of justice that compatriots and co-nationals owe to one another.

In this chapter I shall argue that duties of cosmopolitan justice exist because the condition that gives rise to duties of justice, namely, the appropriate form of association, exists globally. This claim is compatible with the view that we have special duties of justice to compatriots. I shall argue, too, that duties of justice to compatriots do not necessarily take precedence over duties of justice to noncompatriots. Additionally, I shall argue that there are no duties of justice among persons simply by virtue of the fact that they share a common nationality. Finally, I shall apply this per-

spective by analyzing the justice of protectionist trade policies and restricted immigration policies. Readers with an interest in technical aspects
of the claim that duties of justice are associative duties will be especially
interested in the next section. Those whose interests are focused more particularly on policy matters may skip this section without losing the gist of
the main argument.

DUTIES OF JUSTICE

Duties of justice are a subset of all moral duties. Justice is not the whole of
morality; its object and scope are narrower. In order for one to be bound
by a duty of justice to another, that other must be the right sort of thing
and must be in the right relation to the one bound. This accords with certain relatively strong moral intuitions: I am not bound by duties of justice
to rocks and plants to treat them a certain way, but I may be bound by duties of justice to other persons to treat rocks and plants in a certain way—
for example, by not depleting natural resources. Nor am I bound by duties
of justice to intervene into the affairs of intelligent beings with whom we
have no intercourse but only an awareness of their existence—say, intelligent beings on the second planet orbiting some distant star. I may, however, be bound by broader moral duties, for example, to do them no unnecessary harm.

The subject matter under discussion can be narrowed even further. I am
interested in matters of social justice. Matters of social justice concern
whether the principles and institutions that dominate our social and political life are just. For purposes of brevity, however, I shall refer to duties of
social justice simply as duties of justice. If person A owes a duty of justice
to person B, then A has a duty to observe the established institutional principles that ensure B is being treated justly or to advocate for the establishment of just principles. This conception of justice is sometimes called an institutional conception.[2] Because duties of justice are so often not
distinguished from more general moral duties—a lack of distinction that
creates confusion—it is worth emphasizing the distinction. I wish to draw
attention to two distinguishing properties of duties of justice: (1) Duties of
justice are generated by associational relations; and, (2) they are duties requiring action toward persons indirectly insofar as they require obeying or
advocating just institutions or principles to govern the association. There
are other features of duties of justice that are not a concern here. I have asserted that duties of justice are moral requirements of a special sort that we
owe to other persons, but not to all other persons. Why isn't justice owed
to all persons? This question requires an examination of the above stated
distinctive properties of duties of justice.

Associative Duties and Duties of Justice

In one sense the duties of justice are conventional. This is not to say that they are not real. Rather, it is to say that such duties cannot be claimed as entitlements that one person may use to bind all other persons simply by virtue of the nature of her personhood. On the contrary, duties of justice arise between persons when activities such as politics or commerce bring persons into association.

Persons may be brought into association without any of them intending to bring the association about. This is especially the case when economic activity has consequences for those not directly involved with it—in the language of economists, when the activity produces "externalities." For example, C and D may be involved in ongoing commercial activity that causes serious harm to D's neighbors without either C or D knowing it. In this case, C and D are in association with D's neighbors.

An association is more than mere interaction, but the difference appears to be one of degree.[3] Two people may interact on a temporary basis when, for example, one helps the other. They are not thereby in an association. If, however, established social practices or institutions regularly affect the highest order moral interests of a person, that person is in association with all of the others who act within the constraints of those practices or institutions.

That duties of justice differ from other moral duties insofar as they require association is a point made by Hume:

> Suppose, that several families unite together into one society, which is totally disjoined from all others, the rules, which preserve peace and order, enlarge themselves to the utmost extent of that society; but becoming entirely useless, lose their force when carried one step further. But again suppose, that several distinct societies maintain a kind of intercourse for mutual convenience and advantage, the boundaries of justice still grow larger, in proportion to largeness of men's view, and the force of their mutual conexions.[4]

Because associations affect a person's moral interests, they naturally yield moral questions that do not arise between nonassociates, namely, questions about the morality of the principles that govern it or the justice of the association. The fact that persons are associated makes it sensible to question whether the institutions or principles that govern their association are just. No such question is sensible in the absence of an association.[5]

A number of philosophers have had difficulty accepting the claim that associations generate new duties.[6] The view that under conditions of association questions of justice arise is plausible only if it is plausible that persons already have general moral duties to one another. In other words, duties of justice presuppose more general moral duties. General moral duties explain why there are moral duties at all among associates. The fact of association explains why some of these duties are different than those that exist between persons who are not associates.

In sum, then, duties of justice are duties about the nature of an association and about the principles that guide its institutions. Such duties arise if and only if the following two conditions are met: Persons are in association with one another, and persons in general have moral duties to one another.

Duties of Justice and Institutions

Not all associative duties are duties of justice. Duties of justice are directed toward the general institutions of public life. Duties to obey, or construct, just public institutions are particularly important because, in the words of Rawls, the effects of the institutions and principles of association "are so profound from the start." As Rawls puts it,

> The intuitive notion here is that this structure contains various social positions and that men born into different positions have expectations of life determined, in part, by the political system as well as by economic and social circumstances. In this way the institutions of society favor certain starting places over others. These are especially deep inequalities. Not only are they pervasive, but they affect men's initial chances in life.[7]

Institutions that endure and dominate public life are particularly significant because of the profound effect that they have on one's moral interests. Questions of justice are questions about the appropriate rules or principles for governing enduring associations that dominate public life whose benefits, and especially burdens, are not easily avoidable, if indeed they are avoidable at all. For, although the burdens of a specific association dominating a particular public life can be avoided by emigration, this offers no way of avoiding the burdens of associations that dominate public life in general.

Associative Duties and Moral Equality

The claim that we owe some, but not all, persons duties of justice may be said to be inconsistent with a fundamental commitment to the moral equality of all persons. Samuel Scheffler puts the challenge as follows: "If all people are of equal value and importance, then what is it about my relation to my associates that makes it not merely permissible but obligatory for me to give their interests priority over the interests of other people?"[8]

Two persons who are morally equal do not necessarily deserve the same treatment from me. Equality requires, rather, equivalent treatment in equivalent circumstances. I may, for example, have a duty to give the one $50, but not the other. If I borrowed $50 with the promise to repay it, the claim that I have a duty to pay the one $50 but have no corresponding duty to the other does not contradict the principle of moral equality. The latter principle would be violated by the claim that my borrowing from and promising to both under similar conditions generated a duty to one but not to the other. Likewise, duties of justice to some, but not all persons, do not violate the principle of the moral equality of all persons. This principle would, however, be violated by a claim—which I do not make—that our membership in associations only generates duties of justice to some of the persons with whom we are associated. The fact of association plus the entitlement of all of the associates to equal respect produces duties of egalitarian justice. Because of the *assumed* moral equality of all members, there is a strong presumption against establishing the institutions of an association in a way that systematically denies some associates opportunities that are available to others.

Another challenge to this account is that even if egalitarian justice is dependent on the moral equality of all persons and even if associations do produce duties of justice, the existence of the association itself cannot be justified.[9] If the association cannot be justified and if one assumes the moral equality of all persons, then special duties of justice to associates cannot be justified.

It is true that duties of justice do not justify the existence of an association; they assume its existence. It is false, however, to suppose that the association needs moral justification in order to render associative duties consistent with the moral equality of all persons. Consider the following example. Through no choosing of their own, a few people wind up together in a lifeboat in the middle of an ocean. Perhaps they were unconscious when loaded into the lifeboat by the ship's heroic crew. In any case, they have a store of provisions to distribute and ration. Assuming the moral equality of persons on board, each of these persons has a duty to the others to abide by a fair system of rationing. Make no mistake about it, abiding by the system will entail sacrifices on the part of those who could overpower the rest and simply appropriate the rations for themselves. Moreover, the duty to abide by a fair system of rationing is owed only to other members on the lifeboat, not to all persons. Hence, one can start with the normatively unjustified *fact* of association and derive duties limited to associates that are perfectly consistent with the moral equality of all persons. If this is the case, then duties of justice, as associative duties, are not necessarily inconsistent with the moral equality of all persons.

Associative Duties and Attitudes

Duties of justice depend upon two objective factors, general moral duties among persons, such as duties of equal respect, and the fact that there is an association among them. This account of associative duties is contrary to some accounts in contemporary philosophy that require associates either explicitly or implicitly to have certain attitudes in order to have an associative duty. Yael Tamir argues, "Our obligation to help fellow members derives from a shared sense of membership rather than from the specific nature of their actions."[10] Ronald Dworkin holds that the requisite attitudes need only become apparent as the result of interpretative activity, but must be there nonetheless: "The members of a group must by and large hold certain attitudes about the responsibilities that they owe one another if these responsibilities are to count as genuine fraternal obligations."[11]

It is plausible that certain moral duties are generated by their bearers. For example, if I declare my adherence to the terms of a contract, then I have generated a duty to fulfill its terms. The duty here, however, follows not from my attitude of willingness to accept the terms of the contract, but from my declaration that I will. My *attitude* does not generate the duty, nor can it change it if I later find the terms troublesome; rather, the *act* of declaration generates the duty. To take the appropriate attitude of the person bound to be a necessary condition of the existence of a duty is to take duties to be mind-dependent. Mind-dependent accounts of duty seem unable to account for an important fact about the nature of moral duties, namely, that we are bound by duties regardless of whether we happen to believe that we are or want to be. So, a mind-dependent account of associative duties would seem to render them less than duties. This appears to be a problem with Tamir's account.

Dworkin, however, is not claiming that duties are mind-dependent. He requires a certain sort of reciprocity such that duties of justice are dependent not on one's own attitudes, but on the attitudes of those to whom one owes the duty.[12] It is intuitively plausible that certain duties depend upon the attitudes of the person to whom one owes the duty. For example, compare two different cases in which E is helped by F. In one case F helps E because it is in F's self-interest to do so. In another case F helps E because F is concerned for E. It is plausible that E owes a debt of gratitude to F only in the second case.

Even if some moral duties may be dependent upon the attitude of those to whom the duty is owed, there are good reasons to believe that this is not true of duties of justice. If duties of justice required appropriate attitudes (even if these were only implicit) on the part of the person to whom the duty was owed, the kinds of associations that might be criticized as unjust would narrow beyond the limits of what is intuitively plausible. Recall the example of C's and D's commercial activity giving rise to externalities that harm D's neighbors. D's neighbors may not even know of C's and D's existence, and therefore have no particular attitudes towards them, but that does not imply that neither C nor D are bound by justice to compensate them for the harm that they suffered. Likewise, a father may be bound by duties of justice to support his children even if there is no love between them. In sum, taking duties of justice to require the right attitudes among the associates cannot explain our moral intuitions about such duties.

With the distinctions between duties of justice, other associative duties, and general moral duties in hand, in the next section I shall argue that given current global conditions duties of global justice exist.

GLOBAL JUSTICE

Prominent contemporary political philosophers have usually focused their efforts on establishing theories of social justice for states.[13] There are obvious reasons for considering the character of state institutions. States are incontrovertible examples of enduring associations. Until the latter part of the twentieth century, state institutions were the most general political institutions with police powers, and economies were studied as national (or state) economies. Nevertheless, these reasons do not compel us to restrict our attention to justice within a single state. Because the history of the expansion of capitalism indicates that the moral interests of persons throughout the world are affected by an expanding economic association, there are good reasons for the investigation of justice at the global level.

The Global Association

In the history of the relationship among persons in Europe, the Americas, Africa, and Asia, three periods are especially important with respect to the global character of economic association: colonial conquest, early-twentieth-century imperialism, and late-twentieth-century globalization. In the first of these periods, the industrialization of Europe and the development of the New World were paid for with the lives of millions of African slaves.[14] In the second, characterized by the classical theorists of imperialism as the export of capital, financial concerns from European and North American centers traveled to the far corners of the globe in the search for profits.[15] This brought the imperialist states and colonies into even closer association. In the third period, globalization has brought people from around the world into closer economic association. According to the World Bank, foreign direct investment (FDI) reached a record level in 1995 of $90 billion. "Propelling these FDI flows have been the rapid globalization of production, the increasing integration of developing countries in buoyant world trade, and the improved economic policies of recipients."[16] Some analysts contend that globalization has not amounted to much of an increase in the amount of trade around the globe in comparison with the period studied by the classical theorist of imperialism, but it has at the very least caused an increase in the ability to effect economic change at a distance through instant global communication and 24-hour global money markets.[17]

The influence of international financial institutions (such as the International Monetary Fund and the World Bank) over the policies of developing countries has become extensive as the debt of those countries has increased. In 1995 the debt-to-export ratio for developing countries was 150 percent, for Sub-Saharan Africa it was 277 percent. International financial institutions set conditions for loans, which conditions constrain the sort of domestic redistributive mechanisms and institutions that are possible in developing countries. Consider, for example, three constraints that developing countries confront if seeking egalitarian schemes of distribution: the need for foreign capital investment, if the economy is to grow; the general trend of attaching expenditure-cutting requirements as the condition of international loans; and the progressive reduction of trade barriers, allowing capital to be more mobile. The conjunction of these constraints can result in punishment by disinvestment for states that pursue egalitarian courses of development.[18]

Economic association is often thought of as involving a set of principles for the production and distribution of goods. However, goods are not all that is distributed. As of 1990, carbon dioxide concentrations were increasing at .4 percent per year.[19] At that rate, by 2030 the concentrations of carbon dioxide in the atmosphere will be double that of 1990.[20] There is widespread, although not unanimous, agreement in the scientific community that the effects of this doubling will include a global mean temperature rise of 1.5 to 5 degrees Celsius.[21] There is somewhat less agreement about the consequences of such a warming, but many scientists predict significant climatic changes with tremendous costs to current patterns of crop growth and rising sea levels that could cause serious flooding in low-lying regions.[22] Global warming seems to pose a threat to most everyone. In addition to the three periods in the history of capitalism bringing persons around the globe into closer economic association, the distribution of pollutants in the atmosphere has also brought people into an unavoidable association affecting their highest order moral interests.

One may conclude that the global economy has had a substantial impact on the moral interests of persons in virtually every corner of the world. Due to this association, I claim that duties of justice exist between persons globally and not merely between compatriots. The effects of global economic institutions and principles on the life prospects of persons are, in Rawls's words, "profound from the start." To understand the effect that the location of one's birth has on one's life prospects, consider the magnitude of global inequality. For example, Switzerland's per capita gross national product (GNP) of $37,180 is the highest in Europe, and its infant mortality rate is 7 in 1,000;[23] Mozambique's per capita GNP is $80, the lowest in sub-Saharan Africa, while its infant mortality rate is 277 in 1,000.[24] The duties of the globally well-off with respect to such inequality will be the subject matter of Chapter 5.

A Failed Limiting Strategy

The thesis that people have duties of justice to noncompatriots has been criticized because there are no global institutions that enforce such obligations. For reasons that will become clear, I use the awkward compound term *justice-positivism* to refer to this position. The following claims by Brian Barry serve as examples of justice-positivism:

> According to Rawls, a society is a scheme of social cooperation, and from this fact we can generate, via the notion of fair play, principles of justice. But clearly, any actual society simply generates whatever is generated by its actual cooperative practices. If it provides retirement pensions out of social security taxes, it is unfair to be a free rider. And so on.[25]

Barry has reiterated this point: "If I ask why I am obliged to contribute to the old-age pension of someone I have never met and have no particular interest in who lives in Rotherham, but not to the pension of somebody equally distant to me who lives in Rennes, the answer is that I belong to the same scheme of social insurance as the first but not the second."[26] The upshot of these arguments seems to be that duties of distributive justice, conceived of as requirements of fairness at least, arise only within an already existing institutional framework of redistribution.[27] Thus, if the current system of global association does not already contain institutions that enforce duties to noncompatriots, appeals to fairness are insufficient to justify them. Insofar as the international situation contains no such institutions, there are no duties of cosmopolitan justice. Barry's claims are directed only to duties of distributive justice, but I can see no reason why they would not be generalizable to all duties of justice, since the claim is not about the content of the purported duties, but their existence in the absence of established institutions of enforcement.

Barry seems to conceive of the duties of fairness as associative duties and to take the requisite association to be a legal-political framework. I call this position justice-positivism because it is analogous to the position of legal positivists. Legal positivists usually defend an identificatory theory of the law, which holds that something is the law only if it is the product of an accepted rule of recognition. A rule of recognition is what a polity (or its relevant leaders) takes to be the appropriate procedure for generating laws.[28] So, one stands under a legal duty only if there is an institutional procedure accepted by society's leaders that says that one does. Justice-positivism maintains that one stands under a duty of justice only if the institutions have been developed to hold us accountable. Justice-positivism is, however, more radical than legal positivism. Advocates of legal positivism maintain the separability thesis, the view that a rule's legality and its justice are distinct matters.[29] This allows them to invoke moral theory to criticize as unjust prevailing legal convention. Justice-positivism does not have the resources for criticizing prevailing legal and institutional convention since there are no duties of justice in the absence of institutionally required duties. This counterintuitive consequence is the principle weakness of justice-positivism.

As ordinarily understood the requirement of fairness has two aspects: It proscribes shirking, requiring fair play under the principles of social cooperation; and it requires giving each his or her due. We may say that a certain rule is unfair when, for example, it treats equals unequally, or rests on a distinction that is morally arbitrary, or is merely the product of unequal power. The fact that we employ this second aspect of fairness to criticize existing principles of cooperation suggests that it is more fundamental than the first. Barry, however, only sees the first aspect of fairness. It is no criticism of the claims of global justice to observe that institutions of redistribution do not exist, for it is precisely the fairness of existing international institutions and policies of distribution that is in question.[30] If existing institutions do not conform to principles of justice, then the duties of justice require their reform or the construction of alternative ones.[31]

THE QUESTION OF CONSISTENCY

We live in different associations that establish various claims of justice. Some of us live in cities; some of us also live in provinces (or states) with substantial delegated powers. We all live in states (or countries) that claim some final sovereign authority, and we live within the global economy. The existence of multiple associations suggests the possibility of conflicting claims of justice: What one owes in virtue of membership in one association may be incompatible with what one owes in virtue of membership in another. For example, our duties to compatriots may seem to conflict with our duties to noncompatriots.

A frequently employed framework for discussions of this potential conflict is that of general and special moral duties. This permits an analogy between the duties of justice within the state and the moral duties to one's family. Often both are taken to be examples of special moral duties. The task of moral theory then is to reconcile these special duties to the more general demand that morality makes upon us due to the fact that all persons (and even many nonpersons) are the object of moral regard. Sometimes defenders of cosmopolitanism invoke this analogy. For example, Martha Nussbaum claims:

> Politics, like child care, will be poorly done if each thinks herself equally responsible for all, rather than giving the immediate surroundings special attention and care. To give one's own sphere special care is justifiable in universalist terms, and I think this its most compelling justification. To take one example, we do not really think our own children are morally more important than other people's children, even though almost all of us who have children would give our own children far more love and care than we give others'. It is good for children, on the whole, that things work this way, and that is why our special care is good, rather than selfish.[32]

Nussbaum invokes the analogy to render special and general moral duties consistent, showing the former as instances of the latter by invoking an argument that is traceable at least as far back as Henry Sidgwick.[33] More often the analogy is invoked to point to a practical dilemma that requires us to sacrifice the general demands of morality in favor of the stronger special ties of family, state, or nation.[34] If one draws a distinction between duties of justice and other moral duties, and if one quite reasonably supposes that at least some of what we owe families and friends is not characterized by justice, then it follows that there is the possibility of deep conflict within our moral lives. Antigone's plight would have no dramatic purchase on us if we did not recognize that there may be times in which doing right by our families may conflict with duties of justice.

As an account, however, of the source of tension between what we may owe compatriots and what we may owe noncompatriots, the comparison to the tension between duties to one's family and friends and general moral duties is misguided. For if there is tension between the claims of compatriots and of noncompatriots, it is a tension *within* justice, not between general and special morality. The source of the tension is not captured by noting that we have general moral duties to all persons (and many nonpersons) and special duties to those with whom we have special ties. The source of the tension stems from our membership in multiple politico-social associations, each of which yields duties of justice. Failure to appreciate this latter point has sometimes led advocates of cosmopolitanism astray. Barry, for example, delivers a rhetorically powerful blow against statism and nationalism in the name of *universal morality*—which he takes to be the basis of cosmopolitanism—but concludes by asserting that *duties of justice* are owed only to compatriots.[35]

To mistake the source of possible tension between the claims of compatriots and noncompatriots is to be misled about the source of its resolution. Scheffler claims, "Part of what it is to have such [special] responsibilities to one's associates is to be required, within limits, to give their interests priority over the interests of non-associates, in cases in which the two conflict."[36] Perhaps this is what special duties entail. It does not follow, however, that certain responsibilities of justice require that the *interests* of compatriots be given priority over *duties* to noncompatriots. Once the conflict between the claims of compatriots and noncompatriots is recognized as a conflict within justice, there is the basis for a possible resolution. Conflicts within justice are resolved by appealing to more fundamental considerations of justice.

The practice of legal decisionmaking illustrates this point. Consider the matter of contract law. When G and H enter into a contract, say, to exchange goods for money, each of them acquires an entitlement over the other that other persons do not have. Suppose G is the purchaser. She is entitled to the goods contracted from H. Meanwhile, H is entitled to the price of the contract. J is not entitled to either the goods from H or the price of the contract from G. Hence, H and G have duties of justice to each other that they do not have to J. There is no reason to conclude, however, that these additional duties release them from their duties to J. G may not stop paying taxes, some of which is redistributed to J, in order to gather the funds to meet the obligation to H. To generalize, new or local duties of justice are acquired within a background of the more general duties of justice, and as such they may not contravene these more general duties.

When claims of justice made by compatriots and noncompatriots conflict, resolution is often possible by appealing to more fundamental or background considerations of justice. This assertion does not, however, entail that the claims of compatriots invariably trump the claims of noncompatriots or vice versa. It is an assertion about the manner of resolution, not its outcome. There are three possible accounts of the relationship between duties of justice that we owe compatriots and those that we owe noncompatriots. First, accounts may take duties of global justice to be primary and attempt to explain state justice as consistent with this. Robert Goodin adopts this strategy when he takes the duties that compatriots owe each other to be assigned general duties.[37] The duties that compatriots owe each other exist because all persons owe all other persons duties, but the state system is a generally reliable mechanism for ensuring that people enjoy that which they are owed. Because duties of justice to compatriots arise within

the background context of duties of cosmopolitan justice, we are not relieved of the latter duties in order to fulfill the former ones. On the contrary, there exists a standing duty to all persons, which duty requires action
if a state fails to provide persons in some other country what they are
owed. Second, accounts may take the duties of justice at the state level to be
primary and attempt to derive global, or international, duties of justice
against the background of duties of justice within states. Rawls's theory of
justice is an example of this.[38] For purposes of ideal theory at least, the duties of justice that compatriots owe each other can be established without
consideration of the possible competing claims of noncompatriots. After
having settled what justice requires of compatriots, matters of justice between peoples may then be addressed.

The most promising account of the relationship between duties of justice
to compatriots and to noncompatriots is the third, to take neither the duties
of global nor domestic justice in general as primary. According to this account, there is no standing preference for either the global or domestic
claims. This does not mean that there are not background, or fundamental,
commitments of justice that can serve as the basis for resolving disputes between them. Rather, adjudication is on the basis of the basic considerations of
justice implicated by the particular dispute. These might involve arguments
about underlying deeper commitments, consistency of commitment, and priority of commitment, without assuming that such considerations always fall
on the side of the claims of compatriots or those of noncompatriots.

There are problems with trying to establish that the duties we owe either
to compatriots or to noncompatriots are more fundamental. This can be il-
lustrated by revisiting the example of contract law I presented earlier. Why
are we justified in claiming that the duties of justice that G and H owe each
other in virtue of the contract may not trump the noncontractual duties
that both owe to J? The justification can invoke at least two considerations.[39] First, the noncontractual duties of justice that both G and H owe to
J are more general than the contractual duties: The latter duties they owe
only to each other, the former duties they owe to J *and* to each other. Second, the duties that they owe to J are temporally prior to the duties that
they owe to each other as the result of the contract. Considerations of generality and temporal priority both point in the same direction. Hence, there
are compelling reasons for believing that G and H may not leave their pre-
contractual duties to J unfulfilled in order to fulfill their contractual duties
to each other. In other words, the pre-contractual duties to J (and to each
other) provide the background for assessing the duties that they may incur
as the result of contracting with each other.

When considerations of generality and temporal priority conflict, our intuitions are far less clear. Debates about justice in federal states reflect this.
Suppose a federal state brings together formerly independent states. Claims

about what a citizen or resident owes all other compatriots may have the virtue of being more general than what that person owes those in his or her province (or state), but such claims may not be temporally prior. Imagine, for example, that prior to the federation, members of the independent states had duties of justice by virtue of their association, which they did not have with citizens of other states who later became compatriots. Establishing the more fundamental commitments of justice according to which disputes can be adjudicated may be a more complicated matter for federal jurisprudence than for contract law, since merely prioritizing the more general and the prior over the more specific and the later does not provide a distinct answer to the question of what the background considerations of justice are. An answer requires in addition some account of the more basic commitments of justice that are at stake in any particular dispute.

Similar problems arise when considering the duties of justice owed to compatriots and to noncompatriots. Considerations of generality point in favor of noncompatriots, while considerations of temporal priority point in favor of compatriots. On the one hand, the fact of a global economic association entails that citizens and residents may not attend only to the duties that they owe to compatriots, for this would be an arbitrary limitation of the more general demands of justice. On the other hand, citizens and residents of states have duties to compatriots flowing from their political association that they do not have to noncompatriots, since they exist in political association with compatriots but not the other. They may have duties of global justice to extend the scope of political association, but this will not resolve conflicts. Rather, it will produce new conflicts akin to those of federal jurisprudence. Therefore, disputes over what is owed to compatriots and what is owed to noncompatriots cannot be resolved by finding an agreement between considerations of generality and temporal priority.

We are sometimes required to privilege the claims of noncompatriots when doing so is required by background or fundamental commitments of justice. We shall see specific examples of this when discussing protectionism and immigration. Alternatively, we may have duties to compatriots that we do not owe to noncompatriots because of our different associations with them. We shall consider this when discussing patriotism. Appeal to background or fundamental considerations of justice to resolve disputes between the claims of both groups involves appeals to the basic consideration of justice at stake in particular disputes without any reason to believe that in general the resolution will favor the claims of compatriots over noncompatriots, or vice versa. An important methodological point follows from this. Since we may not say that in general the claims of one group override the claims of the other, it is impossible to give an account of the duties owed to members of one of the two groups, in cases of conflicting claims, without considering the claims of members of the other.[40]

The position I have been arguing for in this section is consistent with the approach taken in Chapter 2 that requires the original position to be global from the start.[41] An alternative constructivist approach to global justice would develop the principles of domestic justice in a first sitting of an original position and the principles of global justice in a second sitting.[42] However, this procedure would allow that principles of domestic justice could be derived without considering competing claims from noncompatriots.

THREE OBJECTIONS

Many theorists will want to deny the conclusion I reached in the previous section and maintain the view that the interests of compatriots necessarily trump the interests of noncompatriots. In this section I briefly consider and reject three such arguments. More extensive consideration of the claims of patriotism and nationalism will follow.

Distance

The thesis of the previous section might be denied on the grounds that the force of duties of justice varies inversely with the distance of their object from the person obliged: The greater the distance, the less strong the duty. Because we are in closer proximity to most of our compatriots than to noncompatriots, our duties of justice then are stronger to the compatriots. This criticism fails for two reasons. First, a general principle of compatriot priority cannot be premised on proximity, as many people live near borders and are therefore closer to certain noncompatriots than to compatriots. A U.S. citizen living in San Diego is closer to the Mexican citizen living in Tijuana than to the U.S. citizen living in Anchorage. Proximity would provide little justification for limiting that person's duties of justice at the U.S.-Mexico border.

The second reason that this criticism fails is that there is no good reason to suppose that duties of justice do vary inversely with distance. If the duties of justice have only a subjective basis, they may. In other words, if we suppose that we only have duties of justice to those for whom we believe or feel that we have such duties, and if generally we believe or feel that we have weaker duties to those further away, then it would be the case that our duties of justice vary inversely with distance. However, the supposition that duties of justice have only a subjective basis is implausible because of its counterintuitive implications. If duties of justice are subjective, then it is impossible for us to be mistaken about what we believe or feel our duties to be. Although we might come to change our minds about our duties as our beliefs and feelings change, we could not claim that we changed our minds because our earlier conception of what our duties were was wrong. Our earlier conception would have been right so long as we had it.

The counterintuitive implication could be avoided and the position salvaged if our duties of justice, rather than being subjective, really did vary inversely with distance, even if we happen not to think so. Perhaps duties of justice lose their momentum due to moral friction over great distances. It is unclear, though, what the language of moral friction is a metaphor for. Moreover, if the account of the duties of justice that I provided earlier is approximately correct, then this characterization of them is wrong. We have duties of justice to those persons whose moral interests are affected by our business of living. There may be some correlation between those who we affect and their distance from us, but it is the effect, not the distance, that is the basis of the duty.

Degree of Association

The problems with the first objection suggest a second one. Because of the tighter association of interests that we share with compatriots, we are required to give priority to their interests over those of noncompatriots. There are two responses available to this criticism. One parallels a response to the first criticism, which is to challenge the premise that we share a tighter association of interests with all compatriots than with any noncompatriots. State boundaries have long been unreliable indicators of the boundaries of common interests. Does the fisherman in Maine have more tightly bound interests with the movie producer in Hollywood than with the fisherman in Nova Scotia? As a result of the global economy, there are increasing numbers of noncompatriots with whom our interests are more closely bound than with our compatriots. Debra Satz provides a nice example:

> Consider whether a Detroit automaker really shares a closer relationship with a Vermont cheesemaker than with a Korean autoworker. Even though the Detroiter and the Vermonter share a political state, she and her Korean counterpart are embedded in a web of relationships in which the actions of each can significantly and often directly affect the well-being of the other. Organizing by Korean autoworkers improves not only their own level of well-being but also that of their American counterparts.[43]

Since the criticism relies on a dubious premise, it is itself dubious.

The second response is to challenge the inference. There is no good reason to think that a tighter association should entail that the interests of one's close associates should be given priority over the interests of other associates. Suppose that Johannesburg were to erect restrictions on who may move into the city from the surrounding countryside in order to protect the local jobs for the local people. This would give priority to the interests of local residents over those of other citizens and residents of South Africa. It would also be inconsistent with the equality of all citizens under the law.

Moral Triage

A third objection relies on the notion of moral triage. The idea is that to owe a duty of justice to everyone else in the world would be overwhelming. So, we are justified in expending greater time and resources in fulfilling the duties of justice to our compatriots, especially if time and resources are limited. Such a criticism might be motivated by a concern typically raised against utilitarianism, that its conception of duty would have us maximizing the happiness of sentient beings in far away places and never engaging in activity that makes our personal lives meaningful.[44] In order to have the time and resources for meaningful personal lives, one might assert that it is necessary to focus on fulfilling only duties to persons who are near to us.

I have two responses. First, suppose that it is true that owing a duty of justice to everyone else in the world would leave personal lives crushed under the weight of moral responsibility. It does not follow that triage requires that we give priority to one's compatriots. A justified system of triage involves combining factors such as need with the likelihood of success. Many of those with the greatest need are in the developing countries, far from those with the greatest means in the more developed countries. It might be countered that the likelihood of success is greater when acting on duties to one's compatriots because effective institutions of national justice exist, while effective systems of international justice do not. Indeed this is often the case, but under existing conditions fulfilling duties of justice to noncompatriots frequently involves domestic action—not international action—such as supporting national legislation and policy that does not give priority to the interests of one's compatriots over the duties of justice owed to noncompatriots. So, the existence of institutions of national justice does not cut completely in the direction of helping only compatriots.

The second response is to note that the criticism seems, in many cases at least, to get the duties of justice wrong. There is merit in those criticisms of utilitarianism that contend it requires that personal lives be wholly devoted to maximizing general happiness, leaving neither time nor resources for personal pursuits.[45] This, however, entails only that cosmopolitan justice must not have maximizing demands, that it must not require that one's duty to others be to maximize, say, their welfare. It does not entail that we must ignore our duties to all others in order to live rewarding lives. Effectively acting on duties of justice, unlike other moral duties, requires effective institutions. Typically, states have population sizes that would crush individual lives under the weight of moral responsibility if meeting a duty of justice required a person to carry out distinct actions with respect to each compatriot. Justice does not require this. Rather, in a *just state* we often meet our duties of justice to others by obeying the laws that require us not to violate the rights of others and to contribute to the national treasury through taxation. When injustices exist, our duties of justice to our compatriots require that we play some role in developing just institutions or policies. This may involve as much as organizing and agitating or as little as advocating and voting. The international condition is one in which there are few, if any, effective institutions of justice. So, the duties of global justice require us to play a role in developing just global institutions and to support just domestic policy that affects noncompatriots. Should just global institutions come into being, there is no reason in principle to suppose that fulfilling the requirements they would place on us would prevent individuals from living rewarding lives any more than obeying just state institutions would.

PATRIOTISM

Some defenders of patriotism contend that appropriate love of country places duties on citizens to give preference to the interests of compatriots over noncompatriots, even if this violates duties of impartial justice.[46] Love of country, however, need not be unconditional. There is no contradiction in asserting that the demands of patriotism must be limited by the demands of justice.[47] There is no reason why our love for a person, for example, should cause us to refrain from moral judgment of that person's conduct. If one loves a person, one wants what is best for that person. It does not follow that one will withhold judgment when that person does wrong. Far from requiring one to refrain from morally judging the beloved, love may even encourage this. This is, of course, an old theme. Aristotle says of friends, "They may be said actually to restrain each other from evil: since good men neither err themselves nor permit their friends to err."[48]

There is no reason to suppose, then, that a patriotism limited by the demands of justice is impossible. Indeed, it seems more plausible to maintain that appropriate love of country by no means implies giving priority to the interest of compatriots over duties of justice; rather, it implies that one seek to make one's country just. Suppose that one responds that such a conception of patriotism leaves it denuded because it potentially involves refraining from supporting the policies of one's country when they conflict with the just claims of other states.[49] If love for a person or country does not require that the lover refrain from making impartial moral judgments about the beloved, then it is only blind loyalty, not patriotism, which is denuded by a withdrawal of support for a country when it commits an injustice.

There are more plausible accounts of the duties of patriotism that are based upon the fact that compatriots exist in a common political association.[50] If we have democratic duties to our compatriots, it is quite plausible that we have duties to limit inequalities so that they are consistent with healthy democratic politics. The idea is that sufficiently large socioeconomic inequalities give rise to inequalities in power that corrupt democratic processes, or may render the worst-off either unable to participate, because of educational and other disadvantages, or unwilling to participate, because of a justified loss of faith in the political process. These reasons are not sufficient, however, to justify the view that redistributive claims of compatriots necessarily trump those of noncompatriots.

It might be claimed that my cosmopolitanism is too moderate. Perhaps I have conceded too much in recognizing a class of special claims of justice that can be pressed by compatriots but not by noncompatriots.[51] If state borders are morally arbitrary, why should one's duties of justice be any different to those who are inside them than to those outside them? It is not state borders, however, that are the basis of the distinction I have drawn. Rather, the fact of political association serves to distinguish the different duties. Still, it might be pressed, if state borders are arbitrary then so are the divisions between political arrangements that exist within borders. This may be true, but it does not entail the conclusion that there are no differences of duties to compatriots and noncompatriots. There are two reasons for this. First, earlier I argued that the mere fact of association among persons regardless of the justification of the association can produce duties. The fact of the matter is that compatriots have one kind of association and noncompatriots have another. These generate different duties. Second, states may be effective and efficient institutions, or part of an effective institutional arrangement, for protecting persons' human rights and their claims to a democratic voice in the political institutions that affect them. If so, then there would be duties of justice to compatriots to ensure the equal value of the institutional means for participating in political life.

In the next chapter I shall discuss in greater detail the redistributive claims that noncompatriots may make. By way of comparison with the claims in the name of democratic politics, I mention here only the principle of fair equality of opportunity. Suppose that substantial inequalities in the conditions of adults are morally justified. A theory of justice that permits substantial inequalities in one generation on the basis of desert or permitting consensual transactions will have to neutralize those inequalities for the next generation in order to remain consistent with the moral equality of persons. The fact that a child's parents were more deserving (however that is measured) does not entail that the child should have a head start in life. Alternatively, if it is permissible for autonomous adults who choose, and do not prevent others from choosing, to engage in pursuits that lead to a privileged social status, this must be in part because no one started out with institutionally secured advantages that made their privilege more likely. Hence, even for theories of justice based upon desert or freedom of contract, the moral equality of persons requires a commitment to fair equality of opportunity as one of the principles of justice.[52] Fair equality of opportunity requires that the permissible inequalities in one generation not affect the chances of success in achieving permissible positions of privilege in the next generation.

Fair equality of opportunity is only a minimally egalitarian distributive principle because it merely limits the permissible effects of inequality for subsequent generations, but does not limit the extent of inequality in the present generation. Although fair equality of opportunity is minimally egalitarian, the present global distribution of resources deviates massively from it. If equality of opportunity were realized, a child growing up in rural Mozambique would be statistically as likely as the child of a senior executive at a Swiss bank to reach the position of the latter's parent. Because of differences in educational and health infrastructures and in effective capacities for meeting security and subsistence needs, children in the poorest developing countries are very far from having the same opportunities for success that the privileged children in the developed world enjoy. Achieving fair equality of opportunity globally would require significant wealth transfers from the wealthiest persons of the developed world to the developing world to support educational, health, food, and security programs.

Consider the relationship between the claims that compatriots may make on the basis of democratic duties and those that noncompatriots may make on the basis of fair equality of opportunity. Claims are competitive when fulfillment of both requires drawing on the same stock of resources, usually money. The claims of compatriots to social conditions permitting political equality and of noncompatriots to fair equality of opportunity are competitive. When claims are competitive, establishing a resolution is urgent. In such cases, there are three possibilities for resolution: (1) The background commitments of justice require fulfilling one kind of claim, but not the other; (2) the background commitments of justice require fulfilling both claims and it is economically and politically feasible to generate the resources to do so; (3) the background commitments of justice require fulfilling both claims but it is not feasible to do so, in which case one must be met at the expense of the other or both must be only partially fulfilled.

I have argued that there is no reason in general to suppose that the duties of justice to compatriots that originate from a common political association trump the duties of justice to noncompatriots, or vice versa. Are there reasons in this particular case for believing that justice requires a prior commitment to either compatriots or noncompatriots? Richard Miller argues that giving compatriots privilege is required by a morality of equal respect, because compatriots of all countries (even the per capita poorer ones) should appreciate the importance of maintaining mutual trust and the appropriate incentives for obeying the law, both of which domestic redistribution effects.[53] However, persons in all countries (even the per capita wealthy ones) should also appreciate the importance of ensuring that positions of privilege in the global economy be equally open to all. I see no reason in this case to give privilege to either the claims of compatriots or noncompatriots. If this is right, then the first of the three possible resolutions is unavailable.

If claims are competitive, and if both are required by justice, then it is best for institutions of justice to ensure that both be fulfilled. In the case under discussion, it would be best if wealth in developed countries were directed so as to achieve both a just political system among compatriots and equality of opportunity in the global economy. Suppose that there were compelling evidence that, due to the resistance of those with greater resources, this was unfeasible. This would be a moral loss that should be recognized as such. Moreover, it would be an avoidable loss caused by those resisting, which means that they are responsible for an injustice. Be that as it may, is there some nonarbitrary way to decide which duty should be sacrificed in the supposed circumstance? If we are considering the matter from the perspective of which duties wealthy persons in developed countries should meet, principles of triage would cut in different directions. The greatest need is likely to be among noncompatriots where deprivation is greatest. The most effective response is likely to be among compatriots where extensive state institutions of redistribution exist and can be operated or built upon. Effective response, however, may weigh more heavily than extent of need because what is important is achieving what justice demands. So, there may be reason to prefer compatriots in this circumstance. I wish to stress, however, that this is not a justification for giving priority to domestic duties of justice over global ones. It is merely an attempt to understand what should be done when those with social power refuse to meet their duties.

In fact global distributive justice requires more than merely respecting equality of opportunity: It requires limits on global inequality. I shall discuss this in Chapter 5. If it is the case that a duty of justice to noncompatriots requires limiting global inequalities, then such a duty would compete with the duty of justice to compatriots to redistribute wealth in order to achieve political justice, and the points about competitive claims made in the previous paragraphs would continue to apply.

NATIONALISM

The nationalist positions that challenge the argument I have been making are those that hold that one's co-nationals are to be preferred in matters of justice over those who are not co-nationals. Co-nationals are distinct from compatriots. Compatriots are members of the same system of governance, the vast majority of which are multinational. Co-membership in a system of governance is not a necessary condition for co-nationality. The criteria for judging whether two people are compatriots is wholly objective: It depends upon their citizenship or residency status. This is not true of the criteria for co-nationals. A common view among theorists of nationalism is that in order to be a member of a nation one must identify oneself as such.[54] Not all compatriots then are co-nationals, and some co-nationals may not be compatriots. I shall consider two distinct nationalist challenges to the position that I am defending. Strong nationalism holds that duties of justice arise only among those who share a national culture. Weak nationalism does not limit duties of justice to co-nationals, but holds that co-nationals ought to be given preference over others in matters of justice. Since I take duties of justice to arise out of associations, my view might appear to be particularly vulnerable to these nationalist challenges. Indeed Tamir, for example, argues that duties of justice are associative duties and that nations are associations that generate such duties.[55]

Arguments from the objective good of cultural membership, examined in Chapter 7, may provide the basis for national self-determination, but they do not make the case for preferring one's co-nationals in matters of justice. For example, Will Kymlicka argues that persons require a cultural context in order for options to have meaning.[56] If autonomy without meaningful choice is impossible, then autonomy without a culture is impossible. This claim, however, does not entail that co-nationals ought to be given preference; it is a claim about the objective good of cultural membership. The claim might provide support for state policies to defend national cultures impartially. It does not entail the view that one ought to be partial to one's co-nationals.

Strong nationalism might be thought to follow from the claim that goods are only intelligible from within the context of a culture.[57] In other words, if cultural relativism about justice were true, then one might think that the duties of justice are limited to co-nationals. There are, however, two problems with this view. First, if the claim that the intelligibility of goods requires a cultural framework is entailed by a more general claim that goods are specific to associations, then strong nationalism is false because there is a global association that also has standards of the good that apply cross-culturally. Second, the meta-ethical position of cultural relativism does not necessarily entail limiting duties of justice to one's culture. If it is a cultural belief that duties of justice exist toward persons who are not members of one's culture, then, according to cultural relativism, they do. Cultural relativism alone will not suffice, but in combination with the empirical premise that all national cultures take duties of justice to be limited to co-nationals, it entails the strong nationalist limitation. Even if the meta-ethical claim were true, the empirical one is surely false. For example, at least some of the theoreticians of Afrikaner nationalism seemed to think that they were doing right by Africans through their policy of the "self-determination" of "independent" homelands. Hence, this argument in defense of strong nationalism fails.

Weak nationalism is intuitively more plausible but no less fraught. An analysis of Thomas Hurka's defense of weak nationalism reveals problems characteristic of many nationalist arguments.[58] He employs an analogy to the family, a common argumentative strategy among nationalists. The analogy is meant to show that just as one is morally required to show some preference for one's family members, so one is required to show some preference for one's co-nationals. The first difficulty for all such arguments is that the intimate relations of mutual dependence that often are the basis of familial preference are generally lacking in relations between most co-nationals, the majority of whom are invariably strangers to one another.

Hurka is able to avoid this problem with the claim that neither familial nor co-national preferences are based upon the intimacy of the relationship, but upon a shared history of activity with mutually beneficial results. The truth of this claim would seem to establish nations as associations generative of moral duties. Establishing the claim, however, is problematic. In order to illustrate the shared history of activity, Hurka does what many nationalists do: He blurs the distinction between co-nationals and compatriots.[59] His example of a shared history of activity is the creation of the Canadian health care system. Although commonly referred to as a "national health care system," this merely trades on the ambiguity of the term *nation* in common usage. In fact, the system was created by a state institution, the parliament, is funded by federal taxes, and is available to Canadians no matter what their nationality.

Suppose we grant Hurka, despite his example, that national activity does yield benefits to members analogous to the benefits yielded by familial activity. This would establish nations as associations and, therefore, the existence of special duties to co-nationals. It does not establish that these duties are duties of justice. Recall that duties of justice are directed toward the institutions of public life. These are institutions wielding political and social power. The claim that the (assumed) duties of co-nationals are duties of justice entails that public institutions may have a national character, may enforce certain national conceptions of the good over others, and therefore grant privileges to those who adhere to such conceptions that are not granted to others.

Here a comparison to familial duties is useful. Many people think we have moral duties to family members—whatever the source of such duties—that we do not have to others. This does not entail that political power may be used to grant privileges to family members. Even on the assumption that families or nations generate special moral duties, an additional argument is required to establish that these are duties of justice. The claim that we have some special relationship to, or concern for, another person does not establish the claim that political and social power should favor that person over others.[60] To believe otherwise, is to fail to see that duties of justice cannot simply be assimilated to the broader class of moral duties. Indeed, nepotism is generally regarded as an affront to justice. If national duties are similar to familial ones, then the use of public institutions to favor co-nationals is equally suspicious.

It is possible to generalize the lessons learned from analyzing the claims of weak nationalists. Two problems confront the weak (and if the weak, then also the strong) nationalist position. One is establishing nations as associations at all. Efforts to do this often conflate the distinction between co-nationals and compatriots. The other is establishing that the supposed moral duties we owe associates are duties of justice. If one fails to distinguish between the duties of justice and other moral duties, one may fail to see that duties of justice, unlike others, are directed toward our relations with others as mediated by political and social institutions and policy. In arguing that public institutions and policy should be designed to prefer some class of people over others, it is insufficient to establish that one has certain moral duties to a particular class that one does not have to the others. For what must be established is not just how *individuals* should conduct themselves, but how *public institutions* should operate. In general, equal respect for persons establishes a powerful defeasible presumption against the operation of public institutions to prefer some class of persons governed by them over others; such preferences are tainted with the suspicion of unfair or invidious discrimination. Insofar as nationalists advocate using state power on behalf of co-nationals, they need especially convincing reasons if they are to overcome the presumption against discrimination. Appeals to the special duties of individuals to co-nationals on the analogy of the special duties to family members will not do.

There is a special problem of accounting for the nature of putative national moral duties for those nationalists, such as Tamir, who hold that one's national identity is a matter of individual choice.[61] This view entails that one can opt out of one's duties of justice by changing one's mind about one's identity. As I insisted earlier, generally moral duties are not demands that one can free oneself of merely by changing one's mind. Suppose that a person is convinced by a utilitarian account of morality that entails a duty to maximize happiness, but in the face of circumstances that person decides that this account of the demands of morality is wrong. She may change her mind about what morality requires of her, but this does not imply that what morality really requires has changed.

A possible rejoinder to this criticism is that there are certain duties that one can opt out of by a change of identity. A person resigning from a club can change identity from member to nonmember and is thereby relieved of the duties of membership. In light of the example of philosophical orientation in the previous paragraph, this rejoinder suggests it is necessary to consider whether one's national identity is more like one's philosophical orientation or more like one's status as a member of a club. If nationality were indistinguishable from citizenship, it would be clear that national identity would be more like one's status as a member of a club. In both cases there would be objective processes by which one acquires or sheds one's identity. This is lacking when one adopts or renounces a philosophical orientation. Doing this merely changes how one thinks about the world and one's self. If one takes the primary marker of one's nationality to be subjective, then national identity looks more like a philosophical orientation. As I argued in the previous paragraph, a change in one's philosophical orientation does not change one's duties. Thus, the objection remains that no moral duties can flow from national identity, subjectively construed.

PROTECTIONISM AND IMMIGRATION

The kinds of domestic policy questions that are especially important from the cosmopolitan perspective are those affecting the interests of noncompatriots. Cosmopolitanism is most controversial where it refuses to grant privilege to the interests of compatriots over the duties owed to noncompatriots. Two examples are immigration and protectionist trade policy. Restrictive immigration policies have the effect of denying noncompatriots the opportunities for development and advancement that an economy of a country offers its citizens. Protectionist trade policies increase the costs of importing goods into a country and therefore reduce trade opportunities for other countries—which may have the effect of also reducing employment opportunities and living standards in those countries.

Restrictive immigration policies and protectionist trade policies complement one another. The former policies discourage immigrants from looking for work in a new country, while the latter policies reduce employment opportunities in the would-be immigrants' country. If either is employed by a relatively more developed country against a relatively less developed one (as is typical), it will protect the privileges of the citizens of the more developed country from competition by the citizens of the less developed. Both kinds of policies then raise questions of global distributive justice. More-

over, it seems reasonable to suppose that protectionist trade policies, by reducing opportunities in the targeted country, increase incentives for persons
to immigrate, even illegally, in pursuit of a better life. To this extent the
analysis of restrictive immigration policies may follow that of restrictive
trade policies, but restrictive immigration policies raise several additional
questions. These include the justified limits on the right to move freely, the
rights of states to protect national cultures, and the rights of states to protect their institutions of justice. I shall begin by discussing the relatively
more simple matter of protectionism and build upon that discussion to address the more complicated matter of immigration.

Protectionism

Protectionist trade policies have the name *protectionist* because they
shield domestic goods from foreign competition. If the name is not used
merely pejoratively, it is significant because it suggests that the standards
for measuring whether the policy has been effective and whether it remains necessary are whether the domestic goods have in fact been
shielded from competition and whether they continue to need to be.

Trade tariffs increase the price of imported goods, thereby reducing demand for them and probably increasing demand for local cheaper counter-
parts. Such policies protect the interests of local capitalists whose return on
investment depends upon the profitability of the business in which they are
invested. They also protect the interests of local workers whose jobs may be
threatened if the profitability of their employers is threatened by imports.[62]
This explains the cross-class enthusiasm for "buy locally" campaigns in
many countries around the world.

The losers in the protectionist game are the capitalists and workers in the
countries whose exports have become the object of protectionist tariffs, as
well as the consumers who fail to receive the benefits of marketplace competition. Capitalists lose because they lose market share in another country.
Workers lose because a smaller market share means less production, and
less production means fewer employees. The more urgent claims of injustice are made by the unemployed and poor who suffer more greatly than
the capitalists as a result of protectionist policies.

Protectionist policies violate a principle of fair equality of opportunity.
Such policies create different sales conditions for producers of equivalent
goods, thereby affecting their ability to succeed. If this were to occur between two different domestic producers, it might be described as a failure
of equal protection under the law. Since one's place of birth is morally arbitrary, it should not affect one's life prospects or one's access to opportunities. There is considerable consensus about this if the principle is applied to

compatriots. Citizens of a state ought not to be disadvantaged in the pursuit of their goals simply because of the region of the state in which they were born. Protectionist trade policy exemplifies how domestic public policy can negatively effect the interests of noncompatriots by endowing one's place of birth with moral significance.

Advocates of protectionism typically rest their position on one of three arguments. First, they might assert that because citizens and residents pay taxes to their government they deserve to benefit from its policies. This, however, does not imply that protectionist policies are justified. For there remains the question of what sort of benefits a citizen is entitled to. Payment of taxes alone does not establish such an entitlement. Just because I pay taxes does not mean that I am entitled to be provided with the job of my choice. So, the fact that citizens and residents of one country pay taxes, and those living in another country do not, does not establish an entitlement of the former to be protected against the competition of the latter. The claim to an entitlement generally requires justification independent of taxpaying. Typically, payment of taxes is an obligation incurred by virtue of the provision of the entitlement, rather than the ground of the entitlement.

A second defense of protectionism is that import tariffs are justified because producers in certain other countries have an unfair advantage over local producers. This response is most dubious when what constitutes the alleged unfair advantage is poorer working conditions and environmental standards in foreign countries. As I noted earlier, ordinarily there are two distinct ways of understanding fairness and therefore its denial, unfairness. One way to understand unfairness is as an advantage due to a *violation* of an established rule. The other is as an advantage due to the *enforcement* of an established rule or practice that is unfair. The charge of unfair advantage must be examined in light of both of these senses.

The first sense of unfair advantage conjures up images of a race in which one's opponent has cheated by, say, taking illegal performance-enhancing drugs. This sense of unfairness applies only to the opponent who is not playing by the established principles of the game. In the absence of a common set of constraints, if one producer does not accept constraints imposed upon the other, there is no unfair advantage in the first sense. It might well be better for workers and for the environment if the constraints governing the one governed both, but in the absence of global labor and environmental laws it is not unfair in the first sense that they do not.

If, however, it would be better if all producers adhered to stricter environmental and labor standards—which are not currently in place globally—is it unfair in the second sense if some producers do not? The argument that it is can be put in the form of an analogy. If laws permitting racial discrimination are in place, a beneficiary of those laws has an unfair advantage in the second sense over a victim of those laws. The advantage is unfair because the law itself is unjust. Similarly, the absence of environmental and labor protections in some states is an injustice, giving producers in those states an unfair advantage over producers in other states.

The obvious question for the argument in the preceding paragraph is whether this rather odd analogy is apt. To be clear, it is an analogy between, on the one hand, the victim of racially discriminatory laws and the person in a country with strong environmental and labor laws, and, on the other hand, between the beneficiary of racially discriminatory laws and the worker in a country lacking strong environmental and labor laws. It argues that just as the beneficiary of racially discriminatory laws has an unfair advantage over the victim, so the working person living in a state lacking strong environmental and labor laws has an unfair advantage over the working person living in a state with strong laws. Notice that the victim of racially discriminatory laws is unequivocally disadvantaged by those laws. There are, presumably, employment and educational opportunities that simply are not available to that person. Moreover, the beneficiary of racially discriminatory laws is unequivocally advantaged by these laws, having been freed from possible competitors in the labor market. However, working people in states with strong environmental and labor laws are not unequivocally disadvantaged by these. Many persons living in states without strong environmental and labor laws are not unequivocally advantaged by working in low-paying and unsafe work conditions and living in unhealthy environments. The claim of unfair advantage in the second sense is dubious because the advantages are, at best, mixed blessings. The analogy simply is not apt.

A third defense of protectionism is advanced in the name of egalitarianism. Consider the following claims by Richard Falk:

> The structures of regional and global economic governance are taking root in a variety of settings, including the European Community, NAFTA, the economic summits of the Group of Seven, the nascent World Trade Organization (WTO), IMF/World Bank. The rationale for such frameworks is almost entirely market-oriented and economistic, emphasizing contributions to trade and investment, efficiencies of production and distribution, and procedures for reducing the relevance of sovereign states, especially their intrusion of people-oriented protectionist, social, and local factors that help the weak withstand the strong.[63]

Falk's position seems to be twofold. First, protectionism is in the interests of the disadvantaged and the particularly vulnerable in a country, because it shields them and their employers from global market competition. Second, free market trade serves only the interests of the already privileged capitalists who are able to exploit their superior market access.

The claim that protectionist policies can benefit the disadvantaged may have some force from a parochial perspective, that is, if one is considering only the disadvantaged of a particular country. If local employers are protected from global market competition, then they might employ those whom they would not employ under global competition, or they might employ them at higher wages than they would under global competition. Restricting access to this market involves restricting the access of employers in other countries. So, once the perspective is broadened beyond the borders of one country, it is less plausible that protectionism benefits the disadvantaged.[64]

The second challenge concerns the beneficiaries of free-market trade policies. The claim, if taken as a factual one, is that only the interests of the capitalist class are served by these policies. If my analysis in the previous paragraph is true, this claim is false. Indeed, it is neither the case that only capitalists' interests are served since their employees gain jobs, nor true that all capitalists interests are served since competition requires losers. If the challenge is taken as a normative claim that justice requires a more egalitarian international distribution of wealth than the market produces, I would agree. The global market does not ensure equality of opportunity, let alone limit inequalities. Protectionist policies do not serve this function either and cannot therefore be justified on this basis. If the criticism is that under current regimes of "free trade" the interests of more powerful capitalists in wealthier countries are served because multilateral tariff reduction plans require less-developed countries to be the first to reduce tariffs, this is a powerful indictment of such regimes, but not necessarily a defense of protectionism. The criticism can just as readily support the requirement of a more fair tariff reduction plan.

One important question that is suggested by the Falk quotation is, What counts as protectionism? If a country passes product safety laws that prohibit certain sorts of products and many of the products that would be prohibited by those laws are of foreign origin, does this count as a protectionist law? Increasingly such laws are being challenged within the World Trade Organization (WTO) and even being struck down. The fact that a law restricts certain kinds of dangerous content in goods or goods manufactured under exploitative conditions is not sufficient to make it protectionist. If the law is stated in general terms without identifying specific countries of origin, then it would apply equally to domestically and foreign-produced goods. If it does not single out foreign-produced goods for special restrictions, then it is not protectionist. Additionally, if its goal is to protect public health or to discourage certain kinds of activities of production, then the measure of its success is not in how well it shields local producers from competition, but how well it contributes to these other goals. If the law turns out to be ineffective in meeting such goals, then it would lose its justification, despite the fact that it may protect local producers. So, a criticism of protectionism does not entail a criticism of legislation to ensure product safety and decent working conditions, WTO practice to the contrary notwithstanding. It is sometimes noted that current "free trade" regimes are directed more toward eroding existing legislative measures ensuring health, safety, and decent working conditions, than toward real protectionism.[65] To the extent that this is true, such regimes cannot be justified on grounds of fair equality of opportunity.

The discussion of what counts as protectionism suggests a possible defense of trade tariffs that is not protectionist. The reasoning involves the claim that tariff barriers for products created in states with unsafe environmental practice and exploitative working conditions help to promote fairness for those who live and work in such conditions by providing incentives for change. Sometimes advocates of such policies refer to them as "fair trade" rather than "protectionist" policies.[66] The goal of fair trade policy is to protect the interests of noncompatriots, not domestic interests. This entails a significant difference for the monitoring and evaluation of whether the trade policies remain justified. Protectionist policies would serve their goal as long as the threat of competition existed and the policies reduced that threat. Fair trade policies would serve their goal as long as they were directed toward states with unsafe environments and exploitative working conditions and they could reasonably be thought to be improving those conditions. Contrary to the analogy discussed in the second defense of protectionism, the present account shows the unfairness of freetrade is not in the *advantages* that it confers to those living in countries with unsafe environments and exploitative work conditions; it lies instead in the *disadvantages* to those people, who might be thought of as comparable to the victims of racially discriminatory laws rather than to the beneficiaries.

One might suspect that this amounts to a distinction without a difference. If protectionist policies serve their goal as long as the threat of competition exists and the policies reduce that threat, and if fair trade policies serve their goal as long as they are directed toward states with unsafe environments and exploitative working conditions, the two policies may frequently yield tariffs on the same range of products. For it is states with unsafe environmental practices and exploitative working conditions that often pose the greatest competitive threat. This much is true. However, the feature that distinguishes the protectionist and fair trade rationales for import tariffs is that the fair trade rationale takes such tariffs as justified only if they serve to promote improved conditions in the targeted state. So, even if a competitive threat exists from a country with fewer environmental protections and inferior working conditions, if import tariffs will not improve these conditions then they are not justified, according to the fair trade account.

The fair trade position is superior to the protectionist position since its success is not measured by whether it protects the privileges of compatriots but whether it improves the conditions for those who are (typically) worse off than one's compatriots. It does, however, raise moral problems of its own. Consider the analogy between those persons living in states lacking enforcement of strong environmental and labor laws and those who are the victims of unfair racial discrimination. The problem with this analogy is that those persons living in such states are not unequivocally disadvantaged by the lack of enforcement, while those who are the victims of unfair racial discrimination are. Let's accept that the absence of enforcement constitutes an injustice suffered by persons living without the protection of such laws. This lack of enforcement might nonetheless give them a certain advantage with respect to states that enforce strict environmental and labor laws. It might encourage investment for production and therefore employment, which is precisely what the protectionists are worried about. The fact that the citizens of states lacking strong environmental and labor regulations, unlike the victims of racially discriminatory laws, are not unequivocally disadvantaged indicates a flaw in the analogy between them. Hence, the remedies offered in the two situations contain a disanalogy as well. The victim of racially discriminatory laws is unequivocally advantaged by the destruction of such laws. If the imposition of protective tariffs against countries with exploitative work conditions and unsafe environmental policies helps to improve these conditions, it may also reduce employment in already poor countries as they lose some of their competitive advantage. So, the victims of these conditions are not unequivocally advantaged by successful fair trade policies.

The adoption of *international* environmental and labor standards bears some advantages over *bilateral* approaches to establishing incentives for healthier and less-exploitative production. The adoption of certain basic uniform production standards (allowing for variations in, say, the level of minimum wages among states, but not in standards of basic safety, age of employment, and freedom of association and collective bargaining) may raise production costs in developing countries relative to those of developed countries and reduce some of their competitive advantage, but it need not equalize costs. Moreover, it would reduce opportunities for any one particular state to undercut another by employing substandard conditions.[67] Proper monitoring of such standards by a truly representative international institution could also help to prevent powerful states from merely imposing rules on weaker ones as may more readily occur in bilateral relations. So, again the blessing is mixed, but more positive. Although international labor and environmental standards may increase unemployment as the result of cost increases, they may also produce greater security against being undercut and against being subjected to the wishes of dominant powers.

The problems with fair trade policies identified above suggest that they can at best be only a partial solution to underdevelopment and poor environmental and working conditions in poorer countries. Developing countries need access to a globally financed, sustainable development fund, which would give them the resources for economic growth within the constraints of more favorable environmental and working conditions. Indeed, this is the remedy most consistent with justice for the persons presently living and working in these unfavorable conditions. I shall defend this proposal further in Chapter 4.

A second arguably nonprotectionist defense of trade tariffs is found in the underdevelopment literature. Trade theories of underdevelopment hold that due to the higher wages in certain countries the price of their commodities will be higher, which forces lower-wage countries to pay more for their imports. The result is unequal exchange.[68] Trade tariffs might be advocated in less-developed countries to shield them from the effects of unequal exchange. This justification of trade tariffs more closely resembles protectionism than does the fair trade justification because it serves the interests of compatriots as opposed to noncompatriots. However, the tariffs are employed to protect those in lower-wage countries rather than higher-wage ones. So, arguably they do not violate fair equality of opportunity.

It is debatable whether the unequal exchange account of underdevelopment is correct. One problem with it is that it is based upon the assumption of perfect capital mobility generating equal rates of profit around the world, but a lack of labor mobility that is supposed to generate wage differentials. It is not obvious, however, that wage differentials would come to be in a world of perfect capital mobility.[69] If we assume, however, that the unequal exchange thesis is roughly correct, trade tariffs would establish friction for capital mobility, but they do not present the only remedy to unequal exchange. Indeed, Arghiri Emmanuel, who first developed the thesis of unequal exchange, argued that the remedies to it are economic diversification to send up prices of exports and send down prices of imports, or institutions of global redistribution to compensate persons in low-wage countries for the inequality they suffer.[70] Moreover, global redistribution is more appropriate than tariff erection since it places the responsibility for the well-being of persons within the larger economic association of the global economy rather than the state economy.

Immigration

Immigration restrictions share the problem of inequality of opportunity that taints protectionist trade policies. Because limitations on immigration impose barriers to the pursuit of goals on some people because of where they are born, but not upon others, they have the effect of distributing opportunities for personal advancement in a morally arbitrary way. In addition to this, restrictive immigration policies appear to be a blatant violation of the right to freedom of movement.

Suppose that the charge of violating freedom of movement is challenged in the following way. Freedom of movement is valuable only insofar as it permits people to pursue opportunities. Hence, citing a policy for violating freedom of movement is redundant if it has already been cited for violating a principle of fair equality of opportunity. The premise of this argument, however, does not entail its conclusion. The reason is that a policy may deny pursuit of opportunities (which the premise asserts to be the problem with restricting free movement) to all persons equally. In such a case there is no inequality of opportunity, but there is denial of permission to pursue opportunities. Equality of opportunity is a distributive principle, for it is sensitive to differences in the distribution of opportunities but not to the lack of opportunity per se. So, we can, without redundancy, charge restrictive immigration policies both with violating a principle of equality of opportunity and violating a principle of freedom of movement.

One might try to reject the idea of treating immigration policy as a matter of justice at all. Michael Walzer argues that the effects of immigration controls on would-be immigrants are not a matter of justice, but of charity.[71] If this is the case, then the principles of fair equality of opportunity and freedom of movement simply do not apply. Walzer's view is that the morality of immigration is a question of the demands of moral duty, the duty of mutual aid or charity, but not duties of justice. Charity is both less demanding and more permissive of discretion than is justice. Walzer's argument, though, seems to endorse justice-positivism about duties of justice to noncompatriots. He contends that duties of cosmopolitan justice would arise only if there were already a system of global governance. "If . . . all human beings were members of a global state, state membership would clearly have been distributed equally; and there would be nothing more to do."[72] However, as I argued earlier, the fact that institutions to enforce duties of global justice do not exist in no way entails that the duties do not exist. Hence, Walzer's refusal to view immigration as a matter of justice to noncompatriots is unjustified.

The kernel of truth in Walzer's view is that questions of membership are questions of the demands of mutual aid or charity when the would-be members are not part of a broader association generating duties of justice. If two societies existed in isolation from one another, then persons in the one society would not be under a duty of justice to admit persons of another society. This would, as Walzer believes, be a matter of charity.

There are at least four reasons that might be offered for placing some restrictions on immigration. First, limiting immigration is sometimes a response to demands from citizens and residents, who are taxpayers, for protection against competition from noncompatriots who are not taxpayers.

Paying taxes, so the argument goes, confers an entitlement to be protected that citizens and residents may invoke, and that prospective immigrants may not invoke. As I have argued, paying taxes does not generally establish an entitlement where one does not exist for other reasons. So, in order to defend immigration restrictions, an independent argument is needed.

The second reason for limiting immigration invokes the economic interest of citizens.[73] Current citizens might be economically harmed by immigration in one of two ways. They may lose their jobs to immigrants who underbid them in the labor market, or they may be compelled to accept lower wages in order to compete with immigrants who underbid them. Both of these possibilities assume that immigrants will primarily seek jobs held by current citizens, rather than, for example, start their own businesses and eventually become employers themselves. They assume furthermore that labor unions will be either unwilling or unable to organize immigrants in order to bring their wages up rather than the wages of current citizens down. It is important to make explicit these assumptions, because the force of the criticism diminishes as the plausibility of the assumptions dim.

There are reasons to doubt that immigration has a generally negative impact on the economic well-being of citizens of the state to which immigration is directed.[74] Suppose for the sake of argument that it does. The reason offered for restricting immigration, then, is that it hurts the economic interests of native workers. The reason has merit only if the relevant economic interests are entitlements of justice. Do persons have an entitlement to be protected in their jobs from noncompatriot labor market competition? Assuming that the labor market is a just institution for selecting employees among compatriots, the claim that there is such an entitlement would have to be that market competition from noncompatriots is unjust. However, it is hard to find a reason why market competition for jobs would be justified among compatriots, but not between compatriots and noncompatriots. The same reasons that count in favor of market competition in the one case do so in the other.

Market competition makes employer choice effective, ensuring that control over resources (not necessarily ownership) is effective. Competition helps employers find the persons with the appropriate skills at the best price, thus increasing the efficiency of the enterprise. Competition is not, of course, without its costs. There cannot be competition without losers. Egalitarians point to such costs to make the case that the labor market must be complemented by redistributive mechanisms. If the efficiency benefits of competition are significant, and if costs generally can be ameliorated, then such costs do not outweigh the benefits. Moreover, since effective control over resources and efficient enterprises seem to be necessary for an efficient economy, a lack of competition would probably result in a Pareto inferior distribution of resources.[75]

The advocate of restricted immigration might respond that the losses to efficiency are justified in the name of a greater socioeconomic value, for example either justice or equality. It has often been argued that the labor market is unjust since it rewards persons on the basis of talents and abilities for which they are not responsible. It is sheer luck that one was born with marketable talents or into a family that cultivated abilities. Those who are lucky would appear, then, to be undeserving of any greater share of resources than the unlucky. Assuming that this argument is sound, it still does not make the case for restricting labor market competition to compatriots for two reasons. First, the very same considerations of luck underlie the contention that compatriots should not be privileged in matters of justice over noncompatriots, simply by virtue of being born on the right side of the border—something for which they are not responsible. Second, by arguing against the justice of the labor market in toto, the argument proves too much for the typical advocate of restricted immigration who would like to preserve the market between compatriots, but not between compatriots and noncompatriots.

The argument for limiting immigration in the name of equality fares no better. On the assumption that labor market competition from immigrants will lower wages for native workers (as noted above, this is not obvious), income and wealth differentials within a country may grow as the result of permissive immigration policies. If we suppose that a policy is unjust if it makes the least advantaged even more disadvantaged, then perhaps less efficiency is the cost of ensuring distributive justice. This argument is, however, plausible only if one adopts a parochial perspective that takes the least advantaged to be the least advantaged among one's compatriots. Those immigrants who would underbid current citizens in the labor market are quite plausibly improving their condition by immigrating. Unless the least-advantaged compatriots are less advantaged than potential immigrants, restricted immigration does not protect the least advantaged. (Open immigration does not necessarily serve the interests of the least advantaged either, since often they cannot take advantage of the liberty to immigrate. However, I have been arguing against restricted immigration on the basis of fair equality of opportunity, not the benefit to the least advantaged.)

If either of the previous two arguments in defense of immigration restrictions were sound, governments would be permitted broad latitude in limiting immigration. They could do so whenever current taxpayers demanded it or whenever the economic interests of current citizens and residents were threatened. As we have seen, the arguments are not sound. There are, however, two additional reasons for limiting immigration that would offer far less latitude to governments than the previous two.

A common practice among states is to limit immigration on the basis of nationality. Insofar as the practice is a case of preferring co-nationals over others, it is unjust.[76] An advocate of such a policy might argue that it is justified not because co-national preference is justified, but because the survival of the national culture of a group of citizens within the state justifies it.[77] If we suppose that one's culture provides one with a context in which choices have meaning,[78] then preservation of a culture is required to preserve the liberty of the members of that culture. Moreover, if, as Rawls argues, a theory of justice that takes seriously the freedom and equality of all persons prioritizes liberty over socioeconomic equality,[79] then cultural preservation may be more important from the perspective of justice than equality of opportunity. Hence, an appeal to fair equality of opportunity would not justify open immigration in those cases in which immigration would threaten the survival of a local culture.[80] The benefits of cultural survival, however, would still have to balanced against the costs of limitations on freedom of movement.

Setting aside reasonable concerns about restricting freedom of movement, the force of the claim that cultural survival may trump fair equality of opportunity is significantly more limited than it might appear. Restricting immigration on this basis is justified only if the cultural *survival* of some group of citizens is threatened. Immigration could not be limited simply because citizens wished not to commingle with those of certain racial, ethnic, or national origin, or simply because they wished to maintain cultural purity or dominance. Since there is quite a lot that can be done short of restricting immigration in order to ensure cultural survival, it would be a rare circumstance in which the requirements of cultural survival justified restricting immigration.[81] Additionally, recognition of the good of culture in providing a context for the exercise of meaningful choice does not justify indefinite protection of a culture. It only justifies protection during the lifetime of those members of that culture who are too old to assimilate into another culture.[82] In other words, the trumping power of an appeal to cultural survival is further limited to those rare circumstances in which immigration would threaten the survival of the culture during the lifetime of adult members of that culture. Hence, although cultural survival in principle may provide a reason for forgoing fair equality of opportunity, the circumstances in which it would actually require this with respect to immigration policy are bound to be extremely rare. Even where they exist, freedom of movement may still compete with cultural survival as a reason not to restrict immigration.

A further reason for restricting immigration is to protect just state institutions. If open immigration policies would frustrate the capacity of the basic structure to satisfy the entitlements of justice that citizens and residents are owed, then immigration may be limited to the extent, but only to the extent, necessary for satisfying those entitlements.[83]

Unlike the second argument, this one is not based merely on the defense of the interests of compatriots; it is based on the duties of justice owed to citizens and residents. Why should the claims of protecting the institutions of justice take priority over the claims of noncompatriots to equality of opportunity and freedom of movement? The government's collection of revenue is justified in order that those taxed may fulfill their duties of justice to other persons through the exercise of government policy. Assuming that this is an effective way of ensuring that many just entitlements are protected by states, and assuming further that global institutions exist to protect whatever entitlements cannot be protected by state governments, then each state would be justified in spending its revenue both to support and to protect those state institutions that carry through on the duties of justice that citizens and residents owe each other and to pay its citizens' and residents' share in support of global institutions. State policy could be directed to protecting institutions of justice under these conditions for two reasons. First, this ensures that citizens and residents receive their just entitlements. Second, ex hypothesi noncitizens and residents are likewise receiving their just entitlements from other state and global institutions of justice. Such global conditions would not result in inequality of opportunity since under such conditions opportunity would not be a function of where one was born. Although it would permit some restrictions on freedom of movement, this would not affect opportunities since the requirement of justice would be satisfied in all states and globally effective institutions of justice would exist. Although this would involve some limitations on freedom of movement, restrictions are substantially less evil where those who are limited are not otherwise victims of injustice.

The picture painted above is, however, far from reality. Most states do not ensure that the just entitlements of citizens and residents that they could protect are protected. On the contrary, many states are systematic violators of these entitlements. Moreover, institutions of global distributive justice barely exist at all. Since limiting immigration under actual circumstances enforces inequality of opportunity, the case for it in the name of protecting just state institutions runs perilously close to the protection of undeserved privileges. However, there may be merit in such a policy despite this danger.[84] Limiting immigration may preserve something of value even to those who do not enjoy it, namely, examples of more just institutions. Imagine the case of a state statisfying the principles of egalitarian distributive justice. It may be true that those fortunate enough to be born in such a state have no entitlement to more opportunities than those who are born into bitter poverty in the developing world. However, the loss of an egalitarian model of wealth distribution would not only be a loss for the citizens of these countries, but for humanity in general since we have yet to construct enduring examples of egalitarianism.[85] Moreover, the inequality of opportunity that would be maintained by protecting just institutions may be partially mitigated by the pursuit of other matters of international justice, for example the advocacy of institutions of global distributive justice. Finally, lest it be thought that such compromises reveal the impracticality of the goal of cosmopolitan justice, it is worth noting that this problem exists precisely because justice is lacking in so many states of the world and there are no global institutions of wealth redistribution. If the effects of where one is born were not "so profound from the start," there would be far fewer material incentives to leave one's country of birth.

CONCLUSION

I have defended the existence of duties of justice to noncompatriots and the claim that these duties are consistent with the existence of duties of justice to compatriots as well. Moreover, one cannot rest on arguments in defense of policies benefiting compatriots if those policies violate duties of justice to noncompatriots. Rather, when the justified claims of either compatriots or noncompatriots affect the other, the claims of both groups have to be assessed in light of background considerations of justice that do not categorically weigh in favor of one party or the other. In the next chapter I shall further explore duties of global distributive justice in particular.

FOUR

Global Egalitarianism and Imperialism

National boundaries have become so porous that traditional distinctions between local, national, and international issues have become blurred. Policies formerly considered to be exclusively matters of "national concern" now have an impact on the ecological bases of other nations' development and survival. Conversely, the growing reach of some nations' policies—economic, trade, monetary, and most sectoral policies—into the "sovereign" territory of other nations limits the affected nations' options in devising national solutions to their "own" problems.

—The World Commission on
Environment and Development[1]

In Chapters 2 and 3 I defended principles of cosmopolitan justice and their corresponding duties. The arguments have been mostly concerned with justice taken generally. In this chapter I direct our attention to arguments about distributive justice in particular. It is possible that there may be something exceptional about duties of distributive justice that limit their application. I shall argue that duties of global egalitarian distributive justice exist, respond to skepticism about duties of global distributive justice, and then focus on the principle and object of distributive justice. Later, I apply the conclusions of moral theory to a matter of social theory, the theory of imperialism. Finally, two issues of importance to development are discussed: the indebtedness of many developing societies and the costs arising from global warming.

SKEPTICISM ABOUT DUTIES OF
GLOBAL DISTRIBUTIVE JUSTICE

Consider three possible worlds. In the first an international system of states exists, each in possession of well-working institutions of political and economic justice. Individual rights are upheld, democracy is operative, and global institutions ensure that inequalities around the globe are limited. The second is like the first but without the institutions of global distributive justice. So, although justice, including egalitarian distributive justice, is approximately satisfied within each state, gross inequalities incompatible with egalitarian distributive justice exist between persons internationally.

The third possible world is our own. Many states have imperfect commitments to political justice; many others have no such commitment. A commitment to global egalitarian distributive justice is almost nowhere to be found. Internationally, extreme inequalities exist. The United Nations Development Program notes that the assets of the world's 358 billionaires exceed the combined annual incomes of countries accounting for 45 percent of the world's population,[2] that 1.3 billion people now live on less than $370 a year,[3] and that 89 countries are worse off according to the human development index than they were ten years ago.[4]

These huge inequalities have dramatic effects on the life prospects of persons. One example of this is access to needed medical care. In Uganda the public health budget amounts to $12 per citizen per year.[5] According to one study, only 1 percent of the new medicines patented between 1975 and 1997 were for tropical diseases.[6] Easily curable but deadly diseases such as sleeping sickness go untreated in Africa because the purchasing power of persons there can command only 1 percent of world drug sales.[7] According to the World Health Organization, 8 million children die each year before the age of 5 from curable diseases.[8]

In seeking to remedy the injustices of our world, should we set as our goal the first possible world, which includes a system of just states *and* institutions of global distributive justice, or the second, which contains only just states? There is practical import to deciding whether a commitment to global egalitarianism is appropriate. If it is, then efforts to realize such change must necessarily have an international dimension.

Notice that the difference between the first and second possible worlds is not a difference about the scope of the values of liberty and democracy, nor even equality. If one upholds the second ideal, one takes the universality of the value of equality seriously. Any state that fails to institute principles of egalitarian distributive justice is in that way unjust. Rather, the difference between the first and second ideal concerns the scope of duties of distributive justice. The first ideal maintains, while the second one denies, that persons have duties of distributive justice that extend beyond the frontiers of the state in which they reside. I turn now to an examination of various skeptical arguments concerning the first ideal.

Rawls

John Rawls maintains that a duty of assistance exists to other peoples only if their society requires resources to establish just or decent social and political institutions. According to this account, no duty of distributive justice is owed to persons in other countries, no matter what the inequalities may be, if the social and political arrangements of their state are just or decent.[9] Rawls contrasts this view with a cosmopolitan account of distributive justice that takes persons as the object of duties of distributive justice and their well-being as important. Rawls maintains something akin to the second ideal described above, while cosmopolitans maintain a version of the first.

Rawls's reasons for limiting the duties of distributive justice are not entirely clear, because his chief argument involves drawing conclusions from two hypothetical cases.[10] In the first case, two just or decent societies decide to industrialize at different paces and save at different rates. As a result, although they once had the same level of wealth, over time one is twice as wealthy as the other. In the second hypothetical case, two just or decent societies respond differently to their commitment to equal justice for women, producing differential population growth and resulting, once again, in one being twice as wealthy as the other. In both cases Rawls emphasizes that, because the societies are just or decent, they are free and responsible for their own decisions. Indeed, this seems to be his primary point. Because the various persons are responsible for their differential wealth, it would be wrong to tax the wealthier society to support the poorer. I have three responses to his view.

First, the ability to take responsibility for one's ends is a feature of the model of persons that I defended in Chapter 2; so Rawls's criticism might be thought to have particular purchase on my account of cosmopolitanism. That very model of persons, however, is Rawls's own model for purposes of domestic justice. On the domestic level Rawls thinks that persons are responsible for their own ends *and* that duties of distributive justice exist.[11] Consider the following two cases in the arena of domestic justice, each roughly paralleling one of Rawls's hypothetical cases in international justice. First, imagine two young persons with roughly equal opportunities and native endowments. One elects to pursue a highly pressured and lucrative career, while the other prefers less wealth and greater leisure. Second, imagine two women with roughly equal opportunities but both of modest means. The one elects to forgo motherhood and pursue a career that substantially increases her income and total wealth. The other prefers to have a large family and is thereby unable to improve her economic condition.

Rawls, rightly I believe, does not think that these differences in preferences entail that the more prosperous have no duties of distributive justice whatsoever to the less prosperous. Why is this? Rawls's account of the constructivist procedure of justification places parties behind the veil of ignorance with respect to, among other things, their abilities, dispositions, and conceptions of the good. In light of this ignorance, parties choose principles that require institutions to maximize the life prospects of the least advantaged regardless of their abilities, dispositions, and conceptions of the good. This procedure is justified on the following grounds:

> We do not deserve our place in the distribution of native endowments, any more than we deserve our initial starting place in society. That we deserve the superior character that enables us to make the effort to cultivate our abilities is also problematic; for such character depends in good part upon fortunate family and social circumstances in early life for which we can claim no credit.[12]

If one cannot claim that one deserves those dispositions that cause one to be successful, then one cannot claim the entire fruits of one's success. That which makes one successful can also be put to work for the good of others. "Those who have been favored by nature, whoever they are, may gain from their good fortune only on terms that improve the situation of those who have lost out."[13] Hence, any restriction against redistribution on the basis of one's responsibility for one's character vanishes. Nor would it be consistent with the reasonable pluralism of conceptions of the good to allow social institutions that reward some reasonable conceptions of the good at the expense of others.

If an original position for global justice includes representatives of persons rather than corporate entities, it would seem similar reasoning should prevail. If persons cannot claim responsibility for the abilities and dispositions that when harnessed lead to successful economic development for states, then there is no reason to suppose that those who are successful ought to be able to claim the full fruits of their success. The fact that the success was caused by their talents and dispositions does not relieve them of distributive duties to others. Additionally, if global reasonable pluralism is to be respected, institutions must not allow some reasonable conceptions of the good to flourish at the expense of others.

Second, depending on how one conceives of the goods of distributive justice, it may be a mistake to take Rawls's first illustration (of two societies with apparently different industrialization/leisure preferences) as an example containing inequalities. Although one might suppose that the per capita gross domestic product (GDP) in the one society is higher than in the other, indicating inequality, the amount of leisure time available on average is higher in the poorer society. If leisure is taken to be a primary good (a proposal that Rawls neither endorses nor rejects[14]), then the offsetting averages of wealth and leisure may indicate rough equality between persons.

Finally, whatever persuasive power Rawls's two examples have is due, I believe, to the fact that currently duties of distributive justice are discharged primarily at the state level. If a scheme of distribution and redistribution is just between compatriots and it suits their preferences, then why should a global scheme be imposed upon them? In Chapter 3 I granted that because we exist in political association with our compatriots, we have a duty to them to ensure that they have the means to play an active role in the politics of society. So, there is a place for state-level distributive principles. Duties of distributive justice, however, arise out of economic association. As capitalism globalizes, it makes more sense to take the primary locus of duties of distributive justice to be the planet rather than the state. In other words, institutions of distributive justice increasingly should be global rather than national—in which case, regardless of whether state institutions of distributive justice pre-exist global ones, the morally fundamental duties of distributive justice (apart from those arising from political association) are at the global, not the state level.

Barry

Brian Barry argues that a principle of distributive justice must fulfill the requirement of reciprocity. Intuitively the principle of reciprocity is attractive as a means for ensuring respect for persons. A distributional principle that allows some to gain at the expense of others is one that does not treat everyone with equal respect. This intuitive defense of reciprocity says nothing about the benchmark against which gain is to be measured. Yet, a benchmark is vital for determining whether reciprocity is met. Barry maintains that reciprocity requires that a principle of justice ensures that all parties gain in comparison to a prior state of actual holdings. Given current world conditions, any principle requiring redistribution would not meet this requirement of reciprocity.

> The extent of increased cooperation that would really be mutually beneficial is probably quite limited. In particular, redistribution on the insurance principle seems to have little appeal to rich countries. In the foreseeable future, aid to the needy is going to flow from, say, the United States to Bangladesh rather than vice versa. The conditions for reciprocity—that all the parties stand prospectively to benefit from the scheme—simply do not exist.[15]

If this were the appropriate way to understand the reciprocity requirement, it would look as if no principle of egalitarian distribution could be applied domestically in any of the capitalist societies since the very wealthy would not benefit from redistribution to the poor. Thus, duties of egalitarian distributive justice would be almost completely inapplicable and where (if anywhere) they applied, ironically, would only be in states in which great inequalities requiring redistribution did not exist. In other words, they would be applicable only if they were already approximately satisfied, and inapplicable otherwise. Cases of what most people would think of as indisputable advances of justice, such as the abolition of slavery in the United States and the elimination of apartheid in South Africa, would not satisfy this account of reciprocity.

Is it true that almost all cases of egalitarian distributive justice violate the requirement of reciprocity? The answer depends on the benchmark against which gains required by reciprocity are measured. Barry measures gains against the benchmark of actual holdings of societies prior to redistribution. Alternatively, gain might be measured against the benchmark of equal holdings of individuals. According to this benchmark, a principle of distributive justice violates the requirement of reciprocity only if it permits some to be worse off than they would be under conditions of equality. So, unless the globally wealthy could substantiate the very implausible claim that some principle of global redistribution would leave them worse off than under conditions of equality, they may not claim that redistribution violates reciprocity.

The benchmark of equality among persons has several virtues in comparison to the benchmark of the prior holdings of societies. First, its object of concern is persons, not states, which is consistent with cosmopolitan justice based upon respect for persons. Second, it conforms to many people's intuitive sense that redistributive principles need not ensure that the already privileged benefit. Third, it does not privilege existing holdings, which may be the product of all manner of injustices. Most important, it better conforms to our notions of the moral equality of all persons and of the moral arbitrariness of distinctions of social class, physical and mental prowess, and psychological dispositions. If all persons are morally equal, and if the benefits of the social class that one is born into, one's physical and mental prowess, and one's psychological disposition toward work are all undeserved, then it would make no sense to use actual holdings, which reflect these differences, as a benchmark.

In responding to Barry, Thomas Pogge argues that the appropriate benchmark against which to measure whether reciprocity has been satisfied is the condition of a society if it were "existing in perfect isolation *with a proportionate share of the world's natural assets*."[16] This benchmark has the drawback of measuring the holdings of societies rather than persons; but, because it speaks of "proportionate shares," it can be translated into individualist terms. So, translated it would state that the benchmark is the equal holdings of natural assets between persons, assuming their society existed in isolation. Stated in this way, however, the requirement of societies existing in isolation is superfluous. The key question is whether persons have an equal share of natural assets. The substantive difference then between Pogge's benchmark and mine is that Pogge's involves a comparison against equality of *natural assets* only. To determine whether a distribution of global wealth or resources meets the criterion of reciprocity, why compare it to the condition of individuals, when natural assets alone are equalized? The more appropriate comparison is when all distributed resources are equalized. Justice is to govern the benefits and burdens of an association. Its principles then must govern the fruits of the association, not merely natural assets.

In sum, Barry's claim that principles of egalitarian global distributive justice violate reciprocity is groundless once the appropriate benchmark for measuring reciprocity is established.

Nardin

Terry Nardin's account of international justice is based upon his account of international society, which he takes to be a "practical association of states."[17] He distinguishes between practical associations and purposive associations. Purposive associations establish rules to serve a common purpose. Practical associations establish rules, based upon mutual restraint and toleration of diversity, which enable associates to get along despite lacking a common purpose.[18] With this distinction in mind, one might think that only purposive associations are based upon a conception of the common good, but Nardin thinks not. In practical associations the common good is "not a set of aims to be achieved through cooperation" but "a set of values defined by common laws."[19] Apparently, in practical associations the common good is a set of procedural values none of which is valued primarily for its own sake but each valued insofar as it permits members to pursue their own substantive commitments in a just fashion. International society, because it is so diverse, is more appropriately thought of as a practical association, rather than a purposive one.

Much of Nardin's basic outlook is consistent with the account of cosmopolitanism that I endorse. The cosmopolitan original position does not assume that persons share practical aims. Indeed, a central concern of the cosmopolitan perspective is to establish an institutional framework for ensuring fairness under conditions of a plurality of world views and personal aims. One basic difference, however, between Nardin's account of international justice and cosmopolitanism is that his account of international justice is statist; the international association is an association of states, not of free and equal persons. As it turns out, however, this is not the premise upon which he opposes claims of global distributive justice.

Nardin's case against global distributive justice is based upon the assertion that a strong commitment to egalitarianism is incompatible with a practical association. This is a significant claim because if it is true, there is a fundamental incoherence in the cosmopolitanism I have developed that is based upon fairness to persons with a plurality of aims and that advocates duties of global distributive justice. Nardin's views come out when criticizing socioeconomic rights as reflecting "a purposive conception of society." Here apparently is the reason why: "Although such rights constitute part of the common good, they are nevertheless a subordinate part: substantive or external goods whose pursuit is subject to the constraints of impartiality, noninterference, and mutual accommodation that constitute the core of the common good of formal equals."[20] Nardin's distinctions are not entirely clear, but his view seems to be that claims to a fair share of the object of distributive justice, unlike political and civil rights, are claims to substantial, and not merely procedural, goods.[21]

The view that claims of distributive justice necessarily are claims to a substantial and not merely procedural good is false. The most obvious example is the principle of fair equality of opportunity. Intuitively, its most plausible justification is to establish a fair system of competition for goods. It is not valued for its own sake, but, like liberty, it is valued so that the terms of association may be fair. Later I shall argue that the difference principle is also required if an association is to be treating morally equal persons fairly. Neither egalitarian principle is justified by reference to a particular individual's aim or a substantive account of the good. On the contrary, they are both procedural requirements of a fair mode of association. For this reason Nardin's rejection of global egalitarianism fails.

Goodin

Robert Goodin offers an account of the special duties that we owe to fellow citizens that is premised on the state playing the role of protector of the general duties that all owe to all.[22] The duties of domestic justice are taken to be assigned general duties and can be overridden by the general duties when circumstances demand. He illustrates the position with the example of establishing a lifeguard to fulfill the duty to help others in need. Beachgoers are relieved of helping swimmers, an instance of their general duty to help others in need, because a lifeguard is assigned the role of fulfilling that general duty. By analogy then, citizens of a state are relieved of their duties of justice toward citizens of other states because each state is assigned the role of fulfilling these duties. It is perfectly coherent, then, to acknowledge the universal scope of the values of liberty and equality without being committed to the international scope of duties of justice since individual states assure that justice is done. Goodin allows that citizens of one state may be obliged to fulfill duties to citizens of another state in those cases when the latter state is unwilling or unable to do so, just as beachgoers have some kind of obligation to attempt to save drowning swimmers when the lifeguard is unwilling or unable to do so.

Goodin's model offers a way for someone committed to cosmopolitanism to affirm the instrumental value of the international state system in realizing values with a universal scope. The model might adequately explain how duties such as respect for civil and democratic rights are fulfilled by support for just state institutions. Goodin claims that a consequence of the model is that ordinarily there are no duties of global justice, including apparently distributive justice. "States are assigned special responsibility for protecting and promoting the interests of those who are their citizens. . . . But ordinarily no state has any claim against other states for positive assistance in promoting its own citizens' interests: that is its own responsibility."[23]

The extension of this reasoning to distributive justice, however, is unwarranted. If the duties of distributive justice require a redistributive mechanism, then there must be a pool of resources into which those obliged pay, and from which those who are owed may draw. If one owes, but does not contribute, then one's duty has not been met. State institutions only draw on the resources of citizens and residents of each state; whatever redistribution they effect is only fulfilling the duties that those citizens and residents owe to each other. The resources distributed by the Mozambiquean state do not fulfill a well-off Swiss's duty of distributive justice to a Mozambiquean because that Swiss has not contributed to the pool of resources that the Mozambiquean state is distributing. Only global institutions can carry out redistributive duties among members of a global system.[24] So, Goodin's model of duties to compatriots as assigned general duties cannot justify the claim that ordinarily duties of global distributive justice do not exist.

Walzer

Michael Walzer's criticisms of global distributive justice are based upon his account of distributive justice generally. Distributive justice requires a set of common meanings that are culturally bound,[25] making it, then, in his terms a "thick morality."[26] Political communities are bound by common meanings or thick moralities.

> The only plausible alternative to the political community is humanity itself, the society of nations, the entire globe. But were we to take the globe as our setting, we would have to imagine what does not yet exist: a community that in-

cluded all men and women everywhere. We would have to invent a set of common meanings for these people, avoiding if we could the stipulation of our own values. And we would have to ask the members of this hypothetical community (or their hypothetical representatives) to agree among themselves on what distributive arrangements and patterns of conversion are to count as just. . . . But whatever the hypothetical agreement, it could not be enforced without breaking the political monopolies of existing states and centralizing power at the global level. Hence the agreement (or the enforcement) would make not for complex but for simple equality—if power was dominant and widely shared—or simply for tyranny—if power was seized, as it probably would be, by a set of international bureaucrats.[27]

There are at least three separate but related claims here. First, standards of justice require political communities. Second, the existing global arrangement does not give rise to standards of justice; these would have to be "invented." Third, an arrangement of global redistribution would probably result in tyranny. I shall examine each of these claims.

According to the first claim, standards of justice are immanent in the practices and beliefs of a political community. Since political communities contain a plurality of perspectives on the commitments of the community, there is room for dispute on the basis of the community's values. Walzer provides two kinds of arguments for the first claim. One is that different societies, such as Athens in the fifth century B.C. and medieval Jewish communities, employed different standards of justice.[28] The other is that standards of global justice based upon a constructivist procedure would have no purchase on ordinary people in their particular cultures. "Even if they are committed to impartiality, the question most likely to arise in the minds of the members of a political community is not, What would rational individuals choose under universalizing conditions of such-and-such a sort? But rather, what would individuals like us choose, who are situated as we are, who share a culture and are determined to go on sharing it?"[29]

Neither argument is convincing. Suppose that it is a fact that different political communities employ different standards of justice. It does not follow that standards of justice are limited to political communities. People's conception of what they owe each other may typically be drawn from the cultural framework of their political community, but it does not follow that what they owe each other necessarily is limited to this framework. Justification for duties of justice may historically have been made largely in terms of cultural self-understanding, but this does not rule out a culturally neutral philosophical account of the duties of justice. This is connected to the second argument. Suppose it is true that people rarely employ arguments based upon universal principles to settle claims of justice. It does not follow that they could not or should not. Moreover, in the above quotation Walzer seems to be basing moral argumentation on cultural homogeneity. There are increasingly fewer places in the world where such homogeneity exists. This is one of the strongest reasons to look for impartial principles of justice.

Walzer's second claim, that there is no global standard of distributive justice, is probably meant to follow from the first, with the additional premise that there is no global political community. So, with the first claim drawn into doubt, the second is to that degree weakened. There are further reasons for doubting the second claim. I argued in Chapter 3 that a global economic association exists. If this is true, and if all persons are deserving of equal respect, then we cannot avoid standards of global justice that seek to establish fair terms of association among persons. It may indeed be the case that separate political communities engender particular duties of justice among compatriots, but this is consistent with there being global duties as well.[30]

Walzer's third claim is that a system of enforcing duties of global justice would probably be tyrannical. This is needlessly pessimistic. If a just global situation includes states with the powers to enforce democratic and human rights and a system of global wealth tax and transfer, there would be multiple sites, or spheres, of political power. In addition, the existence of institutions of wealth redistribution at the state level, which are subject to democratic control, gives reason to believe that the scale can be extended. So, Walzer's skepticism about duties of global distributive justice is unfounded.

EGALITARIAN PRINCIPLES

With various skeptical challenges to global distributive justice out of the way, I turn now to the question of which principles of distributive justice apply to the global association. I shall follow Rawls's terminology and consider conceptions of "liberal equality" and "democratic equality."[31] One way to answer the question at hand is by focusing on a different one: Which principles of justice would be chosen by representatives of all persons of the world in an original position that included a veil of ignorance, rendering them ignorant of various matters such as the race, gender, citizenship status, psychological dispositions, physical prowess, and conceptions of the good of the persons whom they represent?

Liberal Equality

Distributive principles of liberal equality hold that the distribution should be to everyone's advantage in the sense that it is efficient, or Pareto optimal,[32] and that the resulting inequalities should be attached to offices that are open to all under conditions of fair equality of opportunity. The re-

quirement of fair equality of opportunity entails more than merely nondiscrimination among applicants for positions of privilege. It requires that a
person's chances for successfully attaining a position of privilege should depend upon neither social fortune, which includes the parents' level of privilege and the country of birth and education, nor certain aspects of natural
fortune, including sex, race, and ethnicity. Fair equality of opportunity is
consistent with the principle of self-ownership in that it permits unlimited
inequalities on the basis of talents and abilities, if the influences of fortune
are neutralized.

Fair equality of opportunity would require significant reforms to the current global economy. As I suggested in Chapter 3, one way to imagine fulfillment of the goal is that a child born in rural Mozambique would be statistically as likely to become an investment banker as the child of a Swiss
banker. In order for this to come about, a great deal would have to be spent
on infrastructure among the world's poor. Educational opportunities would
have to be equalized across the globe and between the sexes, health care access and facilities would have to be approximately equal, and all persons
would have to be free of persecution on the basis of race, ethnicity, gender,
religion, and political affiliation. Fair equality of opportunity is only minimally egalitarian since it allows for unlimited inequalities of outcome
within a generation; but in light of current global inequalities, its requirements would be very demanding.

In a cosmopolitan original position, what sort of considerations would
count in favor of liberal equality? The requirement of Pareto optimality
makes sense since a suboptimal distribution is one in which at least one
person is worse off, and representatives would be loathe to permit this. Fair
equality of opportunity makes sense because representatives will be ignorant of the social and natural fortune of those whom they represent. So,
they will not want the distribution to depend upon these matters.

The underlying idea is that one cannot claim to deserve things such as
place of birth and education, race, or parents' privilege. Hence, these things
should not be the basis of a distribution. This shows why even distributions
of goods according to criteria such as desert or consensual transfers should
include a requirement of fair equality of opportunity. Suppose desert is understood in terms of socially valuable work. A distribution according to
desert could not allow a person's starting positions in developing socially
valuable skills to be determined by, say, the parents' privilege. For in that
case, the distribution would not reflect desert, or not desert alone. Alternatively, if there is to be intuitive appeal to the claim that persons should have
what they would have as the result of consensual transfers, it must be the
case that both those who did well as a result of the transfers and those who
did not started out with the same opportunities. Otherwise the outcome
would be the product not merely of consensual transfers, but undeserved

privileges as well. Hence, once an individual's initial social fortune, sex, race, and ethnicity are recognized as undeserved, fair equality of opportunity becomes a procedural requirement of any system of fair competition for scarce resources.

Democratic Equality

Democratic equality not only equalizes the starting point of competition, through fair equality of opportunity, it also restricts the degree of inequality of outcomes by putting talents and abilities to work not only for their possessors but for others as well. Intuitively this is consistent with the democratic ideal that everyone, regardless of talent and ability, may be equal citizens. Just as the conception of democratic citizenship abstracts from a person's social and natural advantages for the purpose of establishing political entitlements, so the principles of democratic equality abstract from these advantages for the purpose of establishing socioeconomic entitlements.

If the representatives in a cosmopolitan original position are also ignorant of the talents and abilities of those whom they represent, they will want the collective set of talents and abilities to benefit all, not just their possessors. Hence, they will not see inequalities as justified because of a person's talent. Nor, however, will they settle on a requirement of equal distribution, if this is suboptimal. If the representatives have no knowledge of the probabilities regarding how talented those whom they represent are, it would seem to be rational for them to be conservative in their calculations and to look to the advantage of the least well-off. Hence, they would require that institutions structure whatever inequalities of distribution that result from differential endowments of talents and abilities to the maximum benefit of the least advantaged over the course of their life. This is the difference principle.[33]

This conclusion could be reached in a different way.[34] A global economic association exists. Assuming that all persons deserve equal respect, what principles would establish a fair distribution of the benefits of the system? Equal respect demands that all, despite differences of social and natural fortune, should have equal opportunity to benefit. Otherwise the distribution would be influenced by morally arbitrary properties of persons. Equal respect also demands that equality of outcome be the benchmark against which all principles governing the distribution be measured. Principles permitting the talented and able to benefit without limit would permit a distribution on morally arbitrary differences. A principle requiring equality of outcome, however, is less preferable than one that allows inequalities that are to the maximum benefit of the least advantaged. Although this latter principle allows inequalities, it is fully consistent with equal respect for persons:

Those who are least advantaged cannot rationally complain about its application, for they could not do any better; and those who are more advantaged have no moral grounds for demanding more privileges than the principle permits because they may not claim to merit more by virtue of their talent or good fortune. Hence, the principles of global distributive justice constituting democratic equality are superior to those of liberal equality.

If fair equality of opportunity alone requires extensive structural changes in the world economy, its conjunction with the difference principle is even more demanding. Not only must the opportunities between the children in rural Mozambique and Switzerland be equalized, but the inequalities of outcome must be so limited that they are to the maximum benefit of the least advantaged. Recall that the assets of 358 billionaires exceed the combined annual incomes of countries accounting for 45 percent of the world's population. Evidence of inequality, however, is not evidence that the difference principle has not been satisfied. Rather, what is required is some reason to believe that the lot of the least advantaged could be better.

According to various estimates, a 0.1 percent tax on foreign exchange transactions, the so-called Tobin tax, would yield between $56.23 billion and $200 billion a year, which could be directed toward sustainable development initiatives that would produce significant gains for the least advantaged.[35] Invoking the Tobin tax is not meant to suggest that it is the policy that would maximize benefits to the least advantaged, but merely to show that there is reason to believe that current inequalities do not do so.

Realizing the difference principle is unlike realizing fair quality of opportunity insofar as it requires not only wealth transfers for the infrastructure, which ensure opportunities across the globe, but also a global institutional structure that limits wealth inequalities. Perhaps under ideal conditions this could be a system of limited property rights, but in order to remedy existing unjust inequalities some sort of tax and transfer system is probably required.

Two Objections

The above defense of democratic equality as the standard of global distributive justice might be criticized in at least two ways. First, some writers defend a global minimum floor principle instead of the global difference principle.[36] A minimum floor principle, like the difference principle, is focused not on equality of starting positions in competition for privileged positions; rather, it limits the inequalities that might arise in the course of that competition by stipulating a minimal condition that all persons may with justice expect not to fall below. Typically minimum floor principles contain a requirement that basic needs for security, nutrition, and health care be met. In light of current deprivations globally, a commitment to a minimum floor principle would require significant redistribution from the wealthy to the poor in order to meet the unmet basic needs of the latter.

Sometimes the global minimum floor principle is preferred because the difference principle is considered too egalitarian.[37] The case for a minimum floor involves the argument that it is mistaken to employ the benchmark of equality in measuring acceptable inequalities, as the argument for the difference principle does. Only agreements about redistribution made in light of knowledge of current holdings are reasonable.[38] Additionally, the argument maintains that if one starts with a benchmark of current holdings, then a minimum floor principle would be chosen. The problem with this position is that the benchmark of existing holdings, as I argued earlier, insulates from moral criticism holdings that may be the product of all manner of injustice. Since the starting point of deliberations affects the end point, the benchmark of existing holdings allows that morally arbitrary properties, such as social privilege, may affect the ultimate distribution of resources. Additionally, if knowledge of current holdings is permitted to parties searching for agreement on principles of distributive justice, there is no guarantee that a minimum floor will be selected or that any agreement at all will be reached.[39] Why should the parties settle on such a principle? The rich may want something less redistributive, say mere fair equality of opportunity, and the poor may want something more redistributive, for example the difference principle. So, not only is the employment of the benchmark of current holdings inappropriate in determining a distributive principle, there is reason to doubt that its employment would yield any sort of agreement at all.

If the benchmark of equality is employed, there are good reasons for thinking that the representatives in the cosmopolitan original position would choose the difference principle over the minimum floor principle. Absent knowledge about per capita GDP levels and the percentile composition of global inequality, it would be rational for them to choose equality of outcome over the minimum floor since there is no guarantee that the latter would maintain the position of those whom they represent. In other words, the minimum floor could be below equality. Additionally, it would be rational for them to choose the difference principle over equality of outcome since no matter who they represent, the difference principle will allow for improvements over equality of outcome. Assuming transitivity, the difference principle is superior to the minimum floor principle.

Another criticism of the difference principle charges it with being insufficiently egalitarian. Henry Shue defends the minimum floor principle over the difference principle on the following grounds:

> Instead of providing a floor. . . Rawls provides only rope, hitching the worst-off (in a rather loose way) to all the better-off. Whenever the better-off improve themselves, the rope of justice requires that the worst-off should be pulled up-

ward too, by at least a little. But the Rawlsian theory contains no provision that everyone's head must, for a start, be held above the surface of the water.[40]

Shue's metaphor of the rope, however, can be misleading. Although it captures the aspect of the difference principle that requires growth in inequalities to benefit the least advantaged, it does not capture the aspect that requires such inequalities to *maximally* benefit the least advantaged. This is crucial to recognizing the egalitarian nature of the difference principle. If one employs the metaphor then, it should be adjusted so that the rope the difference principle would employ to pull up the worst-off raises them higher than the ropes of any other principle. The upshot of the requirement that inequalities be to the maximum benefit of the least advantaged is that in comparison to other principles, the difference principle most helps the least advantaged.

The second objection to the defense of democratic equality as the principle of global distributive justice is that it places too many demands on individuals to give. Stanley Hoffman puts it as follows: "A donor would have to give, almost automatically, precedence to others, all of the others abroad who are poorer, before using any of his own resources for domestic self-improvement. Before I can spend a penny on the poor in the Appalachians, I have to spend all I can on those who are infinitely poorer in Bangladesh. That is not the way politics can work."[41] Hoffman seems to be supposing that in a distributively just world, institutions would distribute wealth more or less with the results that they achieve now, and that it would be up to individuals to donate their wealth to the poor of the world according to the demands of justice. This, however, mistakes the object of criticism in the claim that the current global distribution is unjust. The injustice does not lie in a failure of people to give (or, a failure of charity); it lies, rather, in a failure of institutions—such as markets—to distribute appropriately (a failure of justice). If the inequalities of the current global distribution are unjust, justice does not require that the rich give more, it requires that the poor get more prior to individual acts of charity. This is the way that the politics of justice work. Politics can work this way at the level of states. So, I see no reason to suppose that it cannot work this way at the global level. Additionally, although, as I argued in Chapter 3, there may be democratic duties to meet certain distributive requirements to compatriots in particular, duties of distributive justice are best seen as duties of global justice, given the existence of a global economic association.

Primary Goods, Capabilities, and Gender Inequality

The Rawlsian conception of democratic equality includes fair equality of opportunity and the difference principles. The defense that I have been offering of these principles does not necessarily entail a defense of Rawls's account of the object or the goods of distribution. According to Rawls, principles of justice govern institutions that distribute primary goods, which include rights, liberties, opportunities, income, wealth, and the social bases of self-respect.[42]

Persons in different circumstances due to disease, educational backgrounds, or even pregnancy, who are equals when measured in terms of primary goods, may nonetheless be unequal in their capacities to convert their holding into freedoms.[43] Because of this remaining inequality, not captured by measuring inequalities in primary goods, Amartya Sen argues that the measure of distributive justice should be capabilities or powers.

> In the context of international policies, the difference introduced by concentrating on primary *powers* as opposed to primary *goods* is rather significant. Calorie and nutritional requirements as well as needs of clothing and shelter vary with climatic conditions. Social developments like urbanization bring about additional needs, and thus a lowering of primary powers given the same availability of primary goods.[44]

It is not clear to what extent there is a principled difference between Rawls and Sen. Rawls admits that equalizing powers of need fulfillment should be a distributional concern at the level of assessing just legislation (assuming principles of justice and a just constitution have been chosen).[45] Generally, Rawls's worries about the capabilities approach seem to be practical. "By embedding primary goods into the specification of the principles of justice and ordering the basic structure of society accordingly, we may come as close as we can in practice to a just distribution of Sen's effective freedoms."[46] Rawls seems to want to keep the theory simple in order to be useable. To simplify matters, persons represented in the original position are assumed to be normally active and fully cooperating members of society with equal capabilities.[47] Primary goods are defined as the social conditions or all-purpose means required to realize the interests of citizens.[48] Thus primary goods are taken as requirements for the exercise of capabilities, much as Sen wants. However, equalizing primary goods only equalizes capabilities if persons are assumed to be in equal conditions.

The difference between Rawls and Sen appears to come down to the following: According to Rawls, the simplifying assumption that citizens have approximately equal capabilities is employed as a matter of practicality so as to keep measurements of equality clear and easy; Sen's point is that what counts as equal under a simplifying assumption is not necessarily what counts as equal in the real world.

One apparent advantage of Sen's view is that in the non-ideal global setting in which we live, it is the case that, due to a variety of circumstances, people with the same resources will have different capabilities of converting these into freedoms. The special burdens of women are a case in point. In Martha Nussbaum's words, "Women who have traditionally not been educated, for example, may well require more of the relevant resources to attain the same capability level."[49] Additionally, according to Sen, the fact that women in Asia and North Africa have higher morbidity and mortality rates than men is evidence of "disparities in the elementary capabilities to avoid escapable morbidity and preventable mortality."[50] The point in both cases is that if men and women of the same social class are compared with respect to the primary good of wealth or income, important inequalities may go unnoticed.

Jean Drèze and Amartya Sen have revealed extensive discrimination against women in parts of the developing world through their "missing women" index.[51] The index takes 1.022 as a base female-to-male ratio, the ratio in the poor countries of sub-Saharan Africa, which have relatively fewer biases against women in the distribution of food and health care. They then calculate the number of women a country would have if its female-to-male ratio were the same as sub-Saharan Africa. The difference between the number of women a country would have according to the base ratio given its population and the number it does have is the number of women missing, presumably due to unequal distributions of food (within families), health care, and infanticide. Pakistan, at 12.9 percent, has the highest proportion of missing women of any country.[52] The primary goods approach, however, is also able to identify women's oppression. Nussbaum's criticism suggests that wealth and income are the only primary goods that Rawlsian justice seeks to distribute. Recall, however, that Rawls recognizes opportunity as a primary good. With that in mind, it would seem possible to identify inequality of opportunity between women and men as the salient moral fact behind the existence of missing women.

The capabilities approach is not free of problems. Sen is not altogether clear whether what is motivating his position is an appreciation of need differentials or differentials in the powers or capabilities to convert resources into freedoms. He sometimes writes in ways that highlight the former: "Such a formulation will be sensitive to differences in people's needs."[53] The difference between the two views might be thought to be minimal, since freedoms might be thought of as freedoms to meet needs.[54] However, one significant liability of introducing needs into the account is that it makes the capabilities approach vulnerable to being collapsed into a kind of welfarism that Sen wants to avoid.[55] A major problem with welfarist approaches is that they do not regard persons as sufficiently responsible for their disadvantages. For example, on an equal distribution of wealth, someone who has cultivated a taste for caviar and champagne may be less happy than another person with tastes for beer and chips.[56] If distributive justice should aim at the distribution of welfare, then these two people with different tastes would have to be made equally happy, rather than equally wealthy. Taking the object of distributive justice to be wealth and income, rather than welfare, holds persons responsible for their ends.[57] A person who develops expensive tastes, say for caviar and champagne, cannot claim more resources to satisfy those tastes. That person is responsible for them, and it is no concern of justice whether they are satisfied. Now, if justice requires attention to all capabilities of need fulfillment, then the capabilities for fulfilling expensive and cultivated needs would be no less important than those for fulfilling basic needs. Hence, the capabilities approach would suffer a similar problem as welfare approaches.

One response available to Sen is to maintain that justice should be directed only to a limited set of basic capabilities for need fulfillment.[58] In various places he offers examples of a few capabilities of need fulfillment that everyone should have equal power to fulfill. These include the following: (1) the ability to meet one's nutritional requirements; (2) the wherewithal to be clothed and sheltered; (3) the power to participate in the social life of the community; (4) the capability to avoid shame from failure to meet social conventions; and (5) the capability to retain self-respect.[59] Part of the problem with this short list, however, is that it is not clear how justice applies to inequalities in conditions once the basic capacities are met. What is the measure of difference among people who all have the capacities for meeting basic needs? At this stage additional capacities must be introduced. The trick is to establish a set of capacities that are not simply basic, but that also do not place cultivated expensive needs on a par with more basic ones.

The problem confronting the capabilities approach can be summarized as follows. The relevant capabilities for distributive justice are either a small set of basic capabilities or a larger set that includes capabilities that may not be essential to life. The first disjunct entails the problem of evaluating distributions once basic needs are all met. The second involves the problem of placing basic needs and expensive, cultivated needs on par. A possible resolution to the problem might be to select a set of capabilities that approximately correspond to Rawls's set of primary goods—in other words, taking the relevant capacities that a theory of distributive justice should be concerned with as the capacities to fulfill the needs associated with converting the primary goods to freedoms. It would also have the virtue of keeping the theory of global distributive justice squarely within the domain of the political conception of justice in the Rawlsian sense. In other words, this may provide the basis of a *rapprochement* between Sen and Rawls.

ANALYZING IMPERIALISM

A defensible account of global distributive justice is of obvious importance to moral theory. What may be less obvious is that it is also of importance to social theory. By applying the conclusions of the above argument in defense of the democratic conception of equality, certain ambiguities in the theory of economic imperialism can be resolved.

Empirical Theories

Empirical theories of economic imperialism, both Marxist and non-Marxist alike, aim to explain the causes and effects of the export of capital. Classical theorists typically see the cause in the development of finance capital that results in the overproduction or underconsumption of goods.[60] The classical theorists view the chief evil consequence of imperialism to be the inevitability of war.[61] The post-World War II theorists, at least those with some connection to Marxism, usually attempt to account for different effects, in particular the role that the export of capital from states with more developed economies to those with less-developed economies has played in the underdevelopment of the lesser-developed economies. Investment theories take the cause of underdevelopment to be the repatriation of the profits accrued in the less-developed economies to the advanced developed economies.[62] Trade theories place the cause of underdevelopment in the higher labor costs of the goods produced in the more developed countries, requiring them to fetch more when they are exchanged with goods produced in the less-developed economies.[63] Both kinds of theories provide reasons for condemning imperialism on the basis of the resulting inequalities.

Not all postwar Marxists, however, agree that the development of the more developed economies was purchased at the price of the underdevelopment of the less-developed economies.[64] Bill Warren, for example, takes imperialism to be simply the spread of capitalism, which, following Marx, he claims is historically progressive on cultural, economic, and political grounds. For example, capitalism encourages individual development, it increases productivity, and it encourages parliamentary democracy. These are empirical claims, and Warren contends that the record of development verifies them. If the claims are true, then a moral evaluation of the above-mentioned goods may find that they amount to evidence for the progressive nature of imperialism. Warren seems to think quite reasonably that these goods are valuable in themselves, and that Marxists ought to find them especially attractive because they both constitute the ethical foundation of socialism and are necessary pre-conditions for it.

The Role of Moral Theory

Although the best known postwar Marxist theories of imperialism aim to condemn it, it is not surprising that there should be some difference of opinion on this matter among those who usually maintain both that capitalism is historically progressive and that it is ultimately to be condemned. Marxists have long disagreed among themselves about the point at which capitalism ceases to play a progressive role and is to be replaced by socialism. It might be thought then that what is at issue between underdevelopment theorists and Warren is straightforwardly empirical: If the facts bear out the existence of underdevelopment, then imperialism is to be criticized. I shall argue that an analysis of the issue shows that it is not resolvable by empirical verification. Progress can be made on these matters, however, by an appeal to moral theory.

There are important ambiguities in the meaning of the term *underdeveloped* that affect how one determines whether it exists. Presumably, for underdevelopment theorists the term does not mean that a certain state is merely less developed than others. Such an interpretation would take the moral, and hence the political, sting out of the term. Nor can the term mean that a state is less developed than it should be. For although this incorporates some moral evaluation, it does not assign responsibility for the morally undesirable condition of certain states to the more developed ones. There are, rather, three possible meanings of the term *underdeveloped* consistent with the moral orientations and political objectives of underdevelopment theorists. It may mean (1) that a national economy is less developed than would have been the case absent economic relations with more developed states; (2) that an economy is subject to unjust economic relations; or (3) that an economy is constrained in its development by unjust relations internationally.

On the first meaning, a theory of underdevelopment would have to give a counterfactual account of why the state's economy would have been more developed in the absence of relations with the more developed economies. Failing such an account there is the possibility that the less-developed economy would be even less developed still without the relations in question. However, it would be difficult to substantiate such an account. Comparing the development history of two different economies, one allegedly underdeveloped and the other not, would be inadequate as there would be too many variables that might be the cause of the different levels of developmental success. The same problem arises in comparing the two different periods in the development of the same economy. Because there are multiple causes for the level of development of an economy and some factors play a role at some point and not others, it would be tremendously difficult to find two periods that were the same in every respect except that in one period there was interaction with a more developed state and in another period there was not. Without isolating for such interaction, there may be multiple explanations for the different levels of development in the two periods. Hence, whatever disadvantages may be suspected, it is possible that the less-developed country would be even worse off without those relations with a more developed country.

None of these problems arise if *underdeveloped* is understood to mean either subject to unjust relations or constrained by unjust relations. Both of these interpretations, however, require an account of why the inequalities are unjust since the mere existence of inequality is not sufficient to claim injustice. In this case part of the identificatory theory of underdevelopment is normative. A theory of global distributive justice is required in order to identify underdevelopment.[65] The theory clarifies when unequal relations constitute underdevelopment. In light of the argument presented earlier in this chapter, if the global distribution of wealth and income violates either the fair equality of opportunity or difference principles, it is unjust. Given the facts regarding international inequality and good reasons to believe that this situation does not maximize benefits to the least advantaged, there are good reasons to believe that the current global distribution of wealth is unjust.

The fact that distributive injustice exists internationally provides important evidence for underdevelopment on either of the last two accounts. On the one account, underdevelopment exists if global distributive injustice exists. On the other, it exists if the injustice exists *and* the inequalities produce developmental constraints. Although the latter account is more demanding since it has empirical as well as normative criteria, it is plausible that the unjust inequalities of the current global economy meet the higher standard. In Chapter 3 I suggested that there are three constraints that developing countries confront if seeking egalitarian schemes of distribution. The first is the need for foreign capital investment if the economy is to grow. The second is the general trend of attaching expenditure-cutting requirements as the condition of international loans. The third is the progressive reduction of trade barriers, allowing capital to be more mobile. These constraints might punish by disinvestment those states that pursue egalitarian courses of development.

So, either of two plausible identificatory theories of underdevelopment, when applied to existing global inequalities, provide grounds for claiming that underdevelopment exists. The account that includes the empirical criteria as well as the normative is arguably more consistent with the tenor of the accounts of underdevelopment since it identifies not only the evils of injustice but also their effect on the development path of a state, which is typically a chief concern of underdevelopment theorists. However, nothing of the moral point is lost if the theory that includes only the normative criterion is adopted.

Both of these identificatory theories of underdevelopment are dependent on a theory of global distributive justice that takes *individuals* as the primary holders of both duties and entitlements. Talk about imperialism, however, usually involves claims that certain *states* are the agents of impe-rialism, and others the victims. The origin of this probably lies with the classical theorists who view imperialism as another stage ("the highest stage") of capitalist development in which competition among capitalists is backed by state-power in the international arena. Although states may in certain ways be agents of imperialism through policies encouraging the export of capital and protecting it after export, it is the impact of inequal-ity on the life prospects of individuals, not states, that is the proper object of moral concern. Also, it is individuals who primarily bear the duties of international distributive justice. If global inequalities are unjust, it is the persons who benefit from them who bear the weight of moral responsibil-ity of imperialism.

A plausible identificatory theory of underdevelopment is neutral to the causal accounts of underdevelopment, but corresponds with the general view of underdevelopment theory that unequal outcomes from the relations between more and less-developed countries are unjust. Although the ac-count of imperialism that I have been arguing for is consistent with the claims of underdevelopment theory, it does not necessarily gainsay War-ren's contention that capitalism still has a progressive role to play in devel-oping the less-developed economies. To see this, one need only compare the role that a moral critique of imperialism plays in a critique of capitalism with the role that the classical Marxist critique of exploitation plays. If cap-italism requires unjust exploitation, remedying exploitation necessarily re-quires doing away with background conditions of differential private own-ership of capital. Remedying economic imperialism, however, requires the establishment of international institutions and policies of wealth distribu-tion that conform to the democratic conception of equality.[66] This does not directly decide the empirical matter of whether the global fair equality of opportunity and difference principles are consistent with global capitalism, nor does it address the matter of property relations within states. It is a matter for empirical theory to judge whether or not differential private ownership of capital is necessary at a particular stage in the development of a national economy or in international society in order to best realize the requirements of democratic equality.

The existence of an economic class that privately controls the lion's share of the world's wealth, however, means that there is a powerful group of people with economic interests opposed to global egalitarianism. It is on the basis of this that Kai Nielsen contends that socialism in Western indus-trialized countries is necessary for effecting the distributions required by principles of egalitarian justice.[67] It is true that a society containing an eco-nomic system in which either profits did not exist or were controlled pub-licly would contain one less source of resistance to international egalitari-anism. However, establishing the existence of a powerful source of opposition to global egalitarianism is insufficient for asserting that doing away with that source will constitute an improvement from the egalitarian point of view. An economic system without the private accumulation of profits may be so inefficient as to provide even less to the least advantaged, even though it may create greater equality. This is why one must rely on empirical theory to establish that socialism would be better than capitalism in realizing the demands of global egalitarian distributive justice.[68]

Reparations

Public discussions of the injustices of colonialism, imperialism, and the slave trade sometimes raise a different kind of moral claim than the one I have been defending: Those living in states that have benefited from past imperialist and colonial relations owe reparations, as a matter of remedial justice, to those living in states or regions who have suffered from that imperialism.[69] Some might think this is a more radically egalitarian demand than the account that I have defended; in fact, such a demand is neither more egalitarian nor more plausible.

If the remedy for imperialism were reparations for past injustices, the duty to correct the injustice would be fulfilled once the compensation for past injustices had been paid. There would be no guarantee that future economic relations would be to the maximum benefit of the least advantaged. Hence, on this account remedying the injustice of imperialism may provide one-time relief for millions of disadvantaged people, but it would not secure long-term prospects for them in the way that institutions governed by democratic equality would. There are very good reasons to believe that after a one-time compensatory payment, inequalities would continue to grow in the *lassez faire* global market. Those who are lucky in certain ways, whether in terms of natural ability or investment timing, benefit from the market, and those who are not so lucky do not. Since the more resources one commands the more one can earn in market economies, the beneficiaries of luck are more likely to be further rewarded. Hence, after a one-time payment of reparations, inequalities would continue. The establishment of international institutions that conform to the democratic conception of equality would be of more lasting benefit for the least advantaged than a one-time payment would.

One might believe that those who live in states that have benefited from injustices in past generations owe a debt of reparation as a matter of justice to those who are descendants of the victims, on the moral ground that successor states are also successors to obligations.[70] There are, however, two main problems with this view. One is identifying the persons harmed to whom reparations could now be paid. Clearly the dead ancestors were harmed, for example those who suffered as a result of the slave trade. It is doubtful, however, that their descendants have been harmed by past injustices, especially on the plausible premise that those now living would not be alive if the injustices had not occurred.[71] Although colonialism and slavery generated racist social and political systems in many states, it is only aspects of these subsequent racist systems that can be said to harm present generations, not colonialism and slavery. The other problem is that claims from past generations may lose their force under changed conditions over time. For example, if the claim was to a patch of property under conditions of plenty, a claim to that same property may not exist under subsequent conditions of scarcity.[72] Hence, there may have been a debt owed by the dead beneficiaries of colonialism to the dead victims that simply cannot be satisfied by a payment from the descendants of beneficiaries to the descendants of the victims.

There are debts outstanding that time will not allow to be made right. When we are confronted with the facts of the African slave trade, the reasons for considerable moral anguish are made even greater by the realization that it is a wrong that can never be made right. History is full of such examples. We may hope, however, that consideration of the countless debts that will never, and can never, be repaid provides motivation for us to adopt principles of justice that will prevent similar injustice from recurring. Although reparations cannot be demanded as a matter of justice for harms done to past generations, they might serve as a symbolic expression of regret for the countries' unpaid, and unpayable, debts.[73]

PROBLEMS OF GLOBAL
DISTRIBUTIVE JUSTICE IN DEVELOPMENT

I have defended the democratic conception of equality for the global arena. Current global economic relations apparently do not realize this ideal. Most people in the twenty-first-century world live in conditions of underdevelopment. Efforts to raise standards of well-being among persons in developing societies encounter many problems due to the relationship between developed and developing countries. I will present a moral analysis of two such problems: the indebtedness of developing countries and the costs arising from global warming.

The Case for Debt Cancellation

One of the ways in which global inequalities get perpetuated is through transfers of wealth from regimes in the developing world to financial institutions in the developed world in order to service the debt of the former. Governments in the developing world maintain very high levels of foreign indebtedness that cause significant outflows of wealth. In 1995 the average debt-to-export ratios of developing countries was 150 percent, for sub-Saharan Africa it was 270 percent.[74] Servicing this debt involves a flow of wealth from the globally poor to the globally wealthy. The debt problem originated with loans from private banks under circumstances that were usually beyond the control of developing countries and extremely adverse. These circumstances included: a long-term decline in export prices of commodities manufactured in developing countries, protectionist policies directed against developing economies in developed countries, large increases in demands for services in developing countries due to rapid urbanization, and increasing costs of imports to developing economies due to oil price increases.[75] As their debts to private banks grew, developing countries took out additional loans from the International Monetary Fund (IMF) in order to have the cash to meet their repayment schedules.

There have been two significant consequence of this process. One is an ever-increasing indebtedness. For example, between 1982 and 1991 the accumulated debt of sub-Saharan Africa grew from $57 billion to $144 billion.[76] This amounted to an increase in the ratio of debt to GNP from 60 percent to 110 percent.[77] It has been estimated that "out of the $1,200 billion which the Third World owed in 1990, only $400 billion constituted the original borrowing. The rest consisted of accrued interest and capital liabilities."[78] The other consequence was the introduction of forms of IMF conditionality known as economic structural adjustment programs on indebted countries as a requirement of loans. These structural adjustments typically involve cutting public spending, exercising monetary restraint, increasing incentives for exports, implementing deflationary economic policies including wage restraint, and devaluating currency.[79]

Structural adjustment programs often have profound effects on economies and the lives of the poor. For example, consider the conclusions drawn by the United Nations Research Institute for Social Development (UNRISD), after fifteen or so years of IMF-required structural adjustments:

> The level of living of the majority of the population in African and Latin American countries has declined markedly over the past decade. Per capita income in most of these countries during the early 1990s was lower than in 1980, and the average income in the poorest strata much lower. Minimum wages stood at half or less than half of their former value. Unemployment in the formal sector was often much higher than at the outset of the debt crisis, although in relatively more successful cases this problem had been resolved in part by generating a great many new jobs which were badly paid.[80]

The working poor and their children have been particularly threatened by the unemployment and erosion of living standards caused by structural adjustment programs. Even though debt servicing has exacted such suffering in the developing world, it amounts to only about 8 percent of the annual income of the largest developed economies.[81]

The economic havoc that structural adjustment programs have wreaked has weakened institutions that are necessary for justice and has paved the way for all manner of intolerance in many parts of the developing world. The UNRISD report continues:

> Multiple survival strategies also weaken the kinds of institutions which modern societies have developed for the defense of group interests. Trade unions, farmers' associations, mutual insurance societies and so forth depend for their effectiveness on the commitment and financial support of their members. As professional or work place identity erodes, however, and as the interests of members become more diffuse, these institutions lose much of their ability to represent their constituents in formal bargaining processes. . . . The erosion of a structure of modern interest groups in many indebted Third World countries affects the strength of political parties and thus the capacity of political systems to create stable governing coalitions. . . . On a deeper level, however, the sharp sense of uncertainty and insecurity generated by recession and restructuring—by the threat of unemployment, the collapse of wages and the deterioration of public services—provides fertile ground for fundamentalism. As many states lose both capacity and legitimacy, there has been a resurgence of regional, religious and ethnic movements, most particularly in Africa and the former Soviet bloc. Sometimes people reactivate traditional ties for very practical reasons: they are the only available way to fill the gap in social service provision left by the withdrawal of the national government.[82]

Fundamentalist and traditionalist world views rarely endorse equal rights and opportunities for women. So, structural adjustment programs pose a particular threat to women. Since it is widely recognized that equality of opportunity for women plays an important role in reducing fertility rates,[83] such threats may contribute to the pressure of global population growth as well.

If the aims of development include increasing the well-being of persons, but especially the least advantaged, and consolidating just state institutions, then, given the evidence of the preceding paragraphs, it seems reasonable to conclude that the cancellation of debt is necessary for the achievement of economic and social development.[84] Additionally, from the perspective of the democratic conception of equality, the inequalities that debt servicing perpetuates cannot be justified. Since the debt burden is unjust by a defensible standard of global distributive justice, and it frustrates the aims of development, there is a compelling moral case for debt cancellation.

One criticism of the case for debt cancellation is that it simply ignores the fact that indebted states find themselves in the position that they are in as the result of a series of consensual agreements. Justice in contracts requires that they honor their debts. The justice of a contract, however, depends not only on whether it is the product of consensus, but on the background conditions in which it is agreed upon. When one party places another in a weaker bargaining position, the contract may be void due to duress. When one party takes advantage of another's exceptionally weak conditions, the contract may be nullified as unconscionable. Aspects of duress and unconscionability, but especially the latter, exist in the relationship between developing countries and financial institutions in developed countries. The globally wealthy are remiss in their obligations of distributive justice to the globally poor. Insofar as the financial institutions have taken advantage of circumstances of extreme deprivation that were largely beyond the control of poorer countries, the resulting contracts are unconscionable. Insofar as these contracts have placed the indebted countries in an even weaker position, subsequent contracts with the same institution are void due to duress. When these conditions exist, there are no moral grounds for enforcing service of the debt that the indebted countries owe financial institutions.

Barry criticizes the call for debt cancellation on two grounds: that it is statist and that it does nothing for the poorest countries.[85] Presumably the claim that it is statist derives from the fact that it is states that would be relieved of the debt. However, this is to misunderstand an important justification of debt cancellation. For the case in favor of cancellation need not be made on the basis of what is owed to states (a statist claim), even though it is their debt that would be canceled, but on the basis of the effect of debt servicing on the lives of persons. Hence, the demand for debt cancellation is fully consistent with a cosmopolitan conception of justice that takes persons as its object of moral concern. The claim that debt cancellation would not help the poorest countries is simply implausible. The most indebted countries are those in sub-Saharan Africa; these are also among the world's poorest countries. Of course, ultimately the question ought to be, would debt cancellation help the poorest people of the world? If it frees national budgets to address poverty alleviation, then it at least has the potential to help the poorest people of the world.

A final criticism of debt cancellation might be extrapolated from Garrett Hardin's account of "lifeboat ethics." Hardin develops a general argument against helping the poor of the world by considering the strain on the global environment of a country such as India that is projected to grow by 15 million people per year. "Every one of the 15 million new lives added to India's population puts an additional burden on the environment, and increases the economic and social costs of crowding. However humanitarian our intent, every Indian life saved through medical or nutritional assistance from abroad diminishes the quality of life for those who remain, and for subsequent generations."[86] The general claim is that any activity, including debt cancellation, of helping some of the world's poor, has unintended perverse consequences of imperiling others in future generations of the poor. This claim is based upon three premises. First, deprivation in the form of starvation, for example, is unavoidable due to environmental limits, in particular a scarcity of food resources. Second, helping some to live increases the number of people in the next generation. Finally, due to environmental limits, an increase in the number of people increases overall deprivation.

Given the data, the first of these two premises appears to be false. Sen, among others, makes a convincing case that there will be no food shortage for the foreseeable future.[87] What is more, debt relief is necessary for development, and there is a well-known correlation between development and declining fertility rates.[88] In other words, it is possible that after debt cancellation, countries will develop and fertility rates will decline, thereby staving off scarcity in coming generations that may be projected on the basis of current fertility rates.

Suppose, again for the sake of argument, that debt cancellation did increase the overall number of people on the planet in future generations. Does this amount to sufficient moral reason not to cancel the debt? It might, but only if those who control the resources that might alleviate suffering may rightfully claim exclusive control over those resources. If, however, those who are now suffering and will suffer have a claim to some of those resources, then there remains a moral reason to cancel the debt. In other words, there may be moral reasons apart from the consequences of debt cancellation for why it should be canceled. If present and future claims that enable resource control are unjustified, then those who lack control may have a moral case. According to the democratic conception of equality, the present day globally wealthy have not met their duties of distributive justice to the globally poor. If debt cancellation helps to redistribute in the right direction, it is justified. However, we are supposing that this results in more poor in the next generation. This does not relieve the present generation of the globally wealthy of their duties, although it would appear to increase the extent of the duties of the next generation.

Imagine the process of redistribution and population growth continuing until the environmental limit, the carrying capacity of the Earth, is reached. Hardin's point would seem to be that the wealthy may with justice protect themselves in an emergency situation. If their control over the resources is not just, however, this simply does not follow. A more plausible conclusion is that triage is called for, a distribution that would allow more people to live adequate lives (assuming that some definition of this is possible), rather than one permitting fewer to live more privileged lives. This conclusion accords better with equal respect for persons and the moral arbitrariness of the existing global distribution of resources.

The Costs of Global Warming

One significant fact of present day global inequalities is that persons in the wealthiest countries of the world amount to 25 percent of the world's population, but use 80 percent of the world's commercial energy resources. On average each person in a developed country consumes 32 barrels of crude oil per year, while each person in a developing country consumes 3.5 barrels per year. One consequence of this is that 40 percent of all carbon dioxide in the atmosphere is the product of 11 percent of the world's population.[89] If the developing countries develop using technology that has resulted in current levels of carbon dioxide emissions, the negative environmental consequences, particularly for global warming, may be extensive. Currently carbon dioxide concentrations are increasing at 0.4 percent per year.[90] At this rate (without significant increases in emissions from the developing world), by 2030 the concentrations of carbon dioxide in the atmosphere will be double that of 1990.[91]

There is widespread, although not unanimous, agreement in the scientific community that the results of this doubling will include a global mean temperature rise of 1.5 to 5 degrees Celsius.[92] To get an understanding of what this means, consider the U.S. National Academy of Sciences explanation:

> The current average global temperature is about 14°C (57°F). A 3°C rise would create conditions that some organisms have not had to contend with in the last 100,000 years. If the temperature rises 4°C, the earth would be warmer than at any time since the Eocene period, 40 million years ago. In the midst of the last glaciation, when much of North America was covered by ice, the average temperature of the earth was only about 5°C colder than it now is. . . . Moreover, the projected rate of warming is 15 to 40 times faster than natural warmings after major ice ages and much faster than what most species living on earth today have had to face.[93]

Although the consequences of the temperature rise are somewhat more controversial than the prediction of the rise itself, many scientists expect significant sea ice melting and a rise in the global mean sea level, as well as extensive agricultural displacement.[94]

Less certain are the economic costs of relocation due to flooding and of changing agricultural yields due to temperature rises.[95] Despite this uncertainty, there are two reasons to expect that the globally poor will suffer the most as a result of global warming. The first is the general problem that when two people experience the same harm, the one with fewer resources suffers the most since a greater percentage of that person's resources (assuming there are any) goes to repairing the harm. The second is that according to some projections, climate change will disproportionately harm the half-billion poorest and hungriest farmers of the world since many of them have been, and others continue to be, forced onto the marginal land with fewer resources to cope with climatic change.[96]

In light of these facts and projections, I wish to defend two related claims about global distributive justice in development. First, it would be unfair for the developing countries to have to absorb the entirety of the costs of the technology for sustainable development, or development that does not result in significant further aggravation of the problems of global warming. Second, persons in the developed countries should subsidize the costs of responding to the effects of global warming for persons in developing countries. I defend each position in turn.

If the process of global warming is not to be accelerated, developing countries, which are currently experiencing the largest increases in population growth, must either develop no further or develop using new and costlier technologies than were used by the developed countries. The first option is morally indefensible. In order to benefit the least advantaged globally and to provide the economic basis for stable democratic regimes, development is necessary. Justice requires development, but an important question of justice remains: Should the developing countries bear the entire costs of sustainable development or should these be subsidized by the developed world?

The answer to this question has already been provided by my defense of the global difference principle. If global inequalities are to be the maximum benefit of the globally least advantaged, then sustainable development in the developing world must be subsidized by the globally wealthy. One way (but perhaps not the only way required by justice) for persons to meet their duties of global distributive justice is for them to contribute to their country's fund that subsidizes sustainable development in developing countries.[97] This is required by the democratic conception of equality; otherwise, developing countries must either develop more slowly due to the burdens of higher costs for cleaner technologies, which will slow the improvement of those living in poverty, or they must develop in a way that accelerates global warming, which is undesirable both because of its effects on the globally least advantaged and its more general effects.

Turning now to the matter of how the costs associated with repairing the damage of global warming should be assigned, consider the following reasonable principle about financial responsibility for the cost of harms suffered: Where causal responsibility for harm can be established, all and only those causally responsible should be made to absorb the costs of the harm in proportion to their causal responsibility. The idea behind this principle is that financial responsibility lies with causal responsibility. Earlier I noted that 11 percent of the world's population is responsible for 40 percent of the current carbon dioxide emissions. Following the above principle, it may seem that this 11 percent ought to underwrite 40 percent of the costs of repairing the damage of global warming in the developing world. Although I defend this position, there are several complicating factors that require sorting out.

One can be seen by way of example. Suppose that a person in a developing country decides to construct a house near an eroding seashore, when the risks associated with doing so should be known to a reasonable person. In this case, such a person has assumed the risk, and the responsibility of others to absorb that person's costs vanishes. So, there may be instances in which, due to the assumption of the risk, those who are harmed as the result of global warming could not reasonably expect to have their costs subsidized. However, cases like this are probably exceptions to the general rule. If so, they do not threaten the general application of the principle that financial responsibility lies with causal responsibility.

Another complicating factor is that, arguably, persons in the developing world have contributed more than 60 percent to the problem of global warming when one considers not merely greenhouse gas emissions but also deforestation. The forests of the world play an important role in absorbing carbon dioxide, and carbon dioxide is released when forests are burnt. One UN study concluded that tropical forests in the developing world are disappearing at a rate of 11 million hectares per year. At that rate tropical rain forests will disappear from seventeen countries within the twenty-first century.[98] The causes of rain forest deforestation are several, including commercial logging and farming, industrial development, and population growth among subsistence farmers, who require the former forest land for farmland and the wood for fuel.[99] In short, deforestation is often the product of poverty and efforts at economic development. Insofar as the current world distribution of resources is unjust, then deforestation is often a strategy for betterment or survival under conditions of injustice. It would not be fair to hold persons in the developing world responsible for the effects of strategies brought on by background conditions of injustice.

There is a final matter that is more troublesome than the previous two complicating factors. Even if persons in the developed world are causally responsible for approximately 40 percent of the global warming, this is the result of more than 100 years of industrialization. So, the class of persons causally responsible is much larger than the class of persons currently living in the developed world.[100] If financial responsibility is supposed to be based upon causal responsibility, it would be putting an extra burden on those currently living in the developed world to make them financially responsible for approximately 40 percent of the costs of global warming. A measure more consistent with that principle would have been to make payments proportional to emissions into an international insurance fund commencing with the dawn of the industrial revolution.

Although the principle that those who are causally responsible should be financially responsible does not require that persons now living in the developed countries should be financially responsible, that principle along with three additional considerations establish good grounds for believing that the 11 percent in the developed world should bear 40 percent of the costs. First, someone must bear these costs. If they are not absorbed by the 11 percent, they will be by the remaining 89 percent of persons in the developing world, either through repairs and relocation or through additional hardships in living. That 89 percent, however, are no more responsible for the historical background of the problem than are the 11 percent. So, the very same considerations that militate against the 11 percent paying 40 percent also militate against the 89 percent paying 100 percent. In other words, the principle that only those who are causally responsible for a harm should be financially responsible in proportion to their causal responsibility also would be violated if persons in the developing world had to pay the full costs of global warming.

Second, given the facts of global inequality, persons in the developed world generally are in a better position to pay than are persons in the developing world. The more the developing countries lay out in covering the costs of global warming, the less they will have to direct toward developmental projects. To make the developing world completely responsible for the costs of global warming could retard development for a long time.

Thirdly, if neither of two given parties are causally responsible for a harm, and if one of the two parties must nevertheless pay, and if allocating the costs to one would seriously affect that party's well-being due to desperate circumstances, then the party in the better position to pay ought to pay. Why? The most minimal reason is that public policy ought not to create undeserved suffering on the part of those who are already suffering the most. One way of seeing the plausibility of this principle is to imagine what is involved in denying it. Suppose that someone asserted that burdens should be assigned so as to create undeserved suffering among those who are suffering most in order that others suffering less or not at all do not have to bear those burdens. Such a claim amounts to asserting that public policy may make the worst-off even worse off. If my earlier arguments are sound, this is incompatible with equal respect for persons. Hence, it seems reasonable to require that the 11 percent of the world's population living in developed countries should be financially responsible for 40 percent of the costs of global warming in the developing countries.

CONCLUSION

I have argued in defense of the first of the ideal worlds that I sketched at the beginning of this chapter. This ideal includes global duties of distributive justice, not merely state-bound duties. The upshot is that there is a duty of distributive justice both to oppose those policies and institutions that are currently wreaking such havoc on the lives of the least advantaged throughout the world, and to engage in a process of transformation to, and construction of, global institutions of egalitarian wealth distribution.

One final point is worth noting. I have adopted an individualist view that the fundamental objects of the duties of distributive justice are persons, not collectives such as states. One consequence of this focus is that, so long as state institutions mediate international obligations between persons, particularly unjust (or even highly inefficient) state institutions may provide reasons for not undertaking the international wealth transfers demanded by justice. Barry has argued otherwise, but this is consistent with his view (at the time, at least) that the fundamental objects of the duties of international justice are states.[101] Just as a reasonable expectation that someone will squander money is not a reason not to transfer money owed according to justice, so, according to Barry's view, an expectation that a state will not distribute money to the needy is not reason not to transfer the amount owed it according to justice. If the fundamental objects of the duties of international justice are persons, then a transfer effected through unjust (or highly inefficient) state institutions may not reach the intended objects but may instead end up topping off already full pockets.

Thus, special problems of non-ideal justice arise when corrupt states mediate the transfers. I accept that such circumstances constitute some reason (although whether or not sufficient reason depends upon the circumstances) to reject otherwise justified transfers. I doubt that there is a non-vague criterion of what counts as sufficient injustice (or inefficiency) for vitiating a duty of global distributive justice. The mere possibility of corruption, however, is no reason for complacency when we have not even yet established the institutions through which such distribution might be effected. Meanwhile, current institutions and policies are daily taking a tremendous toll on the least advantaged of the world.

FIVE

Cosmopolitan Sovereignty and Justified Intervention

There are few questions which more require to be taken in hand by eth-
ical and political philosophers, with a view to establish some rule or
criterion whereby the justifiableness of intervening in the affairs of
other countries, and (what is sometimes fully as questionable) the justi-
fiableness of refraining from intervention, may be brought to a definite
and rational test.

—John Stuart Mill[1]

In previous chapters I have laid out various principles concerning what persons owe one another in the cosmopolitan framework. If all went well
among persons, and just institutions at the state and global level were in
place and functioning, there would be little need to take up the subject matter of this chapter. Whether owing to weakness in the governing structures
or oppressive control over them, the fact is that states often do not establish
principles that ensure these entitlements. Hence, it is necessary to reflect on
what should be done in order to respect these rights. The issue of sovereignty arises in this context. For it is possible that, although persons are not
receiving their due because of weak or oppressive state structures, others
may do nothing about it because the principle of sovereignty protects the
state from intervention by outside parties.

   In this chapter I shall argue that states with unjust basic structures and
those engaged in international injustices are not protected by sovereignty.[2] I
shall present the case for this and look at the problems with a number of

arguments that are critical of the position. The upshot of this, however, is not that outside intervention is justified whenever such injustices exist. On the contrary, I shall defend three additional necessary conditions for justified intervention.

THE CONCEPTS OF SOVEREIGNTY
AND INTERVENTION

Throughout this chapter I use the term *sovereignty* to mean what some writers have referred to as external sovereignty.[3] Sovereignty as a concept of international political morality concerns the authority of a state to rule without the intervention of foreign states or regional or global governmental bodies. To attribute sovereignty to a state in this sense is to say that it has a certain moral status, namely, that there is a domain of influence in which its power ought to be final. Sovereignty is a relational property involving a state, one of its domains, and other governing bodies that may attempt to intervene in that domain. Although some writers limit sovereignty to a relationship of authority over persons, this seems to me to be too narrow.[4] A sovereign state may exercise authority over various domains: certain activities, certain people, or certain territories. When a state is sovereign with respect to some domain, other states may not intervene in that domain without the consent of the state. In other words, sovereignty limits justified state intervention.

Intervention is any nonconsensual activity by another state or regional or global governing body that usurps power over a domain reasonably claimed by a governing state. The requirement that a domain be reasonably claimed excludes, for example, states claiming the right to govern in a territory acquired by unjust conquest. What counts as a reasonable claim over a domain is often a matter of relatively noncontroversial norms of international conduct; for example, a state may not reasonably claim powers to tax citizens of another state who are neither residing nor employed in its territory. This is not to say that what counts as reasonable is always noncontroversial. Disputes over secession typically involve controversial claims over domains by both the established state and the seceding party. Because of the range of state activity, I doubt that a complete and general account can be given of reasonable claims to domains. In any case, this is not my concern in the present chapter.

Countermeasures are retaliatory acts for violations of principles of international law. According to the foregoing definition of *intervention*, such activity is often interventionary.[5] Given certain violations of international law, countermeasures may be justified where, absent those violations, intervention would otherwise not be justified. In this chapter, however, I shall discuss only the morality of interventions that are not warranted by principles of countermeasure. So, when I use the term *intervention* here, I am not referring to activities of countermeasure, which may have different justifications than those discussed in this chapter.

Military intervention into an area reasonably claimed by the state is intervention insofar as it usurps governance of that territory. Likewise, the funding of political parties by a foreign state is intervention if it is contrary to state policies for funding parties. A state may intervene into the domain of another state without intending to do so when, for example, in exercising its police powers it unintentionally pursues a suspected criminal into the territory of another state. This would count as intervention, albeit unintentional, because it usurps the police powers of the latter state.

The account of intervention I propose is nonmoralized; in other words, interference in a domain reasonably claimed by a state is still intervention even if it is justified. Settling the matter of whether an activity is an intervention does not settle the moral matter of whether it is permissible. In contrast, a moralized account of intervention would hold that interference in the domain of a state only counts as intervention if it is unjustified. A moralized conception of intervention is counterintuitive, for it would entail that the prosecution of a just war, surprisingly, would not be an act of intervention. It seems more sensible to hold that whether an act is an intervention is independent of whether it is just.

Sovereignty from the Cosmopolitan Point of View

The cosmopolitan conception of sovereignty holds that an intervention into one of the domains reasonably claimed by a state is a violation of sovereignty if and only if the intervention will not attempt to advance the cause of justice either in the basic structure of the state or in the international effects of its domestic policies.[6] A straightforward argument in defense of this conception can be made by invoking the value of justice. Basic structures that are comparatively just, where the relevant comparison is to the structure that the intervention would effect, and that do not lead to international injustices should be protected since their alteration would come at a cost to justice itself. One way of protecting such arrangements is through the claim of sovereignty. Sovereignty protects such arrangements from the claim that other states or governing bodies have a right to change them. If a principle of international political morality granted that an unjust basic structure was within the domain over which a state has sovereignty, that principle would be protecting injustice. Providing the blanket protection of sovereignty to a comparatively unjust basic structure or policies with unjust international effects is wrong. It may inhibit the cause of justice. It is better that these receive no such protection, for this allows that effort to alter them, even from the outside, may be permissible. Whether the alteration is, in fact, permissible depends upon other considerations as well, which I shall explore.

Most writers on the subject of sovereignty would disagree with the argument in the preceding paragraph. Since I seem to be offering an unpopular view, I shall spend considerable time demonstrating what I take to be the flaws of the various arguments that contradict the cosmopolitan conception of sovereignty.

THE STATIST CONCEPTION OF SOVEREIGNTY

What I call the statist conception of sovereignty holds that a state has moral authority over a domain in virtue of exercising supreme de facto (although not necessarily always unchallenged) authority over that domain. The difference then between the cosmopolitan and the statist conceptions of sovereignty has to do with the warrant for the authority against intervention. The cosmopolitan conception takes the warrant to be justice alone, while the statist conception takes the warrant to be the fact of political control.

The statist conception entails an absolutist interpretation of the principle of nonintervention. According to the view that claims of sovereignty are justified if the claimant controls the domain, there is nothing that the claimant can do, apart from loosing control of the domain, to render the claim null and void.[7] Hence, sovereignty over the domain licenses the state to do as it wishes in the domain. However, conceptions of sovereignty can be partially statist without being absolutist. Some people advocate a restricted statist conception, which allows for a diminution of authority if a limited set of moral requirements is not met, especially if the state is engaged in gross violations of human rights on the order of genocide. This is perhaps best referred to as "a mixed conception" since the authority of the state stems from two sources: the fact that it exercises de facto authority and its adherence to minimal moral requirements.[8] I shall treat mixed conceptions together with statist conceptions, because both differ from the cosmopolitan conception in allowing the fact of political control to provide some warrant for a claim of sovereignty.

The statist conception of sovereignty is not completely antithetical to the goal of justice. It does not block progress toward justice by political processes *within* the state. Rather, it functions as a side constraint to the achievement of a more just order. Pursuit of this end may not involve the intervention of outside agents. Seen in this way, sovereignty is a right that states may claim regardless of their political or moral character.

Recall that sovereignty as moral concept concerns the *authority* of the state to govern without intervention, not the *power* to do so. This is an important distinction, in part because economic developments are eroding the power of states to govern without being subject to a variety of constraints. This is particularly the case in those developing countries pursuing a development strategy called "modernization by internationalization."[9] These developments may encroach on the power of the state vis-à-vis various international actors, and some argue the sovereignty of the state is thereby also reduced.[10] It does not follow, however, that because a state has lost the power to do something it has thereby lost the moral authority to do it. The transfer of power need not involve the transfer of moral authority. The thief who steals my credit card may have the power to use it, but does not possess the moral authority to do so. Indeed, some will want to criticize the loss of state power in the regime of globalization on the basis of the ideal of state sovereignty. So, the fact that states may be loosing power under globalization does not entail that the statist conception of sovereignty is false.

The statist conception of sovereignty enjoys widespread acceptance by statespersons. It is able to garner substantial support from them because it allows that the internal policies of a state shall not compromise its sovereignty. I shall analyze here various arguments offered in defense of the statist conception, or its corollary the absolutist interpretation of the principle of nonintervention—which also amount to challenges to the cosmopolitan conception that I have already defended. To refute these arguments is part of a complete defense of the cosmopolitan conception of sovereignty. The arguments are of two main kinds. One proceeds by appealing to various considerations of justice, the same value appealed to in the cosmopolitan conception. These arguments, I believe, rely on implausible accounts of the elements of justice or of their moral priority. The other kind of argument appeals to some value other than justice as the basis for sovereignty. In response, I shall argue that it is implausible that the other value trumps considerations of justice. The upshot, I hope, amounts to a refutation of the various ways of denying the cosmopolitan conception of sovereignty.

Sovereignty as Dominium

The classical defense of the statist conception of sovereignty is based upon an analogy to property.[11] Just as the right to property entitles the owner to exclude others from using that property and to do whatever is desired with it, so sovereignty entitles the sovereign to be free from interference and to carry out governance as seen fit. In both cases, having the right entitles the bearer to do the wrong thing.[12]

There are two related problems with this analogy.[13] First, a right to property that includes the right to do whatever one wants with it is untenable. The law of nuisance is one example of a widely accepted practice of limiting a property owner's use-rights by the interests of others. Second, and more to the point, property rights are justified to the extent that they protect important moral interests of individuals to live as they choose. Indeed, limits on property rights are justified in terms of balancing the owners' interests against the claims of the nonowners, for example when ownership creates externalities.

The only important moral interests associated with the power of a sovereign are those of self-governance. A ruler who is not an agent of the people has no moral interest in sovereignty to balance against the interests of the ruled, and therefore not even a prima facie claim to sovereignty. A ruler who is the agent of the ruled possesses a prima facie claim to sovereignty that may be balanced against the claims of others falling within the claimed sovereignty. This sort of balancing, however, undermines the statist conception of sovereignty, for it concedes that the sovereign's authority to act is limited by the interests of others.

The Right to Share a Common Life Together

One influential account of sovereignty is based upon the claimed right of states to protect a political order and territory on behalf of its citizens. Michael Walzer defends this account by employing what he calls "the domestic analogy."

> A man has certain rights in his home, for example, even if he does not own it, because neither his life nor his liberty is secure unless there exists some physical space within which he is safe from intrusion. Similarly again, the right of a nation or people not to be invaded derives from the common life its members have made on this piece of land—it had to be made somewhere—and not from the legal title they hold or don't hold.[14]

According to Walzer's account, states have the right to be free from aggression, or the imminent threat thereof, because individuals have the right to share a common life together and the state by the consent of its citizens protects this individual right.[15]

Walzer's account requires an account of justice that either ranks the right to share a common life together above all other considerations of justice or includes only this right. Neither, however, is plausible. Consider the example of a state that, in an effort to preserve a shared way of life for some of its citizens and residents, violates the human rights of others living in its territory by, say, racially discriminating against them. In such a case the right to share a common life together should not trump the rights of those who would be racially oppressed. If the right to share a common life together cannot plausibly be taken as more important than certain other considerations of justice, then it surely cannot be taken as the only consideration.

The fact that the right to share a common life together cannot plausibly rank higher than at least some other considerations of justice does not necessarily reveal a disanalogy between a right to nonintervention and a right to privacy, as asserted by the domestic analogy. On the contrary, the analogy may stand if Walzer also misinterprets the license that privacy allows. For example, just as a right to privacy may not provide license to injustices such as domestic violence, so a right to nonintervention may not provide license to injustices such as racial discrimination.[16] This, of course, is no relief for Walzer's argument since it contradicts the claim that sovereignty is simply a function of the right to share a common life together.

Independence

One influential defense of the statist conception of sovereignty is that it is a requirement of an independent state in an international community of states.[17] This claim, however, is tautologous and begs the question. If being independent is taken to mean that no other state may exercise authority over another sovereign state, then all sovereign states according to either the statist or the cosmopolitan conception are independent. The issue is whether all states should be independent, even those maintaining unjust basic structures.

Perhaps the advocate of independence would want to argue that independence is a value that trumps other considerations of justice. I can see only two reasons for valuing independence. One is that being independent is intrinsically valuable because it amounts to sharing a common life together. However, the value of sharing a common life together, as we have just seen, does not trump other considerations of justice. The second reason is that independence is necessary in order to assure that just institutions are maintained. The idea is that self-governance is the best guarantee of justice. If this is the case, then far from trumping other considerations of justice, independence is valuable only insofar as it serves them. So, according to either account of the value of independence, it is wrong to see it as trumping other considerations of justice.

The Constitution of Moral Personality

An alternative account of sovereignty involves avoiding altogether the claim that state sovereignty rests on the rights of individuals. One argument of this sort has a Hegelian pedigree and involves a central claim—what I call *the constitutive claim*—that moral personhood can only come to be within a state.[18] Mervyn Frost contends that this entails that persons are not prior to states.[19] Frost seems to claim further that the lack of priority of persons means that the claims of persons may not trump the claims of a state (insofar as this norm is a settled one of the sovereign state-system).[20] Furthermore, moral personhood requires not merely a state, but a sovereign state.[21] The corollary to this is supposed to be that intervention into the affairs of a sovereign state cannot be justified on the basis of protecting justice for persons.

This argument requires several responses. First, the conclusion, as stated in the corollary, begs the question. If respect for state sovereignty is morally required, there is no reason why the conception of sovereignty employed must be the statist rather than the cosmopolitan one. According to the cosmopolitan conception of sovereignty, intervention into the affairs of a sovereign state also cannot be justified in the name of protecting persons since sovereign states, by virtue of having just basic structures and policies with just international effects, already generally afford persons protection or at least do them no unjust harm.

Further problems arise from Frost's apparent belief that the constitutive claim entails the claim that persons are not prior to states and that this entails the view that the claims of persons may not trump the claims of states. Remember that the constitutive claim says that moral personhood can only develop within a state. It is not clear whether the constitutive claim is meant to be stating a causal or a logical truth. The claim may mean that states alone bring persons into existence, or that the existence of a person entails the existence of a state. According to the former interpretation, one could imagine persons without states; but it would be a contingent truth, due to certain causal processes, that persons have states. According to the latter interpretation, one could not even imagine a person who is stateless: It would be a contradiction, like trying to imagine human beings that are not animals. It seems unlikely that Frost would be making a claim such as the latter interpretation, for it is very difficult to think of how one might plausibly argue that a stateless person is a contradiction. On the other hand, one could present a more plausible causal argument to the effect that if the rational capacities of persons are to develop, then state processes of recognition are required.

If Frost means that only states bring into existence persons, then it would be true of any given person (P_1) that there would be some state (S_1) to which she was not prior to in two ways. P_1 is not temporally prior to S_1 (P_1 did not exist before S_1 since effects may not proceed their causes); and P_1 is not causally prior to S_1 (P_1 did not cause S_1 since effects do not cause their causes). P_1 may still, however, be either temporally or causally prior to some other state, S_2. In other words, according to the causal interpretation of the constitutive claim, persons may indeed be prior to many states, namely, those states that did not cause them. So, Frost's claim that persons are not prior to states requires a qualification.

Frost's argument about the moral status of persons and states trades on an ambiguity in the term *priority*. Suppose the qualified claim about temporal and causal priority is true, that P_1 is neither temporally nor causally prior to S_1. It does not follow that the moral claims of P_1 may not trump those of S_1. Consider the example of the temporal and causal priority of parents and their children. Children are neither temporally nor causally prior to their parents. Nonetheless, moral claims of children may sometimes trump those of their parents.

Would the inference to moral priority follow any more easily from the less plausible logical interpretation of the constitutive claim? If Frost means that the existence of a person entails the existence of a state and not vice-versa, this means that for any given person (P_1) there would be some state (S_1) to which P_1 was not logically prior since S_1 does not entail P_1. Some persons, though, must still be logically prior to S_1 since there can be no states without persons as citizens. In other words, S_1 entails P_2. So again, only a qualified version of the priority of states would be true. Suppose this qualified claim is true: Persons are not logically prior to states in the sense that S_1 does not entail P_1. It does not follow that the moral claims of P_1 may not trump those of S_1. Consider the following example. The existence of a human being entails the existence of at least one animal, namely, that human being. The existence of an animal does not entail the existence of a human being. It in no way follows that the moral claims of human beings may not trump those of animals.

In sum, regardless of whether the constitutive claim is taken to be asserting that states bring into existence persons or that the existence of persons entails the existence of states, neither interpretation implies that the moral claims of persons may not trump those of states.

The final problem with Frost's view is that he takes the claim that individuals are not morally prior to states to mean that individuals without states have no rights.[22] Intuitively, this seems implausible. Not only does it mean that one encountering the mythical Robinson Crusoe or the Wild Child could not by any deed violate their human rights (since they have none), but also that those who are really without a state have no rights. This would include, for example, the population of countries where, by most accounts, the state has disintegrated. Examples in Africa such as Somalia come to mind.

Frost might respond that it's not an actual state that is required but simply the recognition of sovereignty in a state system. This, however, will not do for two reasons. First, if the constitutive claim has any plausibility at all, it seems to be because real states do have real legal processes that recognize the claims of individuals, thereby in a sense bringing persons into existence.

The assertion that persons may be constituted in the absence of these processes undermines the constitutive claim. Secondly, the response implies that "citizens" of polities that are not recognized as states have no human rights. This would include, for example, the "citizens" of the former Transkei, which was accepted as an independent state only in the propaganda of the apartheid regime in South Africa.

Tolerance and Pluralism

Another charge against the cosmopolitan conception of sovereignty is that it is ill-suited to our world, in which people are organized into states often pursuing different, legitimate, but incompatible conceptions of the social good. In this world the substantive universalism of cosmopolitanism would amount to intolerance of different legitimate conceptions of the social good.[23] This argument either rests on an indefensible view of tolerance or begs the question.

Tolerance is a political virtue requiring the acceptance of, and nondiscrimination toward, ways of life that respect the demands of justice. As such it is a virtue that is constrained by justice. Permission of unjust acts is not tolerance. It is either regrettable as an all-things-considered necessity, or it is a moral failure. In either case, permission of unjust acts is an injustice to those who have suffered. A state is not tolerant if it permits a murderer to murder; nor is international society tolerant when it permits, say, the systematic violations of human rights. Because of the force of these considerations, advocates of tolerance often allow that sovereignty should be limited by respect for human rights.[24] However, if the above argument offers support for constraining sovereignty in order to protect human rights, it would be question-begging not to constrain sovereignty by other components of justice in the absence of an argument that human rights considerations exhaust considerations of justice.[25]

Relativism

The challenge to the cosmopolitan conception of sovereignty in the name of relativism is that because there is no universal standard of justice, an absolutist interpretation of the principle of nonintervention is morally superior to the license that the cosmopolitan conception gives to intervention. Unlike the criticism based upon pluralism, which holds that there are multiple and incompatible conceptions of the social good, the relativist challenge is based upon the claim that moral truth varies with cultural tradition, hence there is no universal standard of justice.

The only issue I take with this substantive meta-ethical claim here is that if the account of persons I offered in Chapter 2 is sound, then relativism is false. Even if the substantive meta-ethical claim about relativism were true, however, an absolutist principle of nonintervention would not follow from it. [26] On the contrary, in order for the principle of nonintervention to be secure, it needs to be based upon a universal moral claim that states ought to be protected against intervention. Suppose that whatever a cultural tradition holds to be the moral truth is the moral truth. If it is a cultural belief in a particular state that it is permissible to interfere with the affairs of another state, then it is permissible for that state to do so. The claim of relativism, therefore, cannot secure an absolutist principle of nonintervention.

Peace

One common defense of the statist conception of sovereignty focuses on the threat to peace that exists when the requirements for sovereignty include the claims of justice. A conception of sovereignty requiring that the demands of justice be met would be inappropriate in principle, so the argument might go, because it would justify too many military interventions; and it would be even more inappropriate in practice because it is much more open to hypocritical abuse by states than one which granted all states sovereign status. Rather than limiting the power for state abuse, as a theory of justice is meant to do, it expands it.[27]

Considering first the question of principle, two responses are in order. First, from the claim that military intervention into a domain over which the state is sovereign suffices to render that intervention unjust, it does not follow that military intervention into a domain over which the state is not sovereign is just. Lack of sovereignty may be a necessary but not a sufficient condition for justified military intervention.[28] Other conditions, such as the reasonable belief in the likelihood of successfully establishing a more just order, may also be necessary. If some ground is given way to permissible interventions, there is no reason to suppose that all ground is lost.

Second, even granting that necessary conditions other than the lack of a claim to sovereignty exist, there may nonetheless be interventions that are justified on the cosmopolitan conception but not on the statist one. Such interventions might be referred to as "humanitarian interventions" because they are justified in part by comparative injustice. The justification of these interventions must rely in part on a claim that justice at least sometimes outweighs peace.[29] Is this a plausible claim?

The value of peace is twofold. First of all, peace is valuable because human life and well-being are valuable. The disruption of peace involves suffering and death. Secondly, peace is also of value insofar as it provides protection to just institutions. This latter value expresses its instrumental value. If this were the only reason for valuing peace, then it would be a simple argument to establish the greater weight of justice. For if peace were valuable only insofar as it served justice, it would have no value in circumstances in which achieving justice required violence. Peace, however, has intrinsic value as well. Because of this, there is room for disagreement on the relative weight of peace and justice.

Pacifists claim that political violence, even if it were to achieve the aims of justice, is not justified. I maintain that it is sometimes justified to kill and cause suffering in pursuit of political values, in particular the value of justice. I shall defend this view in Chapter 7 where I focus on the use of violence for political ends. My argument here will be, of necessity, sketchy and will simply involve appeals to examples.

All that is required to establish the claim that justice sometimes outweighs peace is to demonstrate that there are times when it is right to kill if necessary to prevent or overcome an injustice. Consider, for example, the case of chattel slavery. Those who deny that justice ever outweighs peace would have to maintain that even if the only means by which a system of chattel slavery could be overcome was by violence, there would still be no case for violence because of the greater value of peace. Another, more mundane, example is law enforcement. The person who values peace over justice would have to say that law enforcement must be nonviolent, even if that means that the guilty are not apprehended. Neither of these examples will convince the confirmed pacifist. Any attempt to do that would require addressing the substantive claims of pacifism. I suspect that for a great many people, however, examples such as these demonstrate that, sometimes at least, the value of justice outweighs that of peace.

Perhaps someone will claim that real peace is more than the absence of violence: It includes social arrangements of mutual respect or even mutual caring.[30] To the extent that this is true, it does not take away from the point that I am arguing because it suggests that just, or proto-just, relations are constitutive of real peace. If this is the case, then there is little or no room to oppose the violent pursuit of justice on the grounds of valuing peace, for the pursuit of just relations simply is the pursuit of peace. The advocate of peace may respond that the ends of peace, such as mutual respect, cannot be achieved by violence. This would appear to be an empirical question. It seems to me to be implausible to claim that violence has never served the cause of justice. Was not the military defeat of the Nazi regime an advance for justice? The advocate of peace, however, may maintain that it is not an empirical question after all because the conception of peace may be one of mutual respect and caring, which is more demanding than the appeals to justice that I have cited. I doubt that mutual caring is a feasible, or even desirable, goal for polities the size of states; and equal respect for persons is the very foundation of the account of cosmopolitan justice that I have been defending.

The practical criticism asserts that the statist conception of sovereignty is more appropriate than the cosmopolitan one because it limits the power of states to exercise violence in a world in which states are known to be ready to rationalize their violent practices. The force of this criticism is based on a consideration of the costs of the actual employment of the cosmopolitan conception of sovereignty. What the criticism ignores, however, is that there are costs to the statist conception of sovereignty as well. Even in the absence of hypocritical misuse, the statist conception is insensitive to injustices when in fact intervention could do something about them. So, while the practical criticism may state a truth about the cosmopolitan perspective, there is no reason to think that only the cosmopolitan perspective involves costs when practiced. Moreover, the costs of the two conceptions are importantly different. The criticism of the cosmopolitan conception is that it involves costs when it is *misused* to rationalize unjust interventions. The statist conception involves costs in its *normal use*; it is meant to be insensitive to injustices. Hence, it would not be surprising to find that the practical costs of the statist conception would occur with greater regularity than those of cosmopolitan conception.

Self-emancipation and Paternalism

One defense of the absolutist principle of nonintervention is based upon the principle of self-emancipation. This principle can claim the authority of John Stuart Mill and Karl Marx.[31] Although a just political order is a great good, an outside agent cannot hand it to a people: A necessary condition is that the oppressed themselves bring it into being. The plausibility of this increases if a just order itself requires either constant vigilance in defense of liberty or popular participation in governance. Perhaps the political virtues required for maintaining a just order can only be taught in the school of political struggle.

One can accept the claim that the virtues citizens must have to maintain a just order require participation in struggling for that order without accepting the conclusion that intervention on behalf of the struggle is never justified. Suppose that popular struggle is a necessary condition for the maintenance of just institutions after a victorious struggle. It does not follow that victory without any outside assistance is also a necessary condition. The condition of popular struggle can be met in conjunction with outside intervention. Moreover, history is replete with examples of those who have struggled against oppression and lost. It is implausible to assert categorically that if they had been aided in their struggle, they would not have been able to achieve a more just social order. Consider the Spanish Civil War, the Warsaw Ghetto, the Hungarian uprising of 1956, and so on.

Certainly there may be times when outside intervention would be so manipulative as to render advances for justice impossible or improbable, but this has to do with the character of the intervention, not with the requirement that those struggling win it themselves. The self-emancipation position is unrealistic if it does not recognize that sometimes, perhaps usually, those who lose just struggles do so not for lack of political virtue but for lack of military power. [32]

Thus far I have argued on the basis of the supposition that popular struggle is a necessary condition for the advancement of justice. Although popular struggle may often be required, there is no reason to believe that it is always required. The Federal Republic of Germany, certainly an advance over Nazi Germany from the perspective of justice, came into existence without a popular revolt against the Nazi regime. North Vietnam deposed the genocidal Khmer Rouge in Cambodia in the absence of a popular revolt. So, whatever truth there is in the claim that popular struggle advances the cause of justice, it would be wrong to elevate it to the status of a necessary condition.

An alternative argument with a similar concern is that even if interventions might sometimes achieve a more just order, they remain nevertheless unjustifiably paternalistic.[33] This is, however, to misunderstand the nature of paternalism and thus to miss what is morally troubling about it. Paternalist actions or policies are those performed or enacted on behalf of the interests of others, but not by them, and that deny them the opportunity to choose. If the opportunity to choose is sufficiently important, then paternalism is wrong even if the consequences are good. This wrong can be captured in a Kantian manner by the claim that paternalist actions or policies treat a person merely as a means to the good of the consequences to be achieved. Interventions into the affairs of another state may be paternalistic if they, in fact, deny those citizens suffering the intervention the opportunity to choose their social structures. Humanitarian interventions may however occur in a context in which there is popular dissatisfaction with the policies and institutions of the state but insufficient political or military power to change them. Such interventions would not be paternalistic since they would be supporting popular choice rather than denying it. Humanitarian interventions, then, are not of necessity paternalistic.

A rejoinder to my argument might be that such interventions are nonetheless paternalistic because there will be some individuals who do not share the goals of the popular struggle and are therefore denied the opportunity to choose. However, these "paternalistic" actions are no more troublesome than majority rule in democratic processes. For even these processes deny the minority the opportunity not to be governed by the practice. The mark of paternalism cannot simply be that some disagree with policy since then even the most libertarian policy achieved by a nonunanimous democratic vote would be paternalistic.

Anti-imperialism

The anti-imperialist challenge bears some resemblance to the anti-paternalist one. However, rather than being a concern that intervention will deny citizens the opportunity to choose, it is a concern that intervention will either be contrary to what citizens actually choose or to what justice (especially global distributive justice) demands.[34] Like the argument based upon the value of peace, this one requires both principled and practical responses.

Assume that a necessary condition of justified intervention is a reasonable belief in the likelihood of success in establishing a more just order. Then, most interventions directed toward some aspect of a more just social order, but which are against the popular will, would be unjustified because often it would be unreasonable to believe that an intervention violating the will of the majority could succeed in establishing a lasting, more just order. The wrong of this sort of intervention is not captured by the cosmopolitan conception of sovereignty but by a criterion of justified intervention that complements it. I asserted that most interventions of this sort would be unjustified, not that all would be. Such an intervention might not be unjust if its goal is not an enduring, more just order, but merely the prevention of an immanent injustice.

Consider the case of an intervention that is necessary to stop the imminent threat of a popular but gross human rights abuse against a minority population. The great good of preventing atrocities of this nature in the short term is the goal, not the establishment of an enduring more just order. Although such an intervention might be justified, a criterion of justified intervention complementing the cosmopolitan conception of sovereignty would not generally license imperialist interventions if these are defined as contrary to the popular will of the citizenry. Where such interventions are licensed, it would be due to dire emergencies that necessitate a shorter-term vision of the goal of the intervention.

The cosmopolitan conception of sovereignty also would not generally justify intervening when the goal was contrary to what global distributive justice required, since the intervention would typically not be an advance for justice. Again, exceptions are conceivable to this general rule. Suppose the intervention would *maintain* conditions of international inequality contrary to the demands of international distributive justice, but *establish* a more just domestic order in a particular state, as, arguably, the 1994 intervention in Haiti did. Even though the goal is in one sense contrary to justice, if the likely outcome is a net gain from the perspective of justice (in this case a more just domestic order), then the cosmopolitan conception of justice would allow the intervention, assuming other necessary conditions are met. The fact that an intervention is imperialist, then, does not entail that it is unjust, even though such interventions typically are.[35]

So much for the problems of what the conception would allow in principle. Its actual application raises an additional problem. Militarily weaker countries with colonial pasts may fear that a principle permitting interventions in the name of justice will be used to rationalize military interventions against them that are in fact contrary to the goals of justice.[36] Obviously, the possibility of such duplicity cannot be ruled out by a theory. When we consider the extent to which the United States (ostensibly committed to the statist conception of sovereignty) was able to engage in imperialistic interventions in Latin America in order to prevent popular change,[37] there is no reason to think that the cosmopolitan conception of sovereignty could not be abused or simply ignored.[38] This danger, however, must be weighed against the costs of not permitting an intervention when it would likely result in a more just state of affairs. The costs of not intervening are real and immediate, and the danger that such an intervention will enable other unjust interventions is hypothetical and remote. More important, whether a just intervention would provide the required precedence for a later unjust one is determined by the political and institutional capacity in the future to prevent unjust interventions. This capacity is a function of political organization and power, not moral principle.

Intervention

The cosmopolitan conception of sovereignty entails that a state cannot claim the protection of the principle of nonintervention in one of its domains unless the intervention will not attempt to advance the cause of justice in the basic structure of the state or the international effects of its policies. No doubt a main source of opposition to the cosmopolitan account derives from a worry that it would license far too many interventions since it makes it more difficult for a state to claim protection against intervention on the basis of sovereignty.[39] If we assume that a basic structure is comparatively unjust and therefore cannot claim the shield of sovereignty to prohibit interventions, it does not follow that any sort of intervention against it is justified. Although the cosmopolitan conception of sovereignty may nullify one kind of argument against intervention, there may be several grounds for justified intervention that cannot be met simply by demonstrating that a state may not claim the protection of sovereignty. I shall turn now to the matter of when and what sorts of interventions are justified.

Basic Structures and Government Policies

In discussing the subject of justice, Rawls distinguishes the basic structure of society from other aspects of the state and society. The basic structure includes the constitution and institutions that it mandates as well as the fundamental economic institutions of the state. Government policy on the other hand includes the effects of governmental power (typically) within the limits of the basic structure. Since the basic structure does not cover the whole of social and political life, it is possible for governmental policy to be unjust in the domestic sphere, while the basic structure is not. For example, governmental policy may create a category of victimless crimes that may be unjust.

Intervention that is directed toward overturning only a policy that is unjust in the domestic sphere and not a comparatively unjust basic structure is unjust, even when it is likely to be successful.[40] The reason for this can be seen by reconsidering the arguments about paternalism and the right to share a common life together discussed earlier. These arguments do not apply to the cosmopolitan conception of sovereignty because overturning injustice was not paternalistic when others could not do so themselves; the right to share a common life together cannot trump other considerations of justice. When, however, the domestic injustice that a regime has committed has not altered the justice of the state's basic structure, the opportunity for those aggrieved to rectify matters in the arena of democratic self-governance is still there. It would be paternalistic to impose a just outcome on the citizenry in that case. Moreover, the right to share a common life together in the form of democratic self-governance must include, up to a limit, the right to make moral mistakes together. The appropriate limit is that the mistakes should not produce injustices in basic structure. When they do, the capacity of the citizenry to engage in further acts of self-governance may be limited. At that point it can no longer be claimed that self-governance is harmed by intervention.[41]

These same considerations do not hold with respect to domestic policy that creates injustices in the international sphere. Here the aggrieved do not have a voice in the arena of self-governance. So, there is less reason to suppose that the normal mechanisms of self-governance will arrive at justice, and there is more moral reason to find ways to represent the interests of the aggrieved through interventionary activity. Although intervention may harm self-governance, when self-governance is seriously harming others who have no voice in the process, intervention may be the only realistic way to prevent or remedy the harm.

Conditions of Justified Intervention

Just cause for an intervention exists if and only if the intervention is directed toward advancing justice either in the basic structure of the state or in the international effects of its domestic policies. Just cause is not a sufficient condition of intervention, however, because it does not require that there be good reason to believe that action will remedy the injustice, that such action is necessary to remedy the injustice, and that greater harms will not also be done in the course of attempting to remedy the injustice. This suggests three additional necessary conditions of justified intervention.

First, it must be reasonable to believe that the intervention is likely to succeed. The reason for this with respect to military intervention is due to the prima facie evil of war. The evil of war can be justified only if, on the basis of available information, there are good reasons to believe that it is likely to be successful in producing a morally improved situation. However, analogous reasoning can be applied to nonmilitary interventions. Such interventions are prima facie evils insofar as they usurp what exists of democratic self-governance in a state. A nonmilitary intervention also can be justified only if, on the basis of available information, there are good reasons to believe that it is likely to be successful in producing a morally improved situation. Whether there is a likelihood of success is typically determined prospectively and is based upon conjectures about the balance of forces, the resilience of attitudes to change, and the similarity to other cases.

There are three different ways that an expectation of success may go awry. First, there may be information relevant to the estimation of success that is not available, in which case misjudgment about the likelihood of success is not a culpable error. In this case, it may be reasonable to believe that success is likely even though it is not. Second, there may be sufficient evidence about the likelihood (or lack thereof) of success, but one may misjudge it. In this case one may believe success is likely when it would be unreasonable to believe so. Finally, the outcome may not be as predicted even though there is no error of judgment because the judgment concerns probabilities. In other words, it may be the case that an intervention was in fact likely to succeed, and it was reasonable to believe that it would, but it nonetheless failed. There is no error in judgment in this case, but rather a misfit between what was likely to be the outcome and what came to pass. Since there is no error in judgment, there is obviously no culpable error.

The second necessary condition for justified intervention is that it be of last resort. With respect to military interventions, this criterion ensures that the suffering caused by war is not unnecessary. With respect to nonmilitary interventions, it protects against unnecessary disruptions to what is left of self-government. What counts as a last resort is, however, relative to circumstances. Given an infinite amount of time and no costs associated with delay, no intervention is a last resort. However, there are often significant costs associated with delay, such as loss of opportunity or continued perpetration of injustices. Also there are sometimes reasonable calculations that no noninterventionary means will repair the injustices in the foreseeable future. When a large-scale humanitarian crisis is looming, one where it is reasonable to believe that further diplomacy is likely to fail and where such diplomacy will consume the time necessary for a successful intervention, then an intervention may be considered a last resort even though there is some remote chance of success without it.

Third, interventions must be proportional to the injustice occurring. Military interventions ought not to repair an injustice at costs to human well-being even greater than the injustice itself. Nonmilitary interventions ought not to repair an injustice at costs to what is left of democratic self-government that are even greater than the injustice itself. Determining whether the evil of an intervention is outweighed by the prospect of remedying an injustice is not a simple matter of measuring evils according to a common standard. The evil of intervention may involve things such as loss of innocent life or violations of democratic self-determination, and the evils of injustice may be violations of civil and democratic rights or principles of distributive justice. There does not appear to be a common standard among these evils. The exercise of moral judgment sensitive to the morally salient features of a particular situation is the best that one can expect in these matters. Aristotle's remarks on the importance of a flexible standard for particular cases in matters of equity are relevant here: "For what is itself indefinite can only be measured by an indefinite standard, like the leaden rule used by Lesbian builders; just as that rule is not rigid but can be bent to the shape of the stone, so a special ordinance is made to fit the circumstances of the case."[42]

In defending these three additional criteria of justified intervention, I have considered the similarities in the justifications of both military and nonmilitary interventions. There is also an important difference as well. With respect to military interventions, the evils to be minimized are the loss of human life and well-being. Given the ever-present danger of these evils in military operations, it is reasonable to hold these criteria as absolutely necessary in the justification of military intervention. With respect to nonmilitary interventions, the evil to be avoided is any disruption to the processes of democratic self-governance. Unlike the evil of military interventions, this danger is not always present. When the injustices in the basic structure of a state make democratic self-governance completely impossible, then there is no such danger to be avoided. Hence, the force of these three criteria in restricting nonmilitary interventions varies in proportion to the degree of democratic self-governance that exists within the states.

An additional word needs to be said about the criteria of proportionality and last resort with respect to military interventions. As long as healthy democratic institutions are in place within a state, there is a strong defeasible presumption against military interventions. There are two reasons for this. First, the loss of life incurred would be hard to justify if the injustices were less than the violation of democratic rights. Second, while democratic processes are still in place, generally a society will be open enough for it to be reasonable to hope that nonmilitary means will effect changes in the direction of justice.[43] This presumption is, however, defeasible. For example, democracies are capable of infringing on the rights of minorities. When such infringements are horrible enough and the possibility for nonmilitary change remote enough, then military intervention may be justified.

A case might be made for two additional candidates for necessary conditions for justified intervention: that the intervention must proceed under proper authority and that the intervention must be intended to improve on injustice. The first would proscribe unilateral, and even collective, acts of intervention that were not authorized by the appropriate international body. The main reason in support of this condition is the good of international order. A world in which interventions occurred only if authorized would be a more orderly one than one in which unauthorized, but otherwise just, interventions occurred. The cost of this condition would be that otherwise just interventions would be proscribed if they could not gain proper authority. In other words, this condition would tolerate a loss from the perspective of establishing and maintaining just institutions in order to maintain international order.

The good of order bears some similarity to that of peace. Order is valued, in part, because the order valued is just. Being disorderly in that context disrupts justice. Unlike peace, though, the value of order is entirely instrumental. Consider an orderly unjust society where policies proceed according to the appropriate channels of authority. What sort of loss is there if this society becomes less orderly? The only loss that I can see is that the injustices would become worse, fewer people would get their due, or people would get less of their due. Trade-offs between order and justice then should be made in favor of justice.

Proper authority is quite plausibly good in interventions—especially when the interventions are military ones—although not a necessary condition of justification. Interventions proceeding under proper authority are more likely to be legitimate in the global community.[44] Moreover, when there is proper authority for an intervention, presumably its justification has been subject to multiple levels of review. This might help to ensure that the necessary conditions are satisfied, and that the intervention is not merely serving the interests of the intervening party to the exclusion of justice. These desiderata do not outweigh justice when an otherwise justified intervention fails to receive proper authorization. There is no need to ensure justice when by hypothesis the intervention is just. The value of legitimacy, like the value of order, is a function of whether the legitimate policy or arrangement is just. So, legitimacy should not trump justice.

The second candidate for addition to the necessary conditions for justified intervention is right intent.[45] There are two potential problems with such a requirement: the metaphysical one of the existence of intentions in corporate entities, and the practical one of determining a single intention when there are differing ones within a collective leadership. Perhaps such problems are not insurmountable. Even so, there is a more significant moral problem with requiring right intent. Assume that we can determine the intention behind state action. Although the intent of a state or state institution may play a role in assessing the excellence or virtue of the state, it has no role to play in considering the justice of its actions. The justice of the action or policy of a state is a function of whether or not actions owed to persons are performed, not why they are performed. This is clear when we consider a matter of domestic justice. Whether a scheme for political leadership selection is just depends upon whether citizens participate in a democratic process. A democratic selection process may be enacted with the intention of staving off social unrest, but the process is not therefore unjust. The intentions of the state are of no intrinsic value from the perspective of justice.

One might object that the intentions of the state are nonetheless of instrumental value from the perspective of justice since they indicate the likelihood that the just cause will be realized. Although it may be true that intentions signal the likelihood of achieving ends, there are two considerations that count against requiring right intent. First, the requirement would be redundant since just cause, reasonable belief in the likelihood of success, and proportionality together provide reason to believe that an injustice will be improved upon and that no unnecessary evils will be perpetrated. Second, the requirement is counterproductive since it would prohibit fulfilling duties owed to others if they were not performed for the right reasons. In the above example, the institution of the democratic selection process would not be allowed because the intention was wrong.

To conclude, there are four necessary conditions of justified intervention: (1) An injustice exists in the basic structure or the international effects of policy; (2) it must be reasonable to believe that the intervention is likely to reduce that injustice; (3) the intervention is proportional to the existing injustice; and (4) the intervention is a last resort after diplomatic means have failed.

Permissible versus Obligatory Intervention

Earlier I argued against the view that interventions against unjust basic structures are impermissible. The thrust of my argument seems to commit me to the view that, when all the necessary conditions are met, interventions against unjust basic structures are morally permissible. However, are interventions in such cases merely permissible? Consider what justice demands of compatriots. Citizens and residents must pay taxes to support the police and court system of a country. Payment of taxes for these purposes is a duty of justice that each citizen owes to all others, so that when an injustice occurs the means to stop and remedy it are available. A citizen may not have a duty to help an individual suffering an injustice, but does have a duty to contribute to the justice system that is meant to help. So, a citizen's duty to help may be thought of as discharged through financial support to the state agency that has a duty to help.

In the standard domestic case, when a person has a claim of justice then other co-members of the association that is covered by the principles of justice have a duty to respect that claim. In other words, claims of justice entail duties on others, not merely permissions. If citizens of other states have a claim of justice to be protected against injustices, when the state has failed to provide the protection or is constituting the threat, then there is a corresponding duty on noncompatriots to help remedy the injustice. This duty falls on all noncompatriots, but those who may most easily help are specially obliged to do so. Fulfilling the duty requires action by the states of those who are obliged. The state may be said to have a duty in virtue of its citizens having a duty.[46] Not all duties of states to intervene, however, are duties to intervene militarily.

The conclusion that interventions may be required by duty, not merely permitted, may be challenged in at least four different ways—all of which, I believe, fail. First, it might be argued that fairness requires more of compatriots who, unlike citizens of different states, already participate in the same legal institutions. Fairness might be thought to require the actions called for by the institutions, but no duty of fairness is required in the absence of common legal institutions.[47] This is the position I call justice-positivism in Chapter 3. It is wrong for two closely related reasons. First, it would render unintelligible the seemingly intelligible claim that persons can be under duties to others to construct just institutions, as when political reform or revolution is called for. Second, fairness is not limited to the duty of fair play under existing institutions. Consider the claim that it is unfair for institutions to discriminate on the basis of race. This claim would appear to have substance even when, indeed especially when, institutions are legally permitted to discriminate on the basis of race.

A second reason to believe that interventions under the right conditions are permissible but not obligatory is also based on the fact that well-developed domestic legal institutions exist, but international ones do not. Duties of justice, it might be argued, although owed to other persons, in fact regulate our actions vis-à-vis institutions: We have duties of justice to others to construct and respect just institutions. These are not, however, duties to all other persons, but only to those persons with whom our activity places us in association. If, for example, our commerce affects the moral interests of others, we have a duty of justice toward them. The force of responsibility is directly proportional to the degree of association. Since we are in much closer association with compatriots than with citizens of other countries, we are under duties of justice to the former, but are simply permitted to treat the latter justly.

I shall not take issue with the view that justice is conventional in the sense that the objection states; I defend this in Chapter 3. I do dispute the conclusion drawn from that premise. Although it may be true that we have different duties to persons depending upon our associations, if the association gives rise to any norms of justice, they must be duties, not merely permissions. Consider the claim that we are permitted to treat others justly. This claim is true of all persons (except in cases where doing so would violate duties that we owe to other persons) and not simply those persons with whom we have some association. If association gives rise to norms of justice and a different moral relation to those with whom we associate, these norms must have the force of duties, not mere permissions. If they were mere permissions, they would be no different than the norms governing our relations with those with whom we do not associate.

A third possible reason is that obligatory interventions might require state leaders to act in ways that violate their duties to the citizens of their state.[48] One might maintain this position because one believes that statespersons have special duties to their constituency, and that expending human and material resources on behalf of the cause of justice in other states violates a duty to expend those resources on one's own constituency. The first thing to note about this argument is that it denies even the permissibility of intervening in other states, not just the duty to do so. If expending resources on the cause of justice in other states violates a special duty of leaders to citizens, then doing so is not even permissible. In other words, the argument entails isolationism.

Suppose it is the case that statespersons have special duties to their own constituency. Does it follow that expending resources on the cause of justice in other states violates these duties? It does not, if the expenditures are themselves required by justice. Suppose the statespersons have a kind of fiduciary relationship with their citizens. They are obliged to act on behalf of the interests of those who have put their trust in them. This duty would not necessarily rule out expending resources on behalf of the cause of justice in other states because an agent's duty to act on behalf of those represented is constrained by duties to others. Special duties that one has in virtue of one's office do not amount to license to violate one's general duties. So, if expending resources on behalf of the cause of justice in other states is required by justice, then whatever the content of a statesperson's special duty to the constituency, it does not necessarily trump general duties to expend those resources.

A final reason to believe that interventions under the right conditions are permissible but not obligatory is relevant only to military interventions. The reason is the terrible fact that in military interventions, people die and are seriously injured. A state may not, so the reasoning goes, require certain of its citizens to die for the cause of justice in some other state. This may be granted without damage to the claim that justice may require military interventions in other countries. Consider an analogy to domestic affairs. Perhaps a state may not require certain of its citizens to be police officers and thereby risk life and limb in law enforcement. However, justice may still require that a police force exist and that adult citizens with the means to pay taxes support those who voluntarily become police officers. So, it is possible that conscription to prosecute just military interventions in other states, on behalf of the citizens of those states, is not justified. This does not undermine the claim that there is a duty to intervene.

The claim that there is a prima facie duty to intervene to further the cause of justice is entailed by the claim that persons throughout the world have duties of justice to one another regardless of whether they happen to live in the same country.[49] If persons have duties of justice to those living in other states, then they are obliged to aid with the development and maintenance of just institutions. If no such duties exist, then statespersons are nonetheless permitted to intervene in the affairs of other states. I argued in Chapter 3 that such duties of global justice exist. It follows from the conclusion of that argument, then, that there is a prima facie duty to intervene in the affairs of states either with unjust basic structures or whose domestic policies create international injustices.

INTERVENTION OR ISOLATION

Advocates of the statist conception of sovereignty sometimes contend that intervention is not the only means of effecting change in the direction of a more just order within a state; isolation can also be effective to that end.[50] I have defined intervention broadly as any nonconsensual activity by another state (or regional or global governing body) that usurps power over a domain reasonably claimed by the state.[51] The consequence of this definition is that activities such as embargoes, which might be thought of as examples of isolation rather than intervention, are classified as interventions if they prevent effective control over a domain reasonably claimed by a state.

There are two reasons that count in favor of taking embargoes as acts of intervention. First, given the growth of the global market, participation in it occurs by default for nearly all states. Part of the powers of state governance, for example, is to negotiate trade treaties. It is not the case, then, that thwarting the exercise of that power is a way of "upholding the value of self-determination."[52] Second, the effects of embargoes on citizens within countries may be just as harsh as a military intervention, or even harsher. Thus, embargoes raise many of the same moral issues as do interventions. For these reasons it makes little sense to appeal to isolation—in the form of embargoes—as means by which nonintervention can be respected while pursuing the cause of justice. If intervention into the affairs of a state is impermissible, then an embargo against that state is proscribed.

In the aftermath of the Gulf War, the United Nations has sought to maintain an embargo against Iraq. Arguably just cause for this embargo exists in the lack of democracy and persecution of the Kurdish and other minorities in Iraq and in the threat that its weapons of mass destruction pose to citizens and residents of other states. Thus, the embargo is not a violation of the sovereignty of Iraq. Reasonable belief in the likelihood of success for such a policy is less plausible. Suppose, for the sake of argument, that it is reasonable to believe that given sufficient time, this embargo will succeed in either forcing the leadership into reforms or motivating a popular rebellion against the leadership, thereby improving the injustices in the country. The embargo is nonetheless unjust because the suffering of innocents—especially many children—is disproportionate to the cause pursued.

This embargo, which has slowed or stopped delivery of basic medical supplies, has, as of 1999, raised the infant mortality rate from 3.7 percent before the war to 12 percent, and causes the deaths of some 40,000 children under 5 and some 50,000 older people each year.[53] Compare these figures with all previous deaths from weapons of mass destruction: The atomic bombs of Hiroshima and Nagasaki combined killed 100,000 people, and no more than 80,000 people died from chemical weapons in World War I. This justifies a startling conclusion about the embargo against Iraq:

> If the U.N. estimates of the human damage in Iraq are even roughly correct, therefore, it would appear that—in a so far futile effort to remove Saddam from power and a somewhat more successful effort to constrain him militarily—economic sanctions may well have been a necessary cause of the deaths of more people in Iraq than have been slain by all so-called weapons of mass destruction throughout history.[54]

Unless the Iraqi regime represents an historically exceptional evil, which is of course implausible, the policies that have produced so many deaths of innocents—even if they were not the target—is far beyond the bounds of proportionality and therefore unjust.

CONCLUSION

The cosmopolitan conception of sovereignty holds that an intervention into one of the domains reasonably claimed by a state is a violation of sovereignty if and only if the intervention will not attempt to advance the cause of justice either in the basic structure of the state or in its international policies. There are three additional necessary conditions for justified intervention: It must be reasonable to believe that the intervention is likely to succeed, the intervention must be proportionate to the injustice, and it must be a last resort. There are additional special issues related to the morality of military interventions that will be discussed in Chapter 7.

According to the cosmopolitan conception, the underlying concern about sovereignty is a concern about justice. Perhaps, then, sovereignty is theoretically redundant. Consideration of the four necessary conditions for the justice of interventions, however, suggests that there may still be a reason to use the language of sovereignty when discussing interventions. Without such language, calling an intervention unjust or unjustified would be ambiguous: Would it be a violation of sovereignty or a failure to fulfill one of the other three necessary conditions? Some precision is gained if we reserve the charge of a violation of sovereignty for interventions that do not advance the cause of justice. The reason for utilizing the concept of sovereignty, then, from the cosmopolitan perspective is simply in order to preserve the clarity of political discourse, not because it adds a substantial consideration to our political understanding.

SIX

A Cosmopolitan Account of National Self-determination

Individual well-being depends on the successful pursuit of worthwhile goals and relationships. Goals and relationships are culturally determined. Being social animals means not merely that the means for the satisfaction of people's goals are more easily available within society. More crucially it means that those goals themselves are (when one reaches beyond what is strictly necessary for biological survival) the creatures of society, the products of culture.

—Avishai Margalit and Joseph Raz[1]

In this chapter I shall argue that a constrained right to national self-determination, including secession, is consistent with the basic commitments of cosmopolitanism, namely, that there exist duties of global justice based upon equal respect for persons regardless of their citizenship or national membership. In certain ways national self-determination is similar to sovereignty, including the manner in which it should be constrained. Hence, this account will be no more satisfactory to the nationalist than my account of sovereignty is to the statist. It's not surprising that an account of cosmopolitan justice cannot accommodate the entirety of the nationalist perspective. What might be surprising is how much it can accommodate.

Cosmopolitanism versus Nationalism

In Chapter 3 I argued that nations are not associations that generate duties of justice. An important corollary of that conclusion is that there is a strong defeasible presumption against policies that favor certain persons over others in virtue of their national identity. These two claims constrain an account of national self-determination. Both of them are usually denied by nationalists who seek to justify the political project of constructing state institutions that reinforce (and enforce) the good as defined by a national culture.

The cosmopolitanism that I have been defending in this book is based on the thesis that duties of justice are global in scope. It does not deny that there may be duties of justice generated by smaller associations. In fact, I accept that there are political duties owed to compatriots that are not owed to noncompatriots. The account, then, may appear to be merely contingently antinationalist. If the existence of duties of justice among compatriots is consistent with cosmopolitanism, then perhaps duties of justice among co-nationals could be as well if, contrary to the argument that I presented in Chapter 3, nations were associations generating duties of justice.

However, the cosmopolitanism that I defend is not merely contingently opposed to nationalism. Nationalists propose conceptions of justice that are fundamentally at odds with the basis of my account of cosmopolitanism, namely, that persons have a highest order moral interest in the capacity to revise rationally their conceptions of the good. Policies that reinforce a conception of the good provide disincentives to persons engaged in reflection on the cultural conception of the good that the state policies reinforce; therefore, these policies violate a fundamental commitment of the account of cosmopolitanism that I maintain. Policies that require a sectarian justification are contrary to the highest order interest of persons to propose and abide by publicly acknowledged fair terms of cooperation.

NATIONAL SELF-DETERMINATION

For reasons that will become clearer in this chapter, I accept Will Kymlicka's distinction between nations and cultural groups that come to be as the result of immigration.[2] Nations, unlike immigrant groups, had an existence in the territory of the state prior to the establishment of the state's structures.[3] National minorities typically are made up of descendants of peoples who were conquered and forcibly integrated into the state; less commonly they are made up of descendants of peoples who voluntarily joined an expanding multinational federation.

A nation has a measure of self-determination when it exercises control over some aspect of its political or social environment. Self-determination, then, is a relational property between a nation, some aspect of its political environment, and other political agents. Up to the point of secession, self-determination is a kind of internal devolution of state sovereignty. A nation may be self-determining with respect to certain matters of policy and in relation to certain other nations or the state. A nation possesses the right to self-determination when it has the moral authority to exercise control over an aspect of its political or social environment.

The Problem of Rational Revision

The conception of persons that I have employed to justify the cosmopolitan conception of justice takes a person's interest in the rational revision of the conception of the good to be a highest order interest. State neutrality with respect to national cultural conceptions of the good is a necessary (political) condition of respecting this highest order interest, since state enforcement of such conceptions would place obstacles in the path of those who rationally questioned such conceptions and would constrain those who did not accept them to act contrary to their beliefs. As long as such beliefs are consistent with the demands of justice, respect for the highest order interest in rational revision should permit them.

Kymlicka argues that cultural membership is a Rawlsian primary good.[4] In order for individuals to make rational revisions in their conception of what is of value, they require not only the freedoms of speech and association and a liberal education, but also a context in which life options have meaning to them. This context is a culture in which ways of life get presented to them. In addition, Kymlicka argues that one's own culture is important because cultural contexts are not easily replaced.[5] Although individuals can move from one culture and language to another, for most people this is a burden and not merely an intellectual one. Rather, if Kymlicka is right about the importance of culture for providing the context in which decisions have meaning, it is a moral burden insofar as it may affect the content of one's life plans and the direction in which one may revise them. This is a burden that one can voluntarily assume, as voluntary immigrants do. It is not a burden that, in the absence of some overriding moral interest, citizens should be required to assume. So, although the stability of one's culture is not a necessary (psychological) condition of the ability to rationally revise one's conception of the good, it is highly desirable given the costs associated with assuming a new cultural context. However, this stability may not be purchased at the price of forgoing state neutrality with respect to national cultural conceptions of the good.[6]

Now, it is not obvious how a state can coherently be in the business of both maintaining neutrality and providing for cultural stability. This suggests some tension between the two derivative commitments of the highest order interest of persons in the rational revision of their conceptions of the good. One of the virtues of recognizing a constrained right to national self-determination is the relief that it provides for this tension.

A Non-nationalist Account of National Self-determination

It might be suspected that there is a sort of creeping nationalism in the claims of the previous section. After all, it would seem an easy step from the recognition of the primary good of cultural membership to the claim that states ought to endorse some cultural practices to the exclusion of others. Yael Tamir takes this further step:

> Individuals wish to be ruled by institutions informed by a culture they find understandable and meaningful, and which allows a certain degree of transparency that facilitates their participation in public affairs. When they are able to identify their own culture in the political framework, when the political institutions reflect familiar traditions, historical interpretations, and norms of behaviour, individuals come to perceive themselves as the creators, or at least the carriers, of a valuable set of beliefs.[7]

The mere claim that cultural membership is a primary good, however, does not entail that state policies should preserve or encourage a national culture. On the contrary, both state neutrality and the enjoyment of one's own culture are related to the fundamental value that cosmopolitanism places on the ability to revise rationally one's life plans. State neutrality is required as a political condition of the ability to revise rationally one's life plans. Moreover, the absence of state neutrality poses a threat to all of those cultures that are not represented in the official conception of the good. On the other hand, the enjoyment of one's culture is a desideratum, at least given the psychological claim that it facilitates meaningful choice.

Who Bears the Right to National Self-determination?

The right to national self-determination is a group right. It is ascribed to, and exercised by, nations, not individuals.[8] An individual might claim the right to emigrate or might claim ownership of a piece of land. However, on the assumption that a nation must be composed of at least two co-nationals, one person exercising a measure of control over the political and social environment is not exercising national self-determination.

Both Tamir and Joseph Raz would seem to disagree. They contend that the right to self-determination is a cumulative individual right.[9] In their view, the strength of the claim depends, at least in part, on how many people are making it. The view that the bearer of a right to national self-determination is an individual and not a nation (in Kymlicka's sense) is both implausible and impractical. One person's claim to national self-determination is not merely weak, it is senseless since that person is not a nation. Taking the size of the group to be the determinative property of a justified right, and failing to consider the group's historic relationship to the existing state, establishes incentives to destabilizing actions and unjust policies. For example, it establishes an incentive to persecute a national minority to diminish its numbers through emigration or genocide. Alternatively, any given cultural group has an incentive to promote immigration among its cohorts to strengthen its claim to self-determination.[10]

Although the right to self-determination is a group right, it need not suppose some extraordinary metaphysical status of nations, such as personality. Not only would this be metaphysically dubious, it is also morally troublesome, as it may result in subordinating the moral interests of individuals to groups.[11] It is a group claim only because an individual cannot in the name of national self-determination make a claim against a state. Any justification of such a claim that is to be consistent with the respect for persons must derive from the claim's service to the legitimate interests of individuals.

NONTERRITORIAL-BASED NATIONAL SELF-DETERMINATION

Nonterritorial-based national self-determination assigns constrained authority to nations over certain institutions that typically are vehicles for the transmission of culture, especially educational institutions; but, it does not assign authority over (or within) any particular territory of its own or over other institutions of government. Such an approach to self-determination is particularly appropriate where, due to urbanization and industrialization, there have been significant migrations of people within the borders of the state.

Recall the tension that I described above between the importance of both state neutrality and the existence of stable cultures. One arena in which it may be particularly manifest is the public school system, for it is there that children during the formative years leave the influence of their parents and come under that of public institutions. Supposing that formal education is a powerful transmitter of culture, the state's commitment to neutrality might well seem incompatible with conditions that permit groups to maintain their culture.

One model for reconciling these competing demands involves a distinction between state and national institutions. Citizens are not permitted to opt out of support for, and obedience to, all state institutions, but they may choose certain national ones that they will support and obey.[12] The element of individual choice establishes a quasi-market among nations, leading to competition in the provision of educational services. A person born into one nationality may declare membership of another and vote on the level of national tax to finance the delivery of educational and cultural services. A person may elect national affinity, but may not elect to not support an educational system. Conceivably, one of the options to support would be a state educational system that is nationally neutral; although, at least with respect to the medium of instruction, such neutrality may be impossible. A nation may decide that it is unable to compete with other nations or the state in the delivery of secondary and tertiary education and may choose only to tax its members for primary education and other cultural activities. In this case individuals who identified with this nation would be bound to pay proportional taxes either to another nation or the state for the support of its secondary and tertiary educational institutions.

This model serves commitments both to state neutrality and to the maintenance of stable national cultures. It gets the state out of the practice of transmitting national cultures, preserving neutrality; and it allows individuals wide latitude in deciding which cultures they wish to inhabit and support. Precisely because it is a market model, state coercion is minimized. An individual is, of course, not completely free to inhabit or support the culture of choice: That individual must choose among the national cultures with which sufficient numbers of other citizens of the state identify. A set of options based upon other people's cultural preferences are given, and that person must weigh the importance of being a member of a particular nation that may, say, tax its members more against other goods that are more desirable. A market among relatively equal persons has the virtue of allowing the widest latitude of choice to its members. The latitude of choice under such a market is wider than what a democratic procedure for determining the distribution of state educational resources would allow because under a democratic procedure, even one that includes proportional representation, members of sufficiently small national minorities will be certain to lose and thus not be given the choice to incur higher costs for the maintenance of their culture.

Taking seriously the value of rational revision of one's conception of the good requires more of a state's educational policy than a lack of culturally based oppression. It requires, at the very least, a citizenry aware of its political autonomy as watch-guard against unjust state infringement of its liberties. Additionally, the maintenance of a commitment to cosmopolitanism requires a citizenry that is tolerant and knowledgeable of political and cultural differences that are compatible with justice. Thus, the national market in schools could not be an unregulated one. The state has a legitimate interest in supervising instructional methods and curriculum to ensure that both autonomy and tolerance are promoted.

One objection to this model is that national cultures that are sufficiently fragile could not withstand the kind of competition that it permits. This claim is no doubt true, but its moral force is weak. There may be no way consistent with neutral justice to maintain national cultures that claim insufficient numbers of people wishing to support them. The only remedy would seem to be state support, but there is no satisfactory principle to determine how the state might apportion its support for weak nations *and* preserve its commitment to neutrality. Suppose that the state were to offer support in proportion to national membership. This has the virtue of being a kind of equal treatment to all persons since a nation with more members would receive proportionally more support. However, this would hardly improve the standing of tiny nations. It may even serve to make them less attractive than richer and more dynamic competitors. Alternatively, suppose the state were to allot equal expenditures to each nation, thereby giving the smaller ones help to the same degree as the larger. Under such a plan, the state would seem to be treating persons unequally by giving some more support for their culture than others. Indeed, any scheme of cross-subsidization for smaller nations would suffer from this problem.

A potentially more serious objection to the model is that it might not create a citizen-body sufficiently integrated to address political issues in common and to share the burdens of justice. Allowing so much national self-determination may destroy the political unity of the state. This is an empirical claim that may require the bitter test of experience to verify. If it is true, then there is a contingent incompatibility between national self-determination of this sort and cosmopolitanism. In this case, then, the tension between state neutrality and stable national cultures may either require other measures or be irresolvable. If indeed it is irresolvable, then the value of state neutrality would trump that of maintaining stable cultures. There are two reasons for this. First, the former value is a necessary (political) condition of the rational revision of one's conception of the good, while the latter is desirable but not necessary. Second, the absence of state neutrality poses a threat to the stability of all of those cultures that are not included in the official conception of the good; so, neutrality contributes to cultural stability.

TERRITORIAL-BASED NATIONAL
SELF-DETERMINATION

Territorial-based national self-determination assigns constrained authority to nations over certain institutions within some particular territory of its own. This model is more likely than the previous to produce state institutions with a national flavor, even if their policies are consistent with a neutral justification. For example, state institutions in a self-determining region may require the national language as the official language and may include recognition of historically important dates of the nation as public holidays. If the principles of justice governing the basic structure of the region are neutral with respect to the various reasonable cultural conceptions of the good, then this sort of national self-determination is consistent with cosmopolitanism.

Not everything that a governing nation may wish to do would be permissible given the constraint stated in the antecedent of the previous sentence. Suppose, for example, that a nation wished to permit the practice of female genital mutilation. Permission for such a practice is not within the authority of a nation to grant because the practice may result in severe short-term pain and hemorrhaging and long-term problems ranging from abscesses to sexual dysfunction.[13] There is no culturally neutral account of the benefits of the practice and no justification that would appear consistent with equality between the sexes.

The Right to Secede

The most demanding kind of territorial based national self-determination is secession. In claiming a right to secede, a nation is claiming the right to establish sovereignty over political institutions and a piece of territory. I will examine the right to secede for two reasons. First, if secession, being the strongest kind of territorial-based self-determination, may be justified under certain constraints, then presumably weaker kinds, such as national autonomy within the state, can also be justified. Second, claims to secede are the most controversial claims of self-determination since the state has much more to lose in granting secession than in granting autonomy within an area of its territory. Because struggles around secession challenge the sovereignty of the state, they are more likely than other struggles of self-determination to become violent.

In order to clarify the moral basis of the right to secede, I make the following two assumptions. First, no injustice is being done by the nation seceding, either to those citizens of the state from which it is seceding or to those residing in the territory it is claiming. By this I mean acts that would be considered unjust independently of the act of secession itself, such as the unjust takings of productive resources or violations of human rights. Second, no injustice is being done to the nation wishing to secede by the state from which it wishes to secede. Here I have in mind acts that are sometimes thought to justify secession, acts such as widespread human rights abuses or unjust territorial occupation.

The right of a nation to secede rests in part on the interest of persons in being governed by state structures to which they consent. This interest is derived from the highest order interests of persons to propose and abide by publicly acknowledged fair terms of cooperation; a lack of consent amounts to a lack of agreement on the terms of cooperation. The interest of persons in being governed by state structures to which they consent can often be protected by the right of persons to emigrate and to change citizenship.[14] If this is so, however, why is the right of nations to secede needed? After all, recognizing the rights of persons to emigrate and to change citizenship places some demands upon a state (even demands that some regimes have thought excessive); but the right to secede, which involves a claim to some territory, places even greater demands upon a state. Addressing this question requires invoking a second reason in addition to the value of the consent of the governed: the value of cultural membership, as discussed earlier in this chapter.

The interest of persons in being governed by state structures to which they consent and the value of cultural membership together make up the basis for the justification of the right of nations to secede. Individual members of a nation are part of a cultural group that cannot simply be reconstituted by individual acts of emigration and citizenship changes. If the members of a nation no longer wish to be governed by the current state, and if they do not have the right to secede as a nation, then they are unable to satisfy both their interest in being governed by a state to which they consent and in maintaining their culture. If only emigration and changing citizenship were available to members of a nation who no longer consented to the government, then they would be burdened with a choice between fundamental interests: either maintaining their culture or living under a regime to which they did consent (assuming they could find one). A right of nations to secede is justified because it secures both of these individual interests by making this choice unnecessary.

There is an egalitarian consideration that can be brought to bear on the matter as well. Immigrants are more likely to have the option of continuing membership in their culture after individually emigrating and going back to their country of origin. Citizens of a multinational state who are also members of a nation (in Kymlicka's sense) are burdened more heavily than those who are immigrants when the former citizens are required to choose between preserving their common culture and living under a regime to which they consent. The right to secede may serve to avoid the necessity of such a choice, thereby promoting equality between citizens who are members of nations and citizens who are members of an immigrant group. These considerations, then, do not support the right of immigrant communities to secede.[15] This is a special case in which the existence of differential entitlements is consistent with equal respect. There are also practical reasons for not granting the right to secede to cultural groups that form as a result of immigration. Such a right would establish incentives to immigrate in order to make destabilizing territorial claims on a state and to close borders to forestall such claims.[16]

Constraints on the Right to Secede

Might the right to secede endow minority nations with excessive power? A minority nation might place heavy demands upon the majority, accompanied by the threat of exiting. The majority could, of course, refuse the demands and allow secession to proceed. Perhaps the minority claims natural resources or a manufacturing base, which would leave the majority with a substantially reduced standard of living. Alternatively, the nation might be a majority whose economic power could be used to coerce the minority by threatening to exit unless injustices are accepted.

Each of these examples suggests that the right to secede cannot be unlimited, but needs to be balanced with other considerations of justice. This should come as no surprise. A scheme of individual rights is also a balancing act. The right to freedom of expression is not license to cause harm to another. Even though there is a right to free speech, not all speech is just; so also not all acts of secession are just, even assuming a right to secede. The constraints on the justified exercise of the right to secede protect the legitimate interests of those individuals who do not support the secession.[17] These individuals may be members of two groups: citizens of the original state and persons residing in the territory claimed by the seceding nation.

In justifying the right to secede, I have assumed that the secession would result in no injustice to the citizens left behind in the state. To understand the extent of this assumption, and therefore the constraints on the justified exercise of this right, the legitimate security and material interests of citizens left behind in the remaining state must be adumbrated. These include:

(1) the security of the state before hostile forces
(2) the justified claims of the state to resources
(3) the justified claims of the citizens of the state to distributed resources

In addition, those residing in the territory claimed by the seceding nation must be assured that their rights are secure. These include:

(4) the human rights of the residents of the area claimed by the new state
(5) the equal democratic rights and privileges of all citizens, including national minorities, of the new state.

Clearly much of the above language is contentious, especially interests one through three. It is possible to agree that justified claims must not be violated, as in (2) and (3), without agreeing on what constitutes a justified claim. It is best to understand (2) and (3) as offering guidelines for debates about the justice of a particular secession. These debates will have to pay close attention to the history and pattern of resource distribution in the area. Taken together, these five interests constitute a set of constraints on the right of nations to secede. A secession that would create a new injustice by harming one of these five interests is proscribed, as would be a secession that would preserve a similar already-existing injustice when the likely outcome of preventing the secession would be the rectification of the existing injustice. Assuming a majority wishes to secede, secession is justified if and only if none of these five interests is unjustly harmed.[18]

The second simplifying assumption that I utilized was that the nation wishing to secede was not suffering any injustice at the hands of the state from which it wished to secede. Is the nation's case for secession strengthened if its members are suffering an injustice? In one sense the answer is no. The moral basis of the right to secede is not remedial. It stands regardless of whether the nation is suffering an injustice. However, greater latitude might be given to the seceding nation because of the injustice it is suffering. In particular, I have in mind lifting the constraint corresponding to (1). Reference to a hypothetical example will show that this constraint can, under certain conditions, be lifted. Assume that the geographical area of a nation is occupied by the military of the state, and that the military is imposing restrictions on the civil and political rights of the nation's members. Resistance to such injustice is not itself unjust; this includes armed resistance as a last resort. Furthermore, as I argued in Chapter 5 where individuals can appropriately claim to be suffering an injustice, there is a duty on all others, not only compatriots, to come to their aid in cases in which the other necessary conditions of justified intervention are met. The state forfeits its right to appeal to the constraint associated with (1), if the seceding nation may claim military assistance. However, constraints associated with the interest stated in (2) and (3) are still valuable protection against imperialistic outcomes of the war. The seceding nation and its allies, for example, would be bound to settle on just terms of resource division.

Two Objections

By way of drawing the argument to a close, I shall briefly consider two criticisms that are in certain ways peculiar to my defense of the justice of secession. First, it might be challenged that the right that I have defended has the peculiar character of justifying secession under certain conditions, but of not satisfying secessionists who invariably are nationalists and would want to reject at least the constraint associated with (5). This may be the case, but the aim of the argument is not to justify nationalism; quite the contrary. I wish to show that the right to national self-determination can be defended on cosmopolitan grounds. Nationalists may well reject many of the constraints that I put on secession. With respect to the constraint associated with (5), such a rejection is probably based on a dispute about the value of state neutrality as a political condition for the rational revision of life plans. Hence, nationalists and cosmopolitans may disagree about the conception of persons (or its political implications) that I defended in Chapter 2.

Second, I have maintained that the claim of nations to secede is properly considered a right. It might be objected that such a claim may be considered a strong moral presumption, but not a right. There are two considerations that incline me to support the view that it is a right: The claim protects fundamental interests of persons, and the claim trumps consequentialist considerations when no competing interest of justice is at stake. For example, if secession results in an overall lowering of the GNP for both the new state and the old, but it does so without harming just claims to productive resources, it is not unjust. If one accepts this general line of reasoning, but not the view that the claim is a right, then perhaps there is a controversy about what a rights-claim amounts to. In any case, I do not see a significant practical difference between a constrained strong presumption in favor of secession and a constrained right to secede.

Two Alternative Accounts of the Right to Secede

The right of nations to secede that I have defended is a constrained one. It is constrained by other considerations of justice, but requires no particular conditions of injustice against the nation in order to be legitimately exercised. By analogy one might consider no-fault divorce. A constrained right to no-fault divorce is one that is constrained in its exercise by considerations of justice, for example the financial obligation of one party to another, but need not be motivated by any justifying ground, such as adultery, to be exercised.

Compare my position to two others. One, more permissive, takes the right to secede as absolute, requiring only the will of the majority of the nation to be exercised. The other, more restrictive, requires not only that obligations of justice not be violated, but also that the right be exercised only as a remedy to existing injustices.

Lenin sometimes argues for the right to secede on moral grounds, in addition to its strategic service in building international proletarian solidarity.[19] When he does, he appeals to its democratic value and seems not to see it as constrained by other considerations of justice: "The class conscious workers do not advocate secession. They know the advantages of large states and the amalgamation of large masses of workers. But large states can be democratic only if there is complete equality among nations; that equality implies the *right* to secede."[20]

Some of the difficulties with a more permissive position are clear from the previous section. Secession may unjustly leave the remaining state with fewer natural resources or a lower GNP than the original state. I am not claiming that an act of secession is unjust merely by virtue of its leaving the remaining state in either one of these conditions, but that it may be. When secession is unjust, the will of those who wish to secede should be constrained on behalf of the legitimate interests of those who would be unjustly damaged.[21]

Allen Buchanan argues for a more restrictive right of nations to secede. He contends that one of the following three conditions must exist in order for secession to be justified: (1) persistent and serious violations of human rights, (2) unredressed past unjust takings of territory, or (3) discriminatory redistribution.[22] This more restrictive account seems to place undue burdens on those who wish to secede. A comparison to a system of individual rights helps clarify this. A person's right to speak may be exercised if it does not conflict with the rights of others. To be justified in speaking freely, one need not appeal to some injustice that will be remedied by exercising the right. Restricting a person's exercise of free speech is justified only by its detrimental effects on the rights of others. Since secession protects important individual interests, and assuming that secession results in no injustices either to the citizens of the state from which the nation is seceding or to the individuals residing in the territory claimed, there would appear to be no good reason to limit or prevent an act of secession.

General Challenges to the Right to Secede

There are two challenges to the general view that nations have the right to secede. The first challenge involves the feasibility of the right. The ought-implies-can principle holds that if there are morally justifiable reasons for some course of action, then that action must be possible; conversely, if the course of action is not possible, then it cannot be morally justified. A well-known criticism of the right to secede is that it violates the ought-implies-can principle:

> To put it in the simplest possible terms: there is a very large number of potential nations on earth. Our planet also contains room for a certain number of independent or autonomous political units. On any reasonable calculation, the former number (of potential nations) is probably much, *much* larger than that of possible viable states. If this argument or calculation is correct, not all nationalisms can be satisfied, at any rate at the same time. The satisfaction of some spells the frustration of others.[23]

This criticism calls for two responses. First, the logic of the argument is fallacious. From the fact that all acts of secession by nations are impossible it does not follow that any particular act is. To claim otherwise is to commit the fallacy of division. If a particular act of secession is possible, then the ought-implies-can principle is not violated. On what is, perhaps, a more charitable reading of the above argument, it might be taken as simply signaling a political complication that at some point will arise if too many nations secede from states. Even on this reading the criticism is weak. There are any number of individual rights that would be the cause of severe complications if too many individuals tried to exercise them at once. Consider how difficult everyday life would be if too many people decided to exercise their rights to freedom of assembly by engaging in mass demonstrations. The recognition of a right does not constitute encouragement to exercise that right. Therefore, a worry about the complications that would arise if it were to be generally exercised is not an adequate reason not to recognize it.

A second criticism of the right of nations to secede centers on the problem of identifying nations. It might be argued that, unlike the bearer of individual rights that is not in question, the bearer of national rights is not always so clear. There may be difficult cases. If a nation cannot be adequately distinguished, then ascribing rights to it is impractical. Such an argument is wrong to suppose that the bearer of individual rights, the person, is not in question. Much of the controversy surrounding abortion, euthanasia, and the treatment of animals centers on the nature of personhood. Pointing out the controversy with individual rights is not merely a dodge of the criticism of national rights. The point is that in the case of individual rights we are able to employ the moral concept in a range of noncontroversial cases, even though there are disputes on a number of others. Likewise, there are undisputed examples of nations; in general, the difference between a nation and an immigrant group is clear. If there are difficult cases of identification, say African Americans, this should not discourage the use of national rights in the noncontroversial cases.

CONCLUSION

It is possible to defend the right of nations to self-determination without either assuming that nations generate duties of justice or advocating that state institutions and policies should reinforce a national culture. One resemblance between the right of nations to self-determination and the sovereignty of states is that both are constrained by considerations of justice. The upshot of the constraints on national self-determination is that cosmopolitans and nationalists will no doubt part company on the questions of what a nation may with justice require of those who fall under its authority and of when it may exercise its right to self-determination, but they can agree at least that the right of nations to self-determination in principle may be claimed.

SEVEN

Political Realism, Pacifism, and the Justice of War

To begin with, there never has been, nor is there today, any absence of hostile foreign powers to provoke war. What is worse, the very development of the empire accruing from their incorporation has begotten still worse wars within. I refer to the civil wars and social uprisings that involve even more wretched anxieties for human beings, either shaken by their actual impact, or living in fear of their renewal. Massacres, frequent and sweeping, hardships too dire to endure are but part of the ravages of war. I am utterly unable to describe them as they are, and as they ought to be described; and even if I should try to begin, where could I end?

—St. Augustine[1]

In Chapter 5 I defended four grounds for a duty to intervene into the affairs of a state: comparative injustice, reasonable belief in the likelihood of success, proportionality, and last resort. I defended these with respect to military and nonmilitary interventions alike. There are two challenges to any criteria that set out to limit the justified use of military force. One is the claim of political realism, which states that when it comes to war no considerations of moral obligations to noncompatriots are relevant. The other is the view of pacifism, which holds that the use of military force can never be justified. In this chapter I shall argue that the grounds of justified intervention defended in Chapter 5 are applicable to determining whether a resort to war—international or civil—is justified. I shall defend this view against the claims of political realism and pacifism, and apply it to the Gulf

War and the Kosovo War in order to shed light on both the implications of the view and the moral status of these wars.

POLITICAL REALISM OR
POLITICS WITHOUT MORALS

Political realism developed in the aftermath of the two world wars and became the prevailing orthodoxy in policy circles in the United States. It has both empirical or descriptive aspects and normative or prescriptive aspects. As a normative view, it holds that if there are any relevant moral considerations in the justification of state action in international affairs (including going to war), they are only considerations of what a statesperson owes the represented state. So, political realists may hold either that there are no moral considerations relevant to the deliberations about the use of military force at all or that the only relevant moral considerations are the interests of one's own state or the statesperson's duties to the citizens of that state. Political realists typically maintain that the object of foreign policy, including military policy, should be the pursuit of national interests. On the face of it, political realism would seem an implausible view. War involves the intentional killing and destruction of infrastructure, and results in psychological suffering far beyond the battlefield. How could anyone deliberating about engaging in war not be required to consider whether it is right to treat others in this way?

One way political realism is defended is by the claim that entertaining moral considerations when deliberating about war leads to bad consequences.[2] However, this is straightforwardly self-defeating. Production of bad consequences is only a concern if one has a moral obligation to those suffering the consequences, which is precisely what political realism denies.

Occasionally defenders of political realism will suggest that only national interests can be considered in deliberating about war because there is no international consensus about morality and justice.[3] There is, however, considerable consensus codified by the Geneva Convention about the treatment of enemy soldiers. Political realists might urge that this is consensus about conduct in war, not about when to go to war. Still, even if there is little moral consensus about when to go to war, the conclusion that there are no moral limitations about when to go to war is warranted only if moral principles require actual consensus for their justification. This argument is never made by political realists.

There may be good reasons why political realists do not try to justify the claim that actual consensus is a necessary condition of the justification of moral principles. For such consensus would be a very demanding requirement. It would mean for example, that principles that enjoy widespread but not unanimous support—such as that slavery is unjust—are not justified. Many strong and widely shared moral intuitions would fail this requirement. In addition, the requirement would have a troubling consequence for the logic of moral judgment. One could not claim that any policy not enjoying either unanimous support or unanimous rejection was either just or unjust. However, it seems perfectly sensible to say, and indeed the law of the excluded middle requires us to say, that such policies must be either just or unjust. So, this justification of political realism fails.[4]

There are two defenses that some political realists invoke that have to do with the relationship between individuals and groups. One is the claim that groups, including states, are necessarily more inclined to act on their own interests than individuals.[5] However, unless the claim is that it is impossible for groups to set aside their own interests when they conflict with the interests of others, this only proves that groups are more likely to be evil than individuals, not that their actions are not subject to moral judgment. Reinhold Niebuhr offers several reasons to believe that groups are likely to be more self-interested than individuals, including the claim that when individuals serve groups they project their ego onto the group.[6] What may appear to be altruism then is merely another form of selfish attachment. This is, he believes, particularly apparent in patriotism that "transmutes individual unselfishness into national egoism."[7] This may be an astute account of the psychology of patriotism, but it does not imply that psychological barriers prevent the individual policymaker from seeing beyond the interests of the state. More plausibly, such people simply refuse to give the interests of noncompatriots the same weight as those of compatriots. Additionally, the sociological barriers that Niebuhr invokes are not insurmountable. He argues that the capacity for self-criticism is a necessary condition of ethical action and that states are incapable of it. "Even those tendencies toward self-criticism in a nation which do express themselves are usually thwarted by the governing classes and by a certain instinct for unity in society."[8] However, this analysis puts far too much power in the hands of the "governing classes." Wars in democratic societies often meet with popular resistance, and policymakers may engage in rational evaluation of policy without engaging in public self-criticism. So, none of these reasons are sufficient for believing that it is impossible for states to act on anything but their own interests.

The second claim that realists make regarding the relationship between individuals and groups is that policymakers are entrusted as agents of citizens to act on their interests. George F. Kennan puts the argument as follows: "Government is an agent, not a principal. Its primary obligation is to the *interests* of the national society it represents, not to the moral impulses that individual elements of that society may experience."[9] There is more than one way to interpret Kennan's claim. He may be arguing that acting on interests should trump acting on moral principles because policymakers are entrusted to act on the former but not the latter. Alternatively, he may be saying that policymakers should act on common interests because they are the interests of all and not on moral principles because they are not held by all.

Neither argument is convincing. Consider the first one. If I am given license by another to act on that person's interests in, say, selling a house, this does not justify my defrauding a potential buyer. The reason for this is that the homeowner would not be justified in defrauding a seller; and if the homeowner is not, then the agent is not.[10] Generally the duties of agents to principals (in this example, homeowners) are limited by more general duties of all to all. What would be a violation of a duty to another if performed by a principal is a violation if performed by the agent as well. The second argument must assume that moral principles are binding only if accepted. This assumption would permit an agent to violate a principle simply because the principal does not accept it. However, if this assumption were true, wrongdoing would be reduced to persons acting contrary to principles that they themselves accepted. This would require most of us to alter drastically our sense of when moral criticism is justified. Hence, the assumption is implausible, and the argument that requires it is unconvincing.

Hans Morgenthau's defense of political realism is built on the empirical claim that politics is properly understood only when political agents are taken to pursue power.[11] The reason why this is the sole way to understand politics apparently is that it is *rational* for political agents to pursue power and power alone.[12] The claim that an activity is rational is more than merely descriptive; it is prescriptive as well. Morgenthau's view is that the pursuit of power is not only essential for understanding politics, it alone is what political actors should be about.[13] Hence, by invoking the rationality of the pure pursuit of power, Morgenthau moves from offering an empirical theory of politics to a normative one.[14] Since anything other than the pursuit of power is irrational, states should consider nothing else when deliberating about going to war. Morgenthau emphasizes what he takes to be the moral implication of this position: "While the individual has a moral right to sacrifice himself in defense of a moral principles, the state has no right to let its moral disapprobation of the infringement of liberty get in the way of successful political action, itself inspired by the moral principle of national survival."[15]

The essential, but controversial, point in Morgenthau's account is that only the pursuit of political power constitutes rational action in politics. There are two issues here. Why does the pursuit of power have any claim on rational action in politics? And, why does it lay an exclusive claim? Morgenthau is of little help on these questions, apart from his insistence that the laws of politics have their roots in unchanging human nature.[16]

Perhaps he is relying on an empirical claim that it is in the nature of humans to see the pursuit of political power as a good. Some empirical evidence could be garnered for this claim by noting that political actors have pursued power, often at the expense of other ideals. This was a frequent theme, for example, in the literature and philosophy of ancient Greece. Evidence such as this, however, would be insufficient to verify the empirical claim, for it does not show that those who are not political actors see the pursuit of power as good—and clearly many do not.

An alternative strategy would be to argue that there is some conceptual connection between political power and the good, just as an economist might claim that the good is what we prefer. If it were conceptually true that the pursuit of power were good, then perhaps we could claim that it was rational. However, there are a number of counterexamples to the antecedent. For example, the pursuit of the power to enslave others is surely not good. Perhaps the best way to interpret Morgenthau's view is as a metaphysical one along Nietzschean lines. The claim, however, that the will-to-power is constitutive of human nature would assert too much since Morgenthau wants also to say, "Political realism is based upon a pluralistic conception of human nature. Real man is a composite of 'economic man,' 'political man,' 'moral man,' 'religious man,' etc."[17]

If there are no good reasons to take the pursuit of power as an inevitably rational plan of political action for all persons, then there are no good reasons to take it as solely constitutive of rational political action. Even if one could find some reason to accept the former claim, accepting the latter would be difficult to reconcile with Morgenthau's avowed pluralism. If one sort of pursuit were solely rational in politics, another in economics, and another still in morals, then either the world would have to come to us neatly divided into political, economic, and moral contexts or there would be rational grounds for not pursuing power in certain circumstances. Practical problems, though, cannot be so neatly distinguished. For example, many political and economic matters have a moral dimension. Although Morgenthau might want to claim that a policymaker's role as political agent would be to pursue the goal of power, rather than to do the right thing, that would simply beg the question of why the person with power to act should assume that role when acting. In other words, it provides no way to limit a problem as strictly political rather than as, say, moral. Therefore, Morgenthau's attempt to evade moral norms fails.

The most sophisticated attempt to establish the realist view did not receive as many endorsements in the twentieth century as might have been expected. This is the view that states exist within the state of nature vis-à-vis one another, and in this state moral principles toward others do not apply.[18] Historically the view was first presented by Hobbes and slightly refashioned by Hegel.[19] In essence, the view is that among sovereign states there is no higher authority that can compel them to comply with a principle. Hence, states are in a state of nature with respect to one another, which is to say that they have the right to take up whatever means they choose in pursuit of their interests, even if those means include warfare. This position has been refuted by Charles Beitz.[20] He identifies two main parts of the Hobbesian argument: first, a premise that states are in a state of nature with respect to one another; and second, that this entails that these states have no moral duties to one another. Beitz argues that neither the empirical premise nor the moral inference are warranted. In order for states to be in a state of nature with respect to one another, they would, among other things, have to be independent of one another in the sense that they could order their internal affairs and policies independently. This would mean that each in the pursuit of its own interests could threaten others without the expectation of harm to its internal affairs. Given current levels of economic, political, and military integration, however, this is not the case. Even if states were in a state of nature with respect to one another, they would be warranted in ignoring the moral claims of other states only if one is not morally obliged to do what is not in one's interest. This is because the Hobbesian point is that honoring the moral claims of others in a state of nature may not result in reciprocation and may even result in punishment.

Beitz's first point that states do not exist within a state of nature with respect to one another is convincing, and sufficient for refuting the Hobbesian argument. If the interests of states are in various ways bound up together, then there exists various deterrents to harmful or threatening action. There is, then, reason to believe that action directed toward realizing others' interests may not be punished and may even be reciprocated.

Beitz's second claim is that even if states did exist within a state of nature, they would still be warranted in honoring the moral claims of one another since morality may require forgoing self-interest.[21] There may be wiggle room here, however, for a modification that would preserve at least some of the Hobbesian point. One might allow that morality requires forgoing most of what may be covered under self-interest without allowing that morality requires one to sacrifice one's life. In other words, there may be an agent-relative limit of self-sacrifice up to which, but not beyond, morality can make demands. For example, perhaps my duty to another to keep a promise should be relaxed if it turns out that it would have the unforeseen consequence of costing me my life. Internationally, assuming what Beitz has proved false, namely, that a state of nature exists that licenses war, then perhaps states may be relieved of their obligations to one another if the result of fulfilling them would be serious threats to the lives of their citizens. I do not claim to have proven that this is the case, but it seems plausible to me. If it is, then the case against the Hobbesian political realist must rest entirely on the claim, which Beitz has satisfactorily established, that an international state of nature does not exist.

Having surveyed the arguments in defense of the view that states have no moral obligations to noncompatriots in foreign policy matters, they all appear wanting. Without this claim, political realism loses its force as a plausible position. Moreover, since there are no good reasons to exclude consideration of moral obligations to noncompatriots in the assessment of foreign policy, and assuming that the pursuit of national interests may sometimes be unjust, the political realists' endeavor to justify foreign policy solely by an appeal to national interest is a failure.

PACIFISM

Pacifism presents a different kind of challenge to the criteria that I established in Chapter 5 for justified military intervention. Although there are many kinds of pacifism and a variety of justifications, by pacifism I mean the view that the use of military force for purposes of settling political disputes is wrong.[22] There appear to be two main kinds of arguments that pacifists use to reject just war theory, or the view that the limited use of military force may be justified. Some reject the theory's power to decide cases on the basis of its criteria. Others maintain that the theory is insensitive to a morally condemning feature of military conflict.[23] I shall consider and reject versions of each of these kinds of arguments.

The first kind of argument I refer to as "skeptical pacifism" since the point of this argument is that we simply are not in a position to know whether sufficient justice lies on a given side to justify its war effort. Some of what Gandhi espoused amounts to arguments of this kind. The second kind of argument holds that just war theory misses very important aspects of the morality of war and as a result fails to see the main moral problem with war. I call this "normative pacifism." While skeptical pacifism holds that we cannot know enough about the morality of a situation to justify engaging in war, normative pacifism holds that we can know enough about the morality of virtually any war to judge it to be wrong.

Skeptical Pacifism

If we suppose that political life is sufficiently ambiguous or complex, we might be able to maintain that we cannot know enough about the actions of others, the threats that they pose, or the institutions that they advocate to justify using military force in order to prevent them from achieving their objectives or to overturn an order they have established. One of Gandhi's justifications of *satyagraha*, nonviolence, was along these lines. "Satya-graha is literally holding on to Truth and it means, therefore, Truth-force. It excludes the use of violence because man is not capable of knowing the absolute truth and, therefore not competent to punish."[24] It is not entirely clear what Gandhi means by "absolute truth," but I assume that his point is that in order to employ violence one must know that the other side is wrong and that one's cause is right, and that humans are in principle incapable of having such knowledge.

Gandhi's claim is not a relativist one. He is not claiming that there are many moral truths, nor is he espousing the nihilistic view that there is no moral truth. On the contrary, he seems to suppose that there is a moral truth of the matter in a given situation, but in principle it cannot be adequately known by mere humans. Additionally, he is committed to the view that if the moral truth of the matter cannot be known, then resorting to violence is not permissible. I see two problems with this position. First, the claim that violence is permissible only if the truth is known is itself a moral claim. A thoroughgoing moral skeptic will be unable to invoke such a claim because it cannot be known. A moral skeptic, however, may not be committed to thoroughgoing skepticism, and might, rather, profess skepticism about the moral character of human conduct and institutions, but not about all moral principles. Even if this is an adequate response to the first problem, the second is more severe.

The view that in principle we cannot know the moral truth about any of the actions of others, the threats that they pose, or the institutions that they advocate is simply wrong. One of the moments in Nobel Laureate Rigoberta Menchú's life that lead her ultimately to support the military struggle against the Lucas García regime in Guatemala was the kidnapping, torture, and killing of her sixteen-year-old brother by the Guatemalan army. Here is how she describes his torture before dying:

> Day and night they subjected him to terrible, terrible pain. They tied him up, they tied his testicles, my brother's sexual organs, they tied them behind with a string and forced him to run. . . . My brother was tortured for sixteen more days. They cut off his fingernails, they cut off his fingers, they cut off his skin, they burned parts of his skin. Many of the wounds, the first ones, swelled and were infected. He stayed alive. They shaved his head and pulled it down on either side and cut off the fleshy part of his face. My brother suffered tortures on every part of his body, but they took care not to damage the arteries or veins so that he would survive the tortures and not die. They gave him food so that he'd hold out and not die from his wounds.[25]

When confronted with descriptions such as these, it is hard to see how one might be skeptical of the morality of the army's action. Nothing anyone could do would make that person deserve such treatment. Therefore, it is simply false that in principle we cannot know the moral truth about any of the actions of others, the threats that they pose, or the institutions that they advocate. There may be times in which such knowledge is unavailable, but it would be grossly mistaken to believe that the unavailability of such knowledge is a necessary feature of our moral lives.

Normative Pacifism

Normative pacifism holds that even "just wars" are morally impermissible because they involve the commission of wrongs not captured by the criteria of just war theory. Robert L. Holmes offers an argument of this sort that presents a serious challenge to just war theory. Holmes develops the following argument against all modern wars, including wars that conform with the requirements of just war theory: (1) Killing innocent persons is presumptively wrong, (2) war necessarily involves the killing of innocent persons, therefore (3) war is presumptively wrong.[26] The point of the argument is not to defeat arguments for war in all imaginable circumstances, but to establish a presumption against the justification of a war that all proponents of war in particular cases must defeat. The first premise has basic intuitive appeal. If killing innocent persons is not wrong, then it is difficult to imagine what kinds of killings would be wrong; our intuitions against killing are strong enough not to countenance that. The second premise is somewhat less obvious. An innocent person is a person who has done no wrong relative to the war.[27] This would include all those who are fighting on the side of justice (if there is such a side) and employing just means. It would also include, Holmes argues, some of the combatants and government leaders on the unjust side, since combatants are often forced by conscription to fight and leaders may oppose the war but seek to influence policy from the inside.[28] Hence, even those fighting on the side of justice and employing just means will kill innocents.

Is Holmes's second premise true? Some supporters of just war theory argue that soldiers, or at least those prosecuting an unjust war, are not innocent; so, a just war conducted only against soldiers does not involve killing innocents, or at least not intentionally killing innocents. Elizabeth Anscombe's view is characteristic: "What is required, for the people attacked to be non-innocent in the relevant sense, is that they should themselves be engaged in an objectively unjust proceeding which the attacker has the right to make his concern; or—the commonest case—should be unjustly attacking him."[29] This, however, simply misses one of the strongest points of the pacifist position: It is a fairly strong moral intuition, often codified as a legal precept, that appraisal of guilt or innocence for evil deeds involves more than one's actions; it involves also the mental state in which the action is taken. If one would not perform an action except under conditions of coercion, then one may be doing wrong, but one is innocent of the wrongdoing. Consider the case of someone who is coerced at gunpoint to rob a bank. It is reasonable to excuse such a person of the wrongdoing because of the coercion. The closest case of this in wartime is the conscripted soldier who would not, but for the conscription, fight. Assuming that stiff penalties exist for evading coercion, such a soldier is in a situation pretty similar to the coerced bank robber. Hence, it is reasonable to excuse the soldier of the guilt of fighting in an unjust war.

Holmes also suggests that a government official with some responsibility for the prosecution of an unjust war may be innocent of the wrongdoing if that official is at the same time attempting to reform the government's policy in line with the demands of justice. Although this case is far less intuitively obvious than the case of the conscripted soldier, it may well be that such an official is innocent of the wrongdoing of the war since she would not choose to be involved in prosecuting the war and is attempting to use certain means to halt it.

One problem for Holmes's argument is that it is fallacious. If all of the elements or parts of something have a certain property, it does not follow that the whole or the composite has that property. If all of the team members are good players, it does not follow that the team is good. Or, if all of the parts of my car are lightweight, it does not follow that the car itself is lightweight. To believe otherwise is to commit the fallacy of composition. A whole can be more or less than the sum of its parts. So, even if all of the acts in a war are wrong, one might still question whether the war is wrong. More technically, war might be an organic whole whose overall evaluation is more positive than the evaluation of it parts.[30] Holmes is aware of this, but he contends that sometimes the properties of the parts infect the whole, as when unsafe brakes make the car unsafe.[31] The substantive issue, then, is whether certain wrong acts in war, namely, killing innocents, infect the morality of an otherwise just war.

The fact that Holmes's argument as presented is invalid is not determinative of its final evaluation. For he could easily save the validity of the argument simply by recasting it as follows: (1) If war necessarily involves killing innocents, then it is presumptively wrong; (2) war necessarily involves killing innocents; therefore, (3) war is presumptively wrong. When the argument is stated this way, it is clear that the substantive issue is whether killing innocents in war infects the morality of an otherwise just war.

The most important issue is whether the first premise of this revised argument is true. If war necessarily involves killing innocents, what is its moral status? Three possible answers are most plausible: Either the killing of innocents considered alone is indeterminative of the overall morality of war, establishes the immorality of war, or establishes a presumption that war is immoral. Holmes's position is the third, which, compared with the other two, looks most plausible. To say that the killing of innocents considered alone is indeterminative of the overall morality of war is to give our intuitions about killing innocents too little regard. This suggests that there is nothing morally special about innocent persons that makes killing them especially wrong. If this is the case, however, then the distinction between moral innocence and guilt has no presumptive significance. Given two different sets of facts, one case involving killing the guilty and the other involving killing the innocent, we would have no basis for even a presumptive comparative moral judgment. This does not square with most people's intuitive sense of the matter.

In comparison, the claim that killing innocent persons simply renders the larger process that requires it wrong gives weight to the moral status of innocence. However, it may give too much weight since it supposes that there are no circumstances in which the evil of killing an innocent can be outweighed by a greater good. This supposition does not follow from the assumption that persons have a special moral status. Even if persons have a special moral status, it may be that helping a sufficient number of them avoid some terrible harm or injustice, outweighs the evil of killing an innocent one. For most of us, our intuitions about this sort of thing are not settled. The claim that killing innocent persons simply renders the larger process that warrants it wrong requires that these intuitions be settled, and it is therefore an implausible claim.

The upshot of preceding arguments is that if war necessarily involves the killing of innocents, it is presumptively wrong. The force of the conditional, however, depends upon the strength of the presumption. Recall that Holmes allows that both soldiers prosecuting a war and government officials coordinating it may be morally innocent. What is the strength of the presumption against killing innocents of these sorts?

Consider two cases roughly analogous to the situation of the conscripted soldier and the reforming official. Case 1: In the middle of the night a hatchet-bearing sleepwalker attacks my housemate. I do not know that the attacker is sleepwalking, but I can repel the attack only by killing her. Case 2: A group of armed thugs has already attacked my neighbor once. I see them coming for a second attack. I do not know that one member of the group has been urging restraint. I can prevent the imminent attack only by firing on the group, which will probably kill all of them. Does the innocence of the person in each case prohibit that person being killed? Unless there is an absolute prohibition against killing innocents—which Holmes does not endorse—I can see no reason why, under the circumstances, appealing to their innocence provides sufficient reason to believe that it would be wrong to kill them.

One way to formulate the judgment that killing the attackers in the two cases above is permissable is that, when it is reasonable to suppose that a person is engaged in a potentially deadly, unjust attack on innocent persons and the only means available for preventing the attack is to kill the attacker, then it is permissible to kill. In other words, the activity of unjustly attacking defeats the presumption of the wrongness of killing innocents. This principle justifies treating combatants as legitimate targets in a just war. The normative pacifist may, of course, reject the principle, but in doing so would also have to reject the permissibility of killing the murderous sleepwalker or the conscience-stricken thug. Indeed, Holmes asserts that the killing of innocents by an aggressor is no worse than the killing of innocent aggressors by those who oppose aggression.[32]

Holmes's point seems to be that the defensive attacks against innocent aggressors may not be repelled by deadly force in the name of protecting innocents since it constitutes an attack on an innocent. So, to say that the one sort of attack is justified and the other is not is inconsistent. However, to focus only on innocence obscures a difference, namely, that some are innocent although their action is unjust, while others are innocent and suffering an unjust harm.

The normative pacifist might reply that this still does not justify harming the perpetrator of an injustice in order to halt the injustice, because whether harm should be meted out depends upon whether one is morally guilty. Hence, harm should no more be meted out to the innocent attacker than to the harmed victims. However, whether harm should be meted out to a person is not solely a matter of one's moral innocence. Certain actions may have costs, even though no one is morally responsible for creating those costs. In these circumstances, principles of justice cannot avoid assigning the costs despite moral innocence all around. For some classes of accidents, no one is morally responsible: Everyone took proper care yet someone slipped and fell in a shop, or someone's livestock got loose and trampled someone else's property. Who should absorb these costs: the persons who fell and whose crops were trampled, or the shop owner and the livestock owner? No matter what the answer is, someone will be harmed who is, by hypothesis, morally innocent. If there are certain kinds of activity that are especially dangerous or socially disruptive, even with due care, it may be reasonable to assign strict liability to those engaged in that activity. Strict liability assigns the costs of the accident to the noninjured party, even if care was taken on both sides. In this case, those who engage in the activity may be as morally innocent as those who are made worse off by it when it goes awry, but the former nonetheless should bear the costs of the harm rather than those who are victimized by it. The assignment of costs here is detached from moral guilt or innocence and is, rather, a function of certain norms, which may include the unfairness of making victims absorb costs, the reasonableness of giving incentives for greater care, and even the greater capacity of the one party to absorb the costs.

When an innocent belligerent involved in an unjust war poses credible threat to an innocent person, there will be costs. Either the innocent victim will likely be harmed or the belligerent repelled by deadly force will be harmed. Who should suffer this harm? If the assignment of costs were only a function of moral guilt or innocence, then clearly neither party should; but just as surely, somebody must. If, as I have argued above, in cases where there is no moral guilt assigning costs should be a function of other considerations, it may be reasonable to hold that the innocent belligerent should suffer the harm.[33] Making the belligerent pay through militarily repulsing the attack may encourage governments to think more seriously before engaging in unjust hostilities, thereby affording greater security for innocent victims and just arrangements. If either the innocent belligerents or their victims must pay, then offering greater security to potential victims and just arrangements provides a good reason for making the attackers pay. In other words, making belligerents absorb the costs of their injustices, even if they are innocent, is a way of ensuring that injustice does not pay and that justice does. Hence, the presumptive wrongness of killing innocents in war is defeasible if those innocents are perpetrating injustices by deadly force.[34]

If it is a matter of justice that innocent belligerents, rather than their innocent victims, should pay the costs of the unjust attack, then it would be wrong for innocent victims to have to pay the costs. This is significant as it entails that protecting innocent persons from attacks, where we are able, is not merely permissible but a duty of justice. To fail to offer such protection in the name of pacifism, then, is unjust.

One way that Holmes seeks to avoid the conclusion that the presumption against killing innocents may be overridden in cases in which they are perpetrating injustices by deadly force is by invoking the distinction between killing and letting die. Not letting an innocent person die is supererogatory— it is good to do, but not wrong if one fails to do it—but killing an innocent person violates a duty not to kill that person and is therefore wrong.[35] There are two problems with invoking this distinction. First, we have a duty of justice to prevent certain kinds of wrongs from occurring to others, including civil and democratic rights abuses and violations of egalitarian principles. When we fail to meet a demand of justice, we have violated a duty and not merely failed to meet a standard of supererogation. So, judging the killing of innocent belligerents engaged in an unjust attack against the failure to defend innocent victims involves weighing conflicting prima facie duties against each other, not weighing a duty against a principle of supererogation. Second, if, as I argued above, the presumption against killing innocents is defeasible when necessary to protect innocent victims, then the weighing of the conflicting prima facie duties should favor protecting the innocent victims.

One might worry that, in seeking to justify the defeasibility of the presumption against killing innocents, I have proven too much, for this might also justify the killing of noncombatants in the name of resisting an attack on innocents. This is not the case. The force of the argument that I have been making is specific: It is only that the presumption against killing innocent belligerents involved in an unjust attack may be overridden in order to assign the costs of their attack to them rather than to their innocent victims. From this it does not follow that noncombatants, other innocent persons, may be killed in order to defend against an attack. Since there is a presumption against killing innocents and since noncombatants are not engaged in an attack, there are no costs to assign to anyone on the basis of their conduct. Therefore, there are no grounds for defeating the presumption against killing innocent noncombatants; and my argument is consistent with the principle of noncombatant immunity.

My argument has not shown that the just war position is without moral costs. On the contrary, it has accepted the claim of normative pacifism that even in a just war innocent persons will be killed. There is then some truth in the normative pacifist account: Even a just war comes at significant moral costs. So, too, does the pacifist position, which holds that the military force necessary to protect innocents may not be used. My argument is that justice weighs in favor of assigning the costs of an unjust belligerence to the perpetrators, even if some of them are innocent, rather than to the innocent victims.

Perhaps the normative pacifist would respond that my position takes the existence of unjust belligerence as a given, whereas in fact the pacifist goal is to end all belligerence. The pacifist position is that if its goal were realized, there would be no situations in which the costs of belligerence would have to be assigned to innocents since there would be no warfare. In comparison to an arrangement in which costs necessarily get assigned to innocents—the question is whether they are assigned to those waging an unjust war or their victims—this is a superior ideal. Again, there seems to be some truth in the pacifist position. However, this does not settle the matter, for it says nothing about what should be done when innocent persons are the victims of unjust belligerence. Perhaps the pacifist would reply that if nonviolence had been practiced earlier, matters would not have come to this point. In any given case, of course, this may or may not be true. Assume that it is true. We may conclude then that it would have been better if nonviolence were practiced since it would have prevented innocent persons from being killed. It does not follow from this that resorting to violence is proscribed. Among several alternatives, the fact that one is morally superior does not entail that the second best is proscribed. The foregoing argument established that it was better that the innocent perpetrators of injustice suffer than the innocent victims. So, if the nonviolent alternative has not been employed, an appeal to force is not therefore wrong.

The pacifist may respond, however, that the admission of the superiority of nonviolence clinches the pacifist case in another way. Since it is practically impossible both to prepare for war and for nonviolent resistance, and since nonviolent resistance is superior, then preparations for war should be renounced in favor of the morally superior course of action. This argument bears some analogy to the following. Of several candidates for office, one is clearly the best and another is second best. There is no proscription against voting for the second best. Indeed, in light of all alternatives but the best, one should vote for the second best. Assuming that one can only vote once, one should vote for the best. This version of the normative pacifist argument accepts my conclusions from above, that, in comparison to allowing innocent victims to be killed by unjust belligerents, there are good reasons for defeating the presumptive wrong of killing innocent persons; but since nonviolence can also protect innocent victims, it is preferable to killing the innocent belligerents perpetrating the injustice.

Each of the following three premises of this permutation of the normative pacifist argument require consideration: (1) A society cannot both prepare for violent and nonviolent resistance to injustice; (2) nonviolent resistance would be successful in warding off injustice; and (3) nonviolent means are better than violent ones, assuming both would ward off the unjust belligerents.

The first premise is most reasonably construed not as expressing a logical contradiction between simultaneously preparing for war and nonviolent resistance, but a practical or psychological barrier against doing both. This seems generally plausible, although there may be exceptions. The kind of effort, discipline, and training that would be required to prepare a population for widespread nonviolent resistance to oppression would be enormous. Holmes believes that the tactics required would involve "concerted actions by large numbers" engaged in "mass strikes and boycotts."[36] All of those engaged in these activities would have to be highly disciplined to resist the temptation of answering violence with violence. It is unlikely that such discipline is possible if participants are open to the permissibility of answering violence with violence, and even less likely if some are preparing to do so.

The second premise is required by the argument since in its absence the choice would be between violently and successfully (assuming that the war would be unjust without a reasonable belief in likelihood of success) repelling unjust belligerents or nonviolently but unsuccessfully responding. Under these two scenarios, justice would seem to incline toward making the innocent but unjust belligerents absorb the costs of their injustice, rather than the innocent victims. So, in order to make the case for a nonviolent preparation in anticipation of unjust belligerence, it must be reasonable to believe in the likelihood of the nonviolent response succeeding. In assessing this, part of what has to be considered is whether the populace is prepared to suffer the harms that will be incurred by nonviolently resisting. In other words, the chance for success cannot be calculated abstractly, but must involve considerations of *this* population under reasonably likely conditions of belligerence. It may be that the discipline required for nonviolent resistance to certain kinds of brutal injustice is simply not possible for most people to sustain for very long without losing either patience or hope.

Gandhi complained of those who were not true followers of *satyagraha*.

> All Satyagrahis do not understand the full value of the force, nor have we men who always from conviction refrain from violence. The use of this force requires the adoption of poverty, in the sense that we must be indifferent whether we have the wherewithal to feed or clothe ourselves. During the past struggle, all Satyagrahis, if any at all, were not prepared to go that length. Some again were only Satyagrahis so called. They came out without any conviction, often with mixed motives, less often with impure motives.[37]

The point is that there may well be a tension between the popular demonstrations required to make pacifism work and the demands that a pacifist practice places on its members. If the pacifist position comes down to claiming that success would be possible only if people were more patient and more disciplined than they in fact now are, then it does not offer a serious alternative to military resistance.

The third premise seems true if and only if one is comparing two situations in which everything else is equal but the costs to the innocent belligerents perpetrating injustices. In other words, if the choice were between nonviolently repelling the imposition of a grave injustice and killing the innocent perpetrators to do the same, then the former is preferable. It is doubtful, however, that the only variable is how many innocent perpetrators of injustice will die. A shooting war will no doubt result in some deaths to innocent victims, and nonviolent resistance may result in their deaths as well, perhaps many more. The truth of the third premise is far less obvious if nonviolent resistance is likely to result in more deaths of innocent victims than a violent response to the injustice would. In this case, we must revert back to the question of what seems to be the most reasonable way to assign the costs of the attempted imposition of injustice. Once we think in these terms, it seems more reasonable to assign those costs to the innocent perpetrators than to their innocent victims. In short, the truth of the third premise is contingent on the nonviolent path resulting in no more deaths to innocent victims than the military one. I see no good reasons to suppose that this will universally be the case. Similar conclusions may be drawn, even if the additional costs to the innocent victims are not additional deaths but increased brutality or a long period of oppression. Costs such as these must be weighed against the costs of killing innocent belligerents.

There is enough room for skepticism about the second and third of these three premises that the moral superiority of pacifism is doubtful. This is not a fully conclusive argument against pacifism. However, it does point to problems with its practice that have moral import. Pacifism may be too demanding in practice to garner and maintain popular support. Nonviolent resistance may involve costs on the side of innocent victims at least as great as a military response. In practice these outcomes would be related. For as the costs of nonviolent resistance mount, the morale for maintaining it is likely to wane. Hence, pacifism often may offer no real alternative to a just war.

I have pursued several possible arguments for the superiority of pacifism over just war theory and found them all wanting. There may be others that are better that I have failed to see. In the absence of such arguments, it is reasonable to conclude that despite its moral costs, the just war perspective, employing the criteria that I established in Chapter 5, is morally preferable.

THE JUST USE OF MILITARY FORCE

In Chapter 5 I argued that intervention into the affairs of other states is just if and only if the intervention is directed toward advancing justice either in the basic structure of the state or in the international effects of its domestic policies. This stipulates the nature of just cause in the case of interventions. I call this the cosmopolitan account of just cause. I also defended three additional necessary conditions for the justice of an intervention: reasonable belief in the likelihood of success, proportionality, and last resort. Here, I shall defend and apply these criteria as the requirements that states or parties struggling for state power must meet in order to be justified in resorting to military force.

Traditionally there are two main aspects of just war theory. The grounds upon which force may be resorted to are referred to as the principles of *jus ad bellum*, while the limits of permissible conduct once war has begun are *jus in bello*. The focus of this chapter is on the principles of *jus ad bellum*. The discussion of the four criteria in this section differs from that in Chapter 5 in two ways. In one sense, the focus is narrower since here the criteria are applied only to military matters. In another sense, it is broader since they apply not only to interventions but to any use of military force for political ends, including civil or revolutionary war.

The Statist Account of Just Cause

The statist account of just cause for the use of military force holds that force is permissible only if the state has been harmed. Harm to states is usually understood to be aggression, where aggression is taken to be a violation of territorial integrity or political sovereignty. States, it is claimed, have a right not to suffer aggression. So, aggression justifies a war of self-defense against the aggressor. Recall Article 2(4) of the United Nations Charter, which I discussed in Chapter 1: "All Members shall refrain in their international relations from the threat or use of force against the territorial integrity or political sovereignty of any state, or in any manner inconsistent with the Purposes of the United Nations."[38] This proscribes aggression, but permits states to do as they please in matters of domestic policy without the fear of intervention.

Insofar as the statist account of just cause protects existing states from external threats and gives them license to be unhindered in their dealings with internal threats, it is essentially conservative. It values the relative order and the peace of the *status quo* over the establishment of more just institutions. In a world full of injustice, this is a significant liability of the statist account.

The problem of conservatism is apparent in the justification of the claim that states have rights. Either states have rights independently of the rights of individuals or their rights derive from the rights of individuals. According to the former, the claims of states may trump those of individuals, which leads to the practical problems of abuse of power and conservatism. According to the latter, however, states rights could be limited by the extent to which they serve the rights and interests of individuals. This view suggests the cosmopolitan account of just cause. Michael Walzer might be thought to have dodged both horns of this dilemma by holding that states have rights against aggression by virtue of the right of individuals to share a common life together.[39] However, the sharing of a common life is either more important than other claims of persons to justice or it is not. If it is more important, then the practical problems of conservatism reappear. If it is not as important as the other claims of individuals to justice (which is what I argued in Chapter 5), then the cosmopolitan account of just cause is implied. Hence, Walzer is unable to avoid the dilemma.

The Cosmopolitan Account of Just Cause

According to the cosmopolitan account, just cause for the use of military force exists if and only if the intervention is directed toward advancing justice in the basic structure of the state or the international effects of its domestic policy. Assume that the UN provisions for the legitimate use of force are to be justified by invoking a concern for the promotion or preservation of individual rights, as Walzer argues. The thrust of the argument for the cosmopolitan account then can be put as follows: There is no guarantee that states will respect the requirements of justice; and when in fact they do not, they lose any moral basis upon which to argue against intervention and to demand protection from internal threats. The point of the cosmopolitan account of just cause is that one needs to look at whether the justified claims of persons are met before one accepts that sovereignty provides a shield against the use of military force; and this is precisely what the statist account ignores.

Some might fear that an account of just cause that values justice above de facto sovereignty would be too permissive of third-party interventions in the name of liberation. Intervention does not receive anything like blanket sanction by the full set of criteria that I set forth in Chapter 5. There may be times when intervention would be wrong, even though just cause exists. However, the evil of the intervention would derive not from a violation of the sovereignty of the invaded state, but from the violation of one of the other criteria for justified intervention.

Imperialism and War

One powerful criticism of the justice of a war is that it is imperialistic. There are at least two characteristics of unjust imperialistic foreign policy. One is the goal of benefiting from, or of maintaining, unjust global inequalities. This follows from the analysis of imperialism as unjust global inequality that I developed in Chapter 4. Another characteristic is the violation of democratic self-determination. This captures the sense that imperialist policies often involve overriding or disregarding the will of the local populace. In order for a policy to be unjustly imperialistic, it need not possess both of these characteristics; the existence of either is sufficient.

It has been argued that a policy may be characterized as imperialistic even if it does not pursue either of these two aims, indeed even if it has no direct detrimental effect on weaker states at all.

> When all is said and done, after we take account of all kinds of specific interests, it finally comes down to a naked display of force, just for the sake of it, just for the sake of asserting U.S. hegemony.... The point is that, in today's conditions, we won't necessarily find any specific and concrete objective to military action. We won't find it, simply because the object of the exercise is not necessarily direct control of territory or even resources.[40]

If this were true of a policy, then the moral force of characterizing it as imperialistic is unclear since there would be no misuse of unequal power relations between states. One could stipulate that whatever a dominant power does in the foreign arena simply is imperialistic, but only at the cost of losing any moral punch to the claim. In order to preserve the force of the punch, it is better to require that imperialism be a policy that either effectively maintains or establishes unjust global economic distributions or that maintains or establishes domestic political or economic relations against the popular will of the residents. A war characterized by either of the two characteristics of imperialism is presumptively unjust.

The Gulf War

The justification for the Gulf War, after Iraq invaded Kuwait in 1990, was made on statist grounds. On January 29, 1991, President George Bush delivered a speech containing the following justification of the war: "The community of nations has resolutely gathered to condemn and repel lawless aggression."[41] The focus on aggression, however, ignored the fact that the restoration of the Kuwaiti government would do nothing to advance the cause of justice for most of its residents. In 1990 the government of Kuwait denied citizenship rights to two-thirds of its population because they were guest workers. Neither they nor their children would ever be eligible to become naturalized citizens. These residents earned a fraction of what Kuwaiti citizens earned and, unlike citizens, could not own land. Additionally only male adult citizens were allowed to vote in the 1985 parliamentary elections, the last before the war. Approximately 3.5 percent of the population had the franchise in those elections.[42]

Since there would be no improvement from the perspective of justice by restoring the Kuwaiti regime to power, the war to do so lacked just cause and was therefore unjust. Additionally, since Western powers had allowed aggression carried out by its allies to go unchecked in other parts of the Middle East, it is reasonable to infer that the main cause of Western action was to maintain favorable stability in this strategically important oil-rich region.[43] Such stability facilitates Western economic dominance, but, as we have noted from the demographics of Kuwait, also maintains local political and economic injustices. So, neither the publicly stated cause of action nor the probable underlying cause of action in the Gulf War were just. Rather, the war was an imperialist one of maintenance of unjust (but favorable to the West) economic and political relations.

From the conclusion that the war to restore the Kuwaiti regime was unjust, it does not follow that the Iraqi invasion of Kuwait was just. Justice and injustice with respect to resorting to war are logical contraries, not contradictories: Although two sides cannot both be just, it is perfectly possible for both to be unjust. Given Saddam Hussein's brutal treatment of political, religious, and ethnic minorities inside Iraq, it would have been crazy to assume things would improve much inside Kuwait under Iraqi rule. So, there was no justice to be found on either side in the Gulf War. Some may recoil at the idea that when injustice in war is done, meeting force with force also may not be just, but this follows from the restrictions that we put on resorting to war. It may often be the case that the criteria that judge one side to be unjust will deliver the same verdict on the other side. In such cases, the way to justice is not through supporting one or the other side in the war, but condemning both.

The Kosovo War

NATO's aerial war against the Federal Republic of Yugoslavia was also justified on moral grounds. Javier Solana, the secretary-general of NATO, sought to justify the mission in the following manner: "For the first time, a defensive alliance launched a military campaign to avoid a humanitarian tragedy outside its own borders. For the first time, an alliance of sovereign nations fought not to conquer or preserve territory but to protect the values on which the alliance was founded."[44] The war, however, met with critics from both the political right and left. Critics on the right condemned it as a war on behalf of "a tiny former Ottoman possession of no strategic importance or economic value."[45] For these critics the problem was that the war was about values, not national interests. Critics on the left charged, "The need to protect the Kosovars served as a pretext for NATO's bombardment, but its real aim was to secure its control of this strategic region and to fortify an extensive NATO bridgehead in the heart of the Balkans. This action must be seen in the context of the expansion of NATO to include the larger Western-oriented states."[46] Hence, at least some of the critics on the right take the war to have failed the prescriptions of realism and some of those on the left take it to have satisfied them, and this is why each criticizes the war. Although it might seem surprising that some of the commentators on the right could agree with some on the left about the morality of the war, they agree about this precisely because they disagree about its aim. Since, as I have argued above, the realist demand to excise moral considerations from the evaluation of the war is indefensible, the criticism coming from many on the left is the more important one for the moral evaluation of this war.

In order to assess the criticism that the real aim of the war was to provide NATO with strategic control over the Balkans, we must address two questions. First, is there sufficient evidence to support the claim about the aim of NATO? Second, if there is such evidence, how does it affect the moral assessment of the war? In other words, how does it affect a judgment on the basis of the criteria of *jus ad bellum*?

The claim about the real aim of the war can be read in two different ways. The stronger interpretation is that NATO was exclusively concerned with strategic control in the Balkans. The weaker claim is that strategic control was an aim, perhaps one without which they would not have gone to war, but not their only concern. The former is the stronger criticism because it entails that any humanitarian consequences of the war were strictly unintended, and we should not have been sanguine about expecting them. If, however, one aim among others of the war was strategic, it is possible that among the others there was a humanitarian one, and humanitarian consequences would have been more likely. Since actors often have multiple motives, this would not be surprising. Without, however, prejudging the second question, it may be that in either case the strategic aims of the war infected its moral character.

The aims of states in war policy cannot be perceived; they must be inferred from their actions. Even if leaders, such as Javier Solana, claim certain aims publicly, it is always possible that they intend to deceive or are themselves deceived about the real aims. The only way to infer the aims is to consider which ones best explain the actions taken. So, we need to consider the events and actions that led up to the war.

Ethnic Albanians make up 90 percent of the population of Kosovo. Most of the remaining 10 percent are ethnic Serbs. According to the 1974 constitution of the Socialist Federal Republic of Yugoslavia (SFRY), Kosovo was granted substantial national self-determination under the status of an autonomous province of the Serb Republic (the latter being constitutionally recognized as a republic of the SFRY). This autonomy secured for Kosovo its own national assembly, constitution, high court, police, flag, bank, university, and academy of arts and sciences.[47] So, although not legally a separate republic in the SFRY, Kosovo had most of the trappings of a republic. This arrangement came to an abrupt end in 1989 when Serbia, in a move that ushered in a new phase of Serbian nationalism in the 1990s, unilaterally revoked Kosovo's autonomous status, removing Kosovars from most public offices and thereby disenfranchising the majority of the Kosovo population. This action was met with strong resistance at the time, including a spectacular underground miners strike, but Serbian nationalists won the day.[48] Kosovar resistance to the Serbian revocation of autonomy was largely peaceful until around 1997, when the Kosovo Liberation Army (KLA) stepped up armed resistance largely with weapons obtained as the result of political chaos in neighboring Albania.

The first serious public indication that NATO was prepared to go to war in the region was on October 12, 1998, when it approved an activation order (ACTORD) for air strikes unless Yugoslav President Slobodan Milosevic ceased hostilities, withdrew certain troops that he had dispatched to Kosovo as part of a summer offensive against the KLA, and permitted the placement of several thousand international observers from the Organization for Security and Cooperation in Europe (OSCE) to monitor compliance.[49]

The ostensible reason for ACTORD was to force Serbian compliance with UN Security Council Resolution 1199 (which did not authorize force) that sought to avert the growing humanitarian crisis before the onset of winter.[50] The situation had become critical as a result of Serbia's summer offensive, which had destroyed 200 villages, killed more than 1,000 people, and displaced somewhere around 270,000 people, including 70,000 who had fled the province, and 50,000 who were surviving in the elements.[51] Whether the intentions of Milosevic were to "ethnically cleanse" the province of Albanians or simply to terrorize a population into submission is not clear. However, we knew enough about his practices in Bosnia to be reasonably worried about "ethnic cleansing" in Kosovo. In any case, even if his intent was "merely" to terrorize a civilian population, the conduct was despicable and involved significant human rights violations.

It is, of course, possible that the concern registered by NATO leaders about a humanitarian crisis in October 1998 was merely a pretext and that it was exclusively interested in strategic control in the Balkans. Such an account of NATO's thinking, however, would have to explain why, once it had issued ACTORD, it did not go ahead with the bombings. Possibly this was because of the lack of a UN mandate to use force. The problem with this explanation is that the lack of a mandate for force had not stopped NATO from issuing ACTORD in the first place. It is conceivable that it was hoping for a stronger pretext that would make bombing more acceptable to the rest of the world after having established the threat. However, if this were the case, NATO was handed the pretext by Serbia in January 1999 when the international news broke the story of the discovery of the bodies of forty-five Kosovars apparently killed at close range by Serb forces in the village of Racak.[52] NATO's reaction was not to follow through on ACTORD, but to send naval forces to the Adriatic Sea and to reduce the warning time prior to air strikes from ninety-six hours to forty-eight.[53] According to the thesis that NATO's eventual aerial war was merely a pretext for establishing strategic presence in the Balkans, one would expect a greater enthusiasm for unleashing the war that would make that possible.

In the subsequent Rambouillet peace talks, the West continued to show a willingness to accommodate Milosevic that is hard to square with the thesis that its sole concern was to gain a military foothold in the Balkans. According to one (possibly partial) account of the Rambouillet talks, the Kosovo delegation's prompt and thoughtful responses to the peace terms were ignored for days, while the negotiators waited without response from the Yugoslav and Serb delegation, traveled to Belgrade to consult with Milosevic directly, and then finally engaged intensively with the Yugoslav and Serb delegation, which eventually made a submission that was largely incompatible with the principles of the peace talks.[54] Why such solicitude, if NATO really only wanted to let the bombs fall?

Two other facts might be appealed to as evidence that NATO's real aim was solely to establish a strategic presence in the Balkans. First, at Rambouillet the Western negotiators seemed to insist on making NATO, rather than the OSCE, the occupying force to carry out any agreed upon peace.[55] Second, countless other states, including NATO states such as Turkey, have been involved in comparably despicable actions with respect to national minorities and NATO has done nothing about it.[56] Both of these facts are compatible not only with NATO being exclusively concerned with strategic matters, they are also consistent with it being concerned about strategic matters among other things.

The facts do not bear out the claim that NATO's sole real aim was to establish a strategic presence in the Balkans. Rather, most of the facts are better explained by the hypothesis that NATO was not solely concerned with strategic matters and was not particularly eager to go to war to gain a strategic foothold. The two facts noted in the preceding paragraph are equally well explained by this hypothesis. This is a significant conclusion to draw because it allows that it would not be completely coincidental if the war served humanitarian as well as strategic ends.

If NATO's motives were mixed and included strategic considerations as well as humanitarian concerns, how does this affect the moral character of the war? As one critic of the war warned, "In pursuing a justified cause we should always be alert to the ulterior and vested interests which might distort it, seeking, so far as may be possible, to favor approaches which stymie those interests and motives."[57] There is, however, no good reason to hold that warring parties should have pure motives in a war; we should care less about their motives, indeed not directly about their motives at all, and more about the likely effects of the war and the alternatives to it. This is consistent with the claim of another critic: "Motives do matter, if only because they tell us a lot about what the actor will and will not do, and what the outcome is likely to be."[58] If the war effort, despite the mixed motives of the warring party, is likely to overturn grave injustices that are otherwise without foreseeable remedy, worry about whether the warring party's intentions are pure is inappropriate. Rather, the question to be addressed here is whether in light of NATO's mixed motives, resorting to war satisfied the four criteria for *jus ad bellum*.

Let us accept that NATO's motive for the war was twofold: the establishment of a NATO presence in the Balkans and the prevention of a humanitarian disaster, since to assert only the first is inconsistent with certain facts about NATO's conduct. One can only speculate about the long-term consequences of the former motive, but the great positive consequences of the latter are clear. By the time NATO began the aerial war, the Serbs had been engaged in an offensive in Kosovo for over a month. They had in fact been pursuing a two-pronged strategy: obstruction in Rambouillet and war on the ground in Kosovo. Estimates put the number of people uprooted by the war in that month alone at 65,000.[59] By this time more than 250,000 people had been displaced. The memory of the Racak massacre and the rapes and massacres in Bosnia gave good reason to believe that serious human rights violations were occurring. Later this was at least partially confirmed by the World Health Organization, which estimated that 20,000 women were victims of rape by Serbian forces in Kosovo in the several months prior to the NATO bombing campaign.[60] Grave injustices were going on, but any possible negative consequences of a NATO presence in the Balkans were uncertain, speculative, and distant. It is a mistaken moral calculation to weigh uncertain, speculative, and distant evils over immediate and grave ones. What is more, as I argued in Chapter 5, any protection that Yugoslavia could claim from sovereignty was rendered null and void by the injustices that were being committed. Hence, just cause for the war existed.

Similar reasoning applies to the criterion of proportionality. If injustices such as the destruction of hundreds of villages—rendering thousands of civilians homeless—murder, and rape do not merit an armed response, then it is difficult to imagine what does. It is, however, inconsistent with taking human rights seriously to consider proportionality as strictly a utilitarian calculation. For example, if one were considering a war that simply involved deliberately attacking select civilian Serbian centers to effect terror in the Serbian population, this would not satisfy proportionality, even if the action were likely to stop the humanitarian crisis on the ground. It must be permissible in the first place to kill combatants before one can justify doing so in order to avert injustices to noncombatants.

Proportionality comes into the moral evaluation of war in two distinct places. It is part of the doctrine of *jus ad bellum* when it expresses the requirement that resorting to war be proportional to the injustices occurring. It is part of the doctrine of *jus in bello* when it expresses the requirement that a particular practice in the prosecution of the war be proportional to the justified war aims. So, in concluding that resort to war met the requirement of proportionality here, I am not asserting that all of the means employed in the war effort met that requirement, in particular the bombing of civilian areas in Belgrade.

Were there grounds for a reasonable belief in the likelihood of success in remedying the injustices that Serbia was perpetrating in Kosovo? One might be tempted to say that there obviously were since in fact NATO was victorious, but that answer is too glib for two reasons. First, when the war began, the bombing campaign provoked, and more importantly permitted, Serbian forces on the ground in Kosovo to increase the intensity of the very activity that established just cause for the war in the first place. This proved to be an even greater humanitarian nightmare than what preceded the war. One critic of the war put the point succinctly: "An equally important

NATO goal was to prevent the forced displacement of the Kosovar Albanians. At the outset of the bombing, 230,000 were estimated to have left their homes. By its end, 1.4 million were displaced. Of these, 860,000 were outside Kosovo, with the vast majority in hastily constructed camps in Albania and Macedonia."[61] It is difficult to fathom that NATO intelligence was not aware of this probability. Second, although regular and well-organized hostilities have ceased in Kosovo, if one takes the broader view that the aim was to establish peace and tolerance in the context of a democratic and autonomous Kosovo, this has not occurred and will not occur for the foreseeable future.[62] Kosovo will remain a NATO protectorate inside of Serbia for some time. Revenge attacks and deep mistrust make multinational cooperation and governance nearly impossible. Given the experience of Bosnia being governed as a UN protectorate, the probability of a similar outcome in Kosovo must have been foreseeable.[63]

The criterion of reasonable belief in the likelihood of success is necessarily prospective; it looks forward to the cessation of hostilities. However, the evaluation of it is often retrospective: Would it have been reasonable at the time to believe that success was likely? Given the two complications raised in the previous paragraph, two questions must be addressed: At what point in the future should one project in measuring the likelihood of success? and, What should count as success? The answer to the first question must be that success should be measured at the cessation of the war since one cannot know whether a party has succeeded until it is all over. Whether things will get worse before getting better is irrelevant to the assessment of whether the criterion will be met. As long as it is reasonable to believe that they will get better, the criterion is satisfied. With respect to the second question, success can only reasonably be measured by the justified cause of the war, for this is the goal. To measure it by something else is to shift the goalposts. So, in the case of Kosovo, success should be measured by the halting of the humanitarian crisis. This at least has succeeded. It would have been reasonable to believe that militarily defeating the perpetrators of the injustices would achieve this since there were no other significant causes of the injustice.

Even if the initial increase in the intensity of the attacks on Kosovars and the subsequent establishment of the NATO protectorate do not call into question whether it was reasonable to believe that success was likely, they may threaten the criterion of proportionality. For one might question whether resorting to war—knowing the probabilities of these events— could achieve sufficient goods to outweigh these evils. If those who were displaced are returned as a result of the peace and if the peace renders impossible the continuance of attacks, then the short-term evils are outweighed by the long-term security. Although a lack of democratic self-determination and an atmosphere of suspicion are far from ideal, they are surely better than a condition in which a military campaign is completely disrupting civilian life and sowing the seeds of ethnic hatred.

The final criterion is whether the war was conducted as a last resort. Given an infinite amount of time and no costs associated with delay, no resort to war is a last resort. However, there are often significant costs, including loss of military opportunity or perpetration of injustices, associated with delay. There are sometimes reasonable calculations that no nonmilitary means will remedy the injustices in the foreseeable future. Whether or not a war is one of last resort must be judged in relation to these considerations.

The morality of the war in Kosovo has received criticism on the basis of the criterion of last resort. In light of the account of negotiations between Yugoslavia and Serbia on the one hand and the Contact Group (representatives of the United States, Great Britain, France, Germany, Italy, and Russia) and NATO on the other from October 1998 through most of the Rambouillet conference in February 1999, it seems clear that although NATO was willing to employ the threat of the use of force, they were not particularly eager to make good on it. After the slaughter in Racak, NATO did not use force as might have been expected given ACTORD. Critics of the war argue that if at Rambouillet NATO had not insisted on playing the role of enforcer of the agreement, a settlement would have been possible.[64] In March 1999, when Rambouillet reconvened for a second round, the Kosovo delegation accepted the peace terms of the February conference, which included significant concessions to the principle of special representation for national groups within Kosovo rather than equal rights for all.[65] The Yugoslav and Serbian delegation rejected many of these principles and instead made a proposal that Marc Weller, legal adviser for the Kosovo delegation at the conference, described as follows:

> The draft proposed a formal subordination of Kosovo to Serbia, abolished restrictions on the exercise of Federal functions in Kosovo and correspondingly reduced the functions of the Kosovo assembly. The office of the President of Kosovo would be abolished and the government replaced by a weakened council of Ministers. There would be no Kosovo Constitutional and Supreme Court. In effect, the draft would have introduced a regime of what external observers have described as an institutionalized system of apartheid in Kosovo.[66]

According to at least one eyewitness, then, it was this sort of obstructionism, which involved diversion from the principles of the February conference, and not a dispute about NATO enforcement of the agreement that led to the deadlock.[67] Of course, it should not be forgotten that as the Yugoslav and Serb delegation carried out the obstructionism at the conference, the Serbs were waging an offensive on the ground.

The claim that more should have been done to reach an agreement seems to be flawed in two ways. First, it presumes that Yugoslavs and Serbs were bargaining in good faith. There are good reasons to doubt this. Their actions suggest that they were happy to obstruct deliberations because they were making advances on the battlefield. Second, it ignores the mounting costs of waiting. Recall that in just the previous month's offensive, 65,000 people were rendered homeless. The longer NATO waited, the more time the Serbs would have had to consolidate their position on the ground and the more Kosovar civilians would have been victims of the attack. If the account that I am relying on about the nature of the Yugoslav and Serbian rejection of the principles of peace turns out to be wrong and the determining issue was in fact whether NATO or OSCE enforced the peace, then the claim that the war was not one of last resort has some merit, but the human costs of waiting would still stand. If, however, the account that I am relying on is correct, then it is reasonable to judge the war as one of last resort.

I have argued that NATO's war against Yugoslavia to stop the Serbian atrocities in Kosovo probably meets the four criteria for *jus ad bellum*. It follows from this that resort to war was just. Keeping in mind the distinction between *jus ad bellum* and *jus in bello,* it does not follow that everything NATO did in prosecuting the war was just.

Before leaving the matter of the moral appraisal of the war in Kosovo, there is one final issue to address. The war was fought on behalf of the Kosovars, but largely not by them. The Kosovars were the principals but largely not the agents of the war. This fact suggests the possibility of the existence of principal-agent problems. Such problems occur in war when third parties fighting on the basis of an ostensibly just cause in fact pursue other ends. When these other ends are unjust, the principal-agent problems may vitiate the justice of the cause. When the ends are not unjust, but merely different, the agents would seem to have betrayed the principals. If the cause of the Kosovar's struggle was to put an end to human rights abuses, then no such problem existed in that war. If, on the other hand, the struggle was one of national independence for Kosovo, then NATO betrayed the Kosovars since it not only stopped short of that but pushed an agreement prior to the war that ruled it out for at least three years.

I argued above on the assumption that the cause of the war was to put an end to human rights abuses, but a case could be made that Kosovars had the right to secede. They are a nation that pre-existed the formation of both the Socialist Federal Republic of Yugoslavia and the successor Federal Republic of Yugoslavia. Moreover, they made a declaration of independence in 1991. The KLA held secession as its goal, but NATO and the Contact Group steadfastly refused to take up that goal. Were the Kosovars betrayed by NATO? Assuming that Kosovar secession would neither violate any justified Serbian interest in resources nor establish a regime that violated the rights of any of the residents of Kosovo, they met with unjust resistance from Serbia to exercise their right to secede. In the end, Kosovo representatives in Rambouillet agreed not to secede for at least three years after signing a peace agreement. If they were under no duress by NATO to agree to this, but were merely convinced of its prudence, then there was no betrayal. If NATO placed them under duress, then NATO is guilty of betrayal. Weller does not discuss what went on at Rambouillet with an eye to this matter, nor am I aware of anyone else who does. This means that we do not know enough about the circumstances of this agreement to decide this matter. So, although NATO's war seems to have satisfied the four criteria for *jus ad bellum,* in the end we do not know enough to make a final moral judgment about its conduct in this war.

CONCLUSION

I have argued that the theory of *jus ad bellum,* which includes the cosmopolitan account of just cause, is the best approach for considering the morality of resorting to war. It is superior to political realism, pacifism, and principles of just war, which include the statist account of just cause. Additionally, this theory finds the Gulf War to be an unjust war and finds the war in defense of the human rights of the Kosovars to be just, although there may remain problems with respect to NATO's response to the Kosovars' claims to secession. Cosmopolitanism, of course, looks forward to a just and peaceful world order, rather than one so ravaged by war. I shall speculate about the institutional requirements of such an order in the next chapter.

CONCLUDING REMARKS

Toward an Egalitarian
World Order

*But even if the intended object behind the occurrence we have de-
scribed were not to be achieved for the present, or if a people's revolution or constitutional reform were ultimately to fail, or if, after the latter had lasted for a certain time, everything were to be brought back
onto its original course (as politicians now claim to prophesy), our own
philosophical prediction still loses none of its force. For the occurrence
in question is too momentous, too intimately interwoven with the interests of humanity and too widespread in its influence upon all parts of
the world for nations not to be reminded of it when favourable circumstances present themselves, and to rise up and make renewed attempts
of the same kind as before.*

—Immanuel Kant[1]

PRINCIPLES, INSTITUTIONS, AND AGENTS

I have sought to defend the view that duties of justice are global in scope
and that these duties require adherence to general principles including respect for civil and democratic rights and substantial socioeconomic egalitarianism. I ventured into certain policy areas, but have said nothing about the
institutions of a global order that would satisfy these principles of justice.
This lacuna might be seen as undermining the argument of the book, but
that would be to misunderstand the relationship between the justification of
moral principles and the justification of institutions. The latter justification
requires appeals to what is morally desirable and what is possible in the cir-

171

cumstances. Without a justification of moral principles, any justification of institutions is incomplete, but a preliminary justification of principles can proceed without an account of the institutions that would satisfy them.

It is, however, necessary to underscore the preliminary nature of this justification of the principles of cosmopolitan justice. It would count as a decisive refutation of a moral principle if it were demonstrated that we could never expect to make progress in satisfying it. However, I believe that this would be a very difficult demonstration to make with respect to the principles of cosmopolitan justice. Some tentative thoughts about the institutional requirements of the cosmopolitanism that I have defended will help to round out the picture of its feasibility and therefore its desirability.

What sort of changes to the existing international state system are required in order to progress toward an egalitarian world order? This question appears to beg another one. Would an egalitarian world order contain multiple states or a world-state? Very few people who have thought about these matters at any length have considered the latter a real possibility, and with good reason.[2] The practical problems of directly governing several billion people seem insurmountable, and the threat to human liberty of a bureaucratic state with global reach would be immense.[3] On the other hand, states have, at times at least, been able to ensure that civil and democratic rights are respected. Given the occasional success of states and the problems of a world-state, some role for states in an egalitarian world order seems appropriate. It is equally clear, however, that the establishment and maintenance of justice requires a significant re-conceptualization of the principle of state sovereignty, and the goal of egalitarianism requires a coordinated international response. So, a system of states with statist powers of sovereignty is as unsatisfactory as a global state.

Two different versions of the Kantian pacific federation of states merit consideration.[4] One involves the assignment of responsibilities for meeting the just claims of persons to states, regional governing institutions, and global governing institutions, and for this reason has unflatteringly been dubbed a "new medievalism."[5] International institutions may best ensure global distributive justice, pollution reduction, organized military responses to injustices, and the like. Some of these institutions may be regional in scope, while others may be global, as the issues warrant.[6] For example, regional security arrangements and high courts might best serve the purpose of promoting respect for human rights since there is often a stronger sense of common interests among neighbors. Global institutions are doubtless best suited for ensuring that duties of global distributive justice are met and for the monitoring and enforcement of global pollution reduction plans. Additionally, there may be reasons to believe that the dispersal of some governing powers should be along functional rather than territorial lines.[7] Generally, the case for particular regional or global governing institutions needs to be made on the grounds of the existence of problems salient to justice requiring regional or global attention. Such problems may range from the international effects of domestic policies, to the inability to fulfill entitlements within state-based justice systems, or to the effects of transnational actors.[8] Where regional or global governance is desirable, the powers of sovereignty over the domain of governance should be transferred to the appropriate international bodies. Regardless of which particular international institutions are most appropriate, in order to be consistent with the principles of cosmopolitan justice, regional and global institutions would have to be subject to mechanisms of democratic accountability. This amounts to an extension of the principles of civilian control over the military, and democratic control over policy formation, into the international realm.

An alternative version of the Kantian pacific federation downplays the role for international institutions in favor of building greater democratic accountability into existing and future multilateral agreements or regimes.[9] The idea here is that a degree of democratic accountability is possible without centralized institutions if the various decentralized agreements are public, allow for input and monitoring by nongovernmental agencies, and are susceptible to pressure from global social movements. The decentralized scheme is not very far from present reality. It simply calls for broader input and monitoring over multilateral agreements than exists now.

Although the realism of the decentralized scheme recommends itself as a transitional measure, it hardly provides a satisfactory solution to the problems of global justice. International institutions can most efficiently handle problems that are international in scope because of the action-coordinating and information-sharing capacities of such institutions.[10] More important, as I argued in Chapter 4, duties of global distributive justice cannot be met in the absence of global institutions. Various multilateral agreements, even if susceptible to public scrutiny, are less able to ensure that duties of distributive justice are discharged than is a global institution that administers a tax-and-transfer program. A piecemeal, decentralized approach will provide insufficient guarantees that all persons throughout the world will contribute their share to meet the just claims of the poor to a portion of the global wealth.

In addition, as Hedley Bull observes, a more just distribution of global wealth is probably necessary in order for consensus about the remaining important global issues to be possible.

> While the distribution of wealth, resources, and power in international society remains as unequal as it is at present, the prospects of movement towards a more centralised global structure, based upon a process of consensus, appears slight. It may be argued that if such a movement is eventually to take place, there must first be brought about a redistribution of wealth, amenities of life and power in favour of the states and peoples of the Third World.[11]

Without a more just distribution of global wealth, attempts to arrive at global and even multilateral agreements about matters such as pollution control or the justified grounds of intervention might be viewed suspiciously by the global poor as covert attempts at imperialist control. Because the decentralized scheme is ill-equipped to achieve global distributive justice, its ability to achieve many of the other aims of justice is also in question.

Would an egalitarian world order containing regional and global institutions as well as constitutional democracies be a pacific union, or would it involve threats to peace such as those that characterized old-fashioned "mediaevalism"?[12] There are reasons to be hopeful about the peaceful nature of such an order. There is some reason to believe that constitutional democracies are less prone to go to war with one another than are other types of regimes.[13] U.S. covert operations against democratically elected governments in Chile, Guatemala, Iran, and Nicaragua, however, demonstrate that possession of a constitutional democracy is by no means a guarantee that a state will not suffer a violation of its sovereignty at the hands of another constitutional democracy. The problem is that constitutional democracies with capitalist economies contain a system of incentives for persons with business interests in other states to advocate the use of state power to protect those interests. In other words, such states contain a class of people who have an interest in imperialist wars. Imperialist wars are externalities of a system in which profits accrue to private individuals.[14] The only way to remove these externalities is through the establishment of an economic system that is not primarily based upon the profit motive or one that institutes public control over profits. A system of socialist states may not be a requirement of a distributively just world order (I argued in Chapter 4 that settling that matter requires appeal to empirical considerations), but it would abolish one more incentive for war. For this reason, as well as for egalitarian considerations, socialist states may be a desirable goal of an egalitarian world order.[15] Two other features of this global order would tend to reduce belligerence. A just global distribution of wealth is likely to remove much of the desperation and resentment that is behind the various internecine conflicts in the world. Additionally, an order that can present a credible threat of the use of multilateral force against states with unjust basic structures or against military groups seeking to establish such structures could considerably reduce risky politicking for unjust ends.

A sketch of the institutional structure for an egalitarian world order is unrealistic if there is no reason to believe that there are potential agents of change with an interest in such an order. Politics is by no means exhausted by political morality.[16] In order for a desirable normative goal to be credible, there must be reasons to believe that its advancement will be in the interests of enough people with the power to advance it. One important insight that distinguishes Marx from earlier egalitarian thinkers is his claim that an egalitarian order is possible because it would be in the interests of the working class.[17] When changing an order is likely to meet with resistance from those who benefit from that order, a sufficient number of potential agents of change who have both moral and prudential reasons for wanting to see it brought into existence is required. Only some sort of globalization-from-below, then, presents a realistic strategy for a more egalitarian world order.[18]

In contrast, Thomas Pogge proposes as a strategy for change "teams of outstanding political philosophers and international lawyers. . . to develop mutually acceptable ideas towards a just world order."[19] There are two problems with this suggestion. First, as a means for achieving institutional change, it is unrealistic to suppose that elite agreement rather than social and political power can unseat unjust privilege. Second, any consensus between academic philosophers and lawyers is far too narrow for the establishment of an overlapping consensus meant to stabilize an order based upon the principles of cosmopolitan justice. An overlapping consensus around such principles, which in any case would be subsequent to achieving just institutions through social and political struggle, would require broad social dialogue.

Given the vast inequalities and other injustices of the existing global order, there can be no shortage of potential agents who would find a more egalitarian order in their interests. Demonstrations against the policies and structures of existing international financial institutions such as the WTO and the World Bank suggest that there are real possibilities for change. However, as has sometimes been noted, such demonstrations, particularly when their primary participants are citizens of the richest countries, often express parochial and protectionist demands as much as cosmopolitan ones.[20] For example, demands to save the jobs of workers of any state in particular, and to require developing countries to enforce strict environmental regulations without a significant increase in developmental assistance, are not ones directed toward cosmopolitan goals. In order for demonstrations against the current world order to pursue cosmopolitan objectives, a sense of solidarity that transcends the interests of local colleagues and compatriots must be fostered.[21]

COSMOPOLITAN HOPE

One could perhaps be forgiven for thinking that under present circumstances an egalitarian world order is impossible, especially given the facts of international inequality and the resistance to demands for fundamental change among those who most benefit from such inequalities. There are, however, good reasons to hope for an egalitarian world order. One is that, by their nature, unjust arrangements are unstable. Such arrangements produce resentment and utopian thinking about a more just order, which then motivate acts of resistance. Short of a global totalitarian order, where there is injustice in the global distribution of wealth there will be resistance. This suggests that ongoing peaceful relations among persons globally requires an egalitarian order.

A more just world order would not suffer from the same forms of instability as an unjust order. The least advantaged in such an order would have no reasonable grounds for resentment. If that were the case, then neither would the more advantaged since they cannot plausibly claim to deserve their advantages. Even if resentment per se cannot be eradicated, taking away the justified grounds of resentment would be an advance for the stability of a world order. Additionally, as I argued in Chapter 2, if the conceptions of persons that the principles of justice are constructed on are true, then there are rational grounds for all members of the global society to accept the principles of cosmopolitan justice.

Moreover, the symbolic power of victories over injustice, even if temporary, can be enormously strong. Kant describes this as the power of enthusiasm.[22] If Kant's words in the quotation that opened this chapter are read as a prediction about the symbolic power of republican revolutions that would sweep aside arbitrary rule, he can hardly be accused of being unrealistic. The increased legitimacy given to human rights claims in international affairs suggests that once again arbitrary power is threatened. Perhaps we are witnessing the beginning of an era in which the claims of global distributive justice will gain legitimacy.

In short, the grounds for a realistic hope for an egalitarian world order exist because of the instability of all unjust orders, the greater stability of a more just one, and the symbolic power of advances in justice. This may seem insufficient in light of current inequalities and the resistance of the beneficiaries of such inequalities, but reasons for hope need not be as strong as reasons for belief. It is enough that instability *may* result in advances for justice and that such advances are both inspiring and possibly more stable than injustice. Cosmopolitan hope is rational just so long as the *possibility* of an egalitarian world order exists.

NOTES

CHAPTER 1

1. Ian Brownlie, ed., *Basic Documents on Human Rights,* 3rd ed. (Oxford: Clarendon Press, 1992), 22.

2. It may ultimately be impossible to say very much about the difference between philosophical and legal approaches to justice without begging certain questions about, for example, the claims of natural law theory and legal positivism. The present formulation of the legal approach does not, however, assume a positivist account of the law since the rules that govern institutions and existing practices may be moral rules.

3. The most comprehensive and powerful statement of contemporary positivism is H. L. A. Hart's *The Concept of Law* (Oxford: Clarendon Press, 1986).

4. Ronald Dworkin, *Taking Rights Seriously* (London: Duckworth, 1977) and *Law's Empire* (Cambridge, Mass.: Harvard University Press, 1986).

5. Leland M. Goodrich, Edvard Hambro, and Anne Patricia Simmons, *Charter of the United Nations,* 3rd ed. (New York: Columbia University Press, 1969), 43.

6. Ibid., p.60.

7. Ian Brownlie, ed., *Basic Documents in International Law* (Oxford: Clarendon Press, 1983), 40.

8. Goodrich, et al., *Charter of the United Nations,* p. 50.

9. Ibid.

10. Ibid., p. 55.

11. There is a very extensive debate in the literature about this. For representative samples of the negative answer, see Michael Akehurst, "Humanitarian Intervention," in Hedley Bull, ed., *Intervention in World Politics* (Oxford: Clarendon Press, 1984), 95–118; and Ian Brownlie, "Humanitarian Intervention," in *Law and Civil War in the Modern World,* ed. John Norton Moore (Baltimore: The Johns Hopkins University Press, 1974), 217–228. For representative samples of the affirmative answer, see Richard B. Lillich, "Humanitarian Intervention: A Reply to Ian Brownlie and a Plea for Constructive Alternatives," in *Law and Civil War in the Modern World,* pp. 229–251; and Fernando R. Tesón, *Humanitarian Intervention,* 2d ed. (Irvington-on-Hudson, N.Y.: Transnational Publishers, Inc., 1997).

12. Goodrich, et al., *Charter of the United Nations*, p. 293.

13. This point is emphasized by, among others, Gian Luca Burci, "United Nations Peacekeeping Operations in Situations of Internal Conflict," in *The New World Order*, ed. Mortimer Sellars (Oxford: Berg, 1996), 237–272; and Michael Glennon, "Glennon Replies," *Foreign Affairs* 78:4 (July–August 1999): 120–122.

14. Thomas Franck sees this as carving out a role for the collective promotion of justice under 2(7). See Thomas Franck, "Break It, Don't Fake It," *Foreign Affairs* 78:4 (July–August 1999): 116–118.

15. Michael W. Doyle argues that "threats to peace has come to be so liberally interpreted, however, as to allow interventions to rectify human rights violations." See his "The New Interventionism," *Metaphilosophy* 32: 1–2 (January 2001): 221.

16. Goodrich, et al., *The Charter of the United Nations*, p. 25.

17. Ibid., p. 355.

18. Ibid., p. 380.

19. See Brownlie, *Basic Documents on Human Rights*, pp. 21–27.

20. Ian Brownlie, *Principles of Public International Law*, 4th ed. (Oxford: Clarendon Press, 1990), 570.

21. Richard B. Lillich and Hurst Hannum, *International Human Rights*, 3d ed. (New York: Little, Brown and Company, 1995), 166.

22. Brownlie, *Basic Documents on Human Rights*, pp. 114–124.

23. Ibid., pp. 125–143.

CHAPTER 2

1. Robert Nozick, *Anarchy, State and Utopia* (Oxford: Blackwell, 1974), 183.

2. John Rawls, *The Law of Peoples* (Cambridge, Mass.: Harvard University Press, 1999), 24.

3. John Rawls, *A Theory of Justice*, rev. ed. (Cambridge, Mass.: Harvard University Press, 1999), xiv–xvi.

4. John Rawls, *Political Liberalism* (New York: Columbia University Press, 1993), 18–19.

5. Ibid., pp. 23–25.

6. Ibid., pp. 25–26.

7. Ibid., p. 12.

8. Rawls, *The Law of Peoples*, p. 32.

9. Ibid., p. 23.

10. Ibid., pp. 4, 90.

11. Ibid., pp. 32–33.

12. Ibid., p. 29.

13. Ibid., p. 40.

14. Ibid., p. 37.

15. Ibid., pp. 27, 37–38, 80–81.

16. Ibid., pp. 40–41.

17. Ibid., pp. 23–30.

18. Thomas Franck, "The Emerging Right to Democratic Governance," *The American Journal of International Law* 86:1 (January 1992): 85.

19. Rawls, *The Law of Peoples*, pp. 44–54.

20. Ibid., pp. 49–51.

21. Ibid., pp. 4, 63.

22. Ibid., p. 65.

23. Ibid., pp. 105–120.

24. Ibid., p. 14.

25. Ibid., p. 50.

26. Ibid., p. 14, especially footnote 5.

27. Ibid., p. 14.

28. Rawls, *Political Liberalism*, p. 4.

29. Ibid., p. 5.

30. Rawls, *Theory*, pp. 65–73.

31. John Rawls, "The Law of Peoples," *Critical Inquiry* 20:1 (autumn 1993): 43–44.

32. Rawls, *The Law of Peoples*, p. 38. Emphasis added.

33. Ibid., footnote 45.

34. Ibid., pp. 64–67.

35. Immanuel Kant, "Perpetual Peace: A Philosophical Sketch," in *Kant's Political Writings*, ed. Hans Reiss, trans. H. B. Nisbet (Cambridge: Cambridge University Press, 1970), 118. Emphasis in original.

36. This is consistent with Rawls's view that the principles of justice should be chosen as if reasonably favorable conditions for their acceptance exist. If such conditions, in fact, do not exist, then the principles are not altered, rather long-term political reform is required. See John Rawls, "Reply to Habermas," *The Journal of Philosophy* XCII:3 (March 1995): 152.

37. Rawls, *The Law of Peoples*, pp. 48–51.

38. Bruce Ackerman, "Political Liberalisms," *Journal of Philosophy* XCI:7 (July 1994): 382–383.

39. Rawls, "The Law of Peoples," p. 40.

40. Rawls, *The Law of Peoples*, p. 82.

41. Ibid., pp. 82–83.

42. Ibid., p. 35.

43. Rawls, "The Law of Peoples," pp. 42–43.

44. I shall develop the point further in Chapter 3, but one virtue of the construction under consideration is that it allows us to weigh the claims of compatriots and noncompatriots in the same procedure. For reasons that I hope become clear in Chapter 3, I agree with Henry Shue's contention that "it is impossible to settle the magnitude of one's duties in justice (if any) toward the fellow members of one's nation-state—or whatever one's domestic society—prior to and independent of settling the magnitude of one's duties in justice (if any) toward nonmembers." "The Burdens of Justice," *The Journal of Philosophy* LXXX:10 (October 1983): 603.

45. See R. G. Peffer, *Marxism, Morality, and Social Justice* (Princeton: Princeton University Press, 1990), 14; Rawls, *Political Liberalism*, p. 7; and Henry Shue, *Basic Rights* (Princeton: Princeton University Press, 1980), 22–29.

46. Ibid., p. 29.

47. Rawls, "Reply to Habermas," p. 179. See also Rawls, "The Law of Peoples," p. 55.

48. A similar point is made by Jürgen Habermas, *The Inclusion of the Other* (Cambridge, Mass.: The MIT Press, 1998), 99.

49. Rawls, *Political Liberalism*, p. 28.

50. Charles Beitz points out that even if the conceptions of person in the original position are more congenial to the self-conceptions of citizens of liberal democracies, the conceptions themselves may still have universal application. Charles Beitz, "Cosmopolitan Ideals and National Sentiment," *The Journal of Philosophy* LXXX:10 (October 1983): 596.

51. Rawls, *Political Liberalism*, p. 64. Elsewhere Rawls asserts that there are three kinds of justification of the political conception of justice in political liberalism. These are *pro tanto* justification, full justification, and public justification. See his "Reply to Habermas," pp. 142–144.

52. Rawls, *Political Liberalism*, pp. 64–65.

53. *Political Liberalism*, p. 74.

54. Ibid.

55. Ibid., p. 19.

56. Harry Brighouse makes this point nicely. "A person who understands the meaning of the idea of the good life would seek one. This almost tautologous claim can be understood from within almost any conception of the good." "Is There Any Such Thing As Political Liberalism?" *Pacific Philosophical Quarterly* 75:3–4 (September/December 1994): 330.

57. The first two are Rawls's conception of the circumstances of justice, and the third is his account of the burdens of judgment. See *Political Liberalism*, pp. 66 and 56–57 respectively.

58. John Stuart Mill urges, "It is always probable that the dissentients have something worth hearing to say for themselves, and that truth would lose something by their silence." "On Liberty in Utilitarianism," in *On Liberty, Essay on Bentham*, ed. Mary Warnock (New York: Meridian, 1962), 176.

59. See Rawls, *Political Liberalism*, pp. 11–12, where he sets out the second and third conditions. However, he is also concerned that the first condition obtains in order to make an overlapping consensus possible. See also *Political Liberalism*, pp. 140–144.

60. This point is also made with respect to the principles of justice by David Estlund, "The Insularity of the Reasonable: Why Political Liberalism Must Admit the Truth," *Ethics* 108:2 (January 1998): 252–275.

61. Rawls, "Reply to Habermas," p. 150.

62. Rawls, *Political Liberalism*, p. 129.

63. Ibid., p. 157.

64. Henry Sidgwick, *The Methods of Ethics* (Indianapolis: Hackett Publishing Co., 1981), 461. J. A. Mirrlees also argues that utilitarians may have good reasons for rejecting strict utilitarian justice in favor of compromise. See his "The Economic Uses of Utilitarianism," in *Utilitarianism and Beyond*, eds. Amartya Sen and Bernard Williams (Cambridge: Cambridge University Press, 1982), 81–82.

65. Rawls, *Political Liberalism*, pp. 156–157.

66. See Ronald Milo, "Contractarian Constructivism," *The Journal of Philosophy* XCII:4 (April 1995): 181–204.

67. See Paul Horwich, *Truth* (Oxford: Basil Blackwell, 1990), chap. 1 for an account of the minimalist conception of truth.

68. Rawls, *The Law of Peoples*, p. 59.

69. Rawls, *Political Liberalism*, p. 60.

70. Ibid., p. 37.

71. Ibid., pp. 10, 154.

72. Ibid., p. 152.

73. Will Kymlicka, *Liberalism, Community, and Culture* (Oxford: Clarendon Press, 1989), chap. 8.

74. Ibid., p. 169.

75. Rawls, *The Law of Peoples*, p. 63.

76. Ibid., p. 61.

77. Rawls, "The Law of Peoples," p. 66, footnote 55. I have been arguing that the problem with Rawls's account of toleration in his law of peoples is that it takes the object of tolerance to be the ideologies and practices of peoples. In contrast, liberals usually extend tolerance only to the opinions and practices of persons. The problem, as I see it, is not with the political character of Rawls's liberalism. For an interesting attempt to argue that the political character of Rawls's liberalism is the source of his misguided account of toleration, see Kok-Chor Tan, *Toleration, Diversity, and Global Justice* (University Park: The Pennsylvania State University Press, 2000), 38–45.

CHAPTER 3

1. Immanuel Kant, "Idea for a Universal History," in *Kant's Political Writings*, ed. Hans Reiss, trans. H. B. Nisbet (Cambridge: Cambridge University Press, 1970), 47.

2. Thomas W. Pogge, "Cosmopolitanism and Sovereignty," *Ethics* 103:1 (October 1992): 50.

3. Judith Lichtenberg employs the concept of *world* to argue for a similar thesis and notes that worlds "can have fuzzy edges" in "National Boundaries and Moral Boundaries," in *Boundaries*, eds. Peter G. Brown and Henry Shue (Totowa, N.J.: Rowman and Littlefield, 1981), 85.

4. David Hume, *An Enquiry Concerning the Principles of Morals*, ed. J. B. Schneewind. (Indianapolis: Hackett Publishing Co., Inc., 1983), 26.

5. Charles Beitz makes a similar point. See "Social and Cosmopolitan Liberalism," *International Affairs* 75:3 (July 1999): 539.

6. Many of the reasons for this are presented with some clarity in Samuel Scheffler, "Families, Nations, Strangers," The Lindley Lecture, University of Kansas, 1994.

7. Rawls, *A Theory of Justice*, p. 7.

8. Samuel Scheffler, "Liberalism, Nationalism, and the State," in *The Morality of Nationalism*, eds. Robert McKim and Jeff McMahan (New York: Oxford University Press, 1997), 204.

9. See David Miller, *On Nationality* (Oxford: Clarendon Press, 1995), 61.

10. Yael Tamir, *Liberal Nationalism* (Princeton: Princeton University Press, 1993), 102.

11. Ronald Dworkin, *Law's Empire* (Cambridge, Mass.: Harvard University Press, 1986), 199.

12. Ibid., pp. 198–199.

13. There are, of course, several notable and valuable exceptions to this rule, including (but not limited to) Charles Beitz, *Political Theory and International Relations* (Princeton: Princeton University Press, 1979); Judith Lichtenberg, "National Boundaries and Moral Boundaries," pp. 79–100; Kai Nielsen, "Global Justice, Capitalism and the Third World," in *International Justice and the Third World,* eds. Robin Attfield and Barry Wilkins (London: Routledge, 1992), 32–33; R. G. Peffer, *Marxism, Morality, and Social Justice* (Princeton: Princeton University Press, 1990), especially pp. 404–412; Thomas Pogge, *Realizing Rawls* (Ithaca: Cornell University Press, 1989), chap. 21; Henry Shue, *Basic Rights* (Princeton: Princeton University Press, 1980); and Fernando R. Tesón, *A Philosophy of International Law* (Boulder: Westview Press, 1998).

14. Basil Davidson, *The African Slave Trade* (Boston: Little Brown and Co., 1980), especially chap. 3, section 4.

15. See Nikolai Bukharin, *Imperialism and World Economy* (London: Merlin Press, 1976); Rudolph Hilferding, *Finance Capital* (London: Routledge and Kegan Paul Ltd., 1981); J. A. Hobson, *Imperialism: A Study* (London: James Nisbet and Co., 1902); V. I. Lenin, *Imperialism: The Highest Stage of Capitalism*, in *Collected Works*, vol. 19, (Moscow: Progress Publishers, 1964); and Rosa Luxemburg, *The Accumulation of Capital* (London: Routledge and Kegan Paul Ltd., 1963).

16. World Bank, *Debt Tables Extracts* http://www.world%20bank/world%20Debt%20Tables%20Extracts%201996.

17. See Anthony Giddens's extracted speech in "Essential Matter," *UNRISD News* 15 (autumn 1996/1997).

18. The developmental path constrained by conditions such as these is sometimes referred to as "modernization by internationalization." See Adam Przeworski, et al., *Sustainable Democracy* (Cambridge: Cambridge University Press, 1995), 4. Allen Buchanan makes a similar point in "Rawls's Law of Peoples: Rules for a Vanished Westphalian World," *Ethics* 110:4 (July 2000): 702.

19. National Academy of Sciences, *One Earth, One Future: Our Changing Global Environment* (Washington, D.C.: National Academy Press, 1990), 65.

20. Ibid., p. 68.

21. Ibid., p. 69.

22. Ibid., pp. 78–102.

23. UNICEF, "The Progress of the Nations: Statistical Profile, http://www.UNICEF%20/stat/statistical%20profile%20%20Europe.

24. Ibid.; http://www.UNICEF%20/stat/statistical%20profile%20%20Sub-sahara.

25. Brian Barry, "Humanity and Justice in Global Perspective," in *Ethics, Economics, and the Law*, Nomos XXIV, eds. J. Roland Pennock and John W. Chapman (New York: New York University Press, 1982), 232.

26. Brian Barry, "Statism and Nationalism: A Cosmopolitan Critique," in *Global Justice*, Nomos XLI, eds. Ian Shapiro and Lea Brilmayer (New York: New York University Press, 1999), 59.

27. Barry has tried to argue for international redistribution on the basis of justice as equal rights to natural resources. See his "Do Countries Have Moral Obligations? The Case of World Poverty," in *The Tanner Lectures on Human Values,* ed. Sterling M. McMurrin (Salt Lake City: University of Utah Press, 1981), 34–39.

28. H. L. A. Hart, *The Concept of Law* (Oxford: Clarendon Press, 1986), 92.

29. For example, see Jules L. Coleman, "Negative and Positive Positivism," in *Ronald Dworkin and Contemporary Jurisprudence,* ed. Marshall Cohen (Totowa, N.J.: Rowman and Allenheld, 1983), 28.

30. Thomas Pogge makes a similar point. "Institutions demand moral reflection most clearly when they, like slavery, *establish* morally objectionable positions or distinctions—as in the case of feudal and caste systems, patriarchal societies, or slavery. But institutions may also be faulted on the basis of deprivations and inequalities they *engender.*" "Rawls and Global Justice," *Canadian Journal of Philosophy* 18:2 (June 1988): 228. Emphasis in original.

31. According to Rawls's view, principles of justice are chosen regardless of actual institutions and even the felicity of actual conditions to construction of just institutions. If infelicitous conditions, in fact, do not exist, then the principles are not altered, rather long-term political reform is required. See John Rawls, "Reply to Habermas," *The Journal of Philosophy* XCII:3 (March 1995): 152.

32. Martha C. Nussbaum, "Patriotism and Cosmopolitanism," in *For Love of Country,* ed. Joshua Cohen (Boston: Beacon Press, 1996), 13.

33. Henry Sidgwick, *The Methods of Ethics* (Indianapolis: Hackett Publishing, Co., 1981), 435–436.

34. Alasdair MacIntyre, "Is Patriotism a Virtue?" The Lindley Lecture, University of Kansas, 1984.

35. Barry, "Statism and Nationalism: A Cosmopolitan Critique," pp. 12–66.

36. Samuel Scheffler, "The Conflict Between Justice and Responsibility," in *Global Justice,* Nomos XLI, pp. 92–93. Scheffler goes on to report (without endorsing) that, "It is, of course, this feature of special responsibilities that leads them to be invoked in opposition to claims of global justice."

37. Robert E. Goodin, "What Is So Special About Our Fellow Countrymen?" *Ethics* 98:4 (July 1988): 663–686.

38. The original position for domestic justice assumes that a domestic society is self-sufficient. See John Rawls, *A Theory of Justice,* rev. ed. (Cambridge, Mass.: Harvard University Press, 1999), 4. So, assessing claims of justice among compatriots does not require consideration of possible conflicts with noncompatriots. The original position for international justice comes only after duties at the state level have been independently established. See Rawls, *The Law of Peoples* (Cambridge, Mass.: Harvard University Press, 1999), 30–35.

39. There is a third consideration as well, namely that justice in contract requires some basic commitments of justice in order to assess the morality of contracts, and quite plausibly this involves what G, H, and J owed each other prior to any contracts. If a contract is to be just, then it may not violate these commitments. In this example, this consideration lines up with the other two. Since my point is to show the greater ease of adjudicating disputes when the first two considerations coincide, I do not invoke this consideration here.

40. This methodological conclusion seems also to be entailed by Scheffler's claim that reconciling the duties of justice to compatriots with those to noncompatriots, if both are taken to be associative duties, entails seeing both as mutually constraining and practically competitive. See "Liberalism, Nationalism, and the State," p. 204.

41. Thomas Pogge also takes this position. See "Rawls and Global Justice," pp. 227–256.

42. This is Rawls's procedure. See Rawls, *The Law of Peoples*, pp. 30–35.

43. Debra Satz, "Equality of What Among Whom?" in *Global Justice*, Nomos XLI, p. 75.

44. Bernard Williams, "A Critique of Utilitarianism," in *Utilitarianism For and Against,* eds. J. J. C. Smart and Bernard Williams (Cambridge: Cambridge University Press, 1995), 93–107.

45. Sidgwick's escape route is that "it would not under actual circumstances promote universal happiness if each man were to concern himself with the happiness of others as much as with his own." Sidgwick, *Methods of Ethics*, p. 431.

46. MacIntyre, "Is Patriotism a Virtue?"

47. In various ways, and with different nuances, this claim is defended by all of the following: Barry, "Statism and Nationalism: A Cosmopolitan Critique"; Jürgen Habermas, "Citizenship and National Identity: Some Reflections on the Future of Europe," *Praxis International* 12:1 (April 1992): 1–19; and Stephen Nathanson, "In Defense of 'Moderate Patriotism,'" *Ethics* 99:3 (April 1989): 535–552.

48. Aristotle, *Nicomachean Ethics*, trans. H. Rackham (London: The Loeb Classic Library, 1934), 483, at 1159b6–7.

49. MacIntyre, "Is Patriotism a Virtue?" p. 6.

50. See, for example, Richard Miller, "Cosmopolitan Respect and Patriotic Concern," *Philosophy and Public Affairs* 27:3 (summer 1998): 202–224; and Satz, "Equality of What Among Whom?" 67–85.

51. Charles Jones, for example, refuses to make this concession. See his *Global Justice: Defending Cosmopolitanism* (Oxford: Oxford University Press, 1999), 134–149.

52. Simon Caney defends a global equality of opportunity principle in his "Cosmopolitan Justice and Equalizing Opportunities," *Metaphilosophy* 32:1–2 (January 2001): 113–134.

53. Miller, "Cosmopolitan Respect and Patriotic Concern," pp. 214–215, 218.

54. See Tamir, *Liberal Nationalism*, p. 65; and David Miller, *On Nationality* (Oxford: Clarendon Press, 1995), 22. Sidgwick sees a distinguishing feature of nationhood to be "a consciousness of belonging to one another." Henry Sidgwick, *Elements of Politics*, 4th ed. (London: Macmillan and Co., Ltd., 1919), 224.

55. Tamir, pp. 95–116.

56. Will Kymlicka, *Multi-Cultural Citizenship: A Liberal Theory of Minority Rights* (Oxford: Oxford University Press, 1995), chap. 4, especially pp. 42–44.

57. Although not arguing for strong nationalism, David Miller makes this point. See Miller, *On Nationality*, p. 75.

58. Thomas Hurka, "The Justification of National Partiality," in *The Morality of Nationalism*, p. 153.

59. David Miller is also guilty of this when describing nations as active communities. See Miller, *On Nationality*, p. 24.

60. Tamir bases her view on the special care existing between co-nationals. See Tamir, *Liberal Nationalism*, pp. 104–112. David Miller invokes the special feelings that we have for co-nationals in *On Nationality*, p. 70.

61. Tamir, *Liberal Nationalism*, pp. 22–32.

62. There is, of course, the proletarian internationalist claim that protectionist policies are not in the long-term interest of the working class because they undercut the basis of international proletarian solidarity.

63. Richard Falk, "Revisioning Cosmopolitanism," in *For Love of Country*, ed. Joshua Cohen (Boston: Beacon Press, 1996), 57.

64. Traditionally, egalitarians with an internationalist orientation have favored free trade. See Karl Marx, "Speech on Free Trade" (1848), in *Selected Writings*, ed. David McLellan (Oxford: Oxford University Press, 1977), 269–270; V. I. Lenin, "The Economic Content of Narodism" (1895), in *Collected Works*, vol. 1 (Moscow: Progress Publishers, 1960), 436; and V. I. Lenin, "Re the Monopoly of Foreign Trade" (1922), in *Collected Works*, vol. 33 (Moscow: Progress Publishers, 1966), 457. More recently, both John Roemer and Philip van Parijs conclude that capital exports to less-developed countries is generally egalitarian from the global perspective. See John Roemer "Egalitarian Strategies," *Dissent* (summer 1999): 74; and Philip van Parijs, "Comment: Citizenship Exploitation, Unequal Exchange and the Breakdown of Popular Sovereignty," in *Free Movement,* eds. Brian Barry and Robert Goodin (College Station: The Pennsylvania State University Press, 1992), 155–167. Thomas Pogge also criticizes protectionism on global egalitarian grounds. See his "Priorities of Global Justice," *Metaphilosophy* 32:1–2 (January 2001): 13.

65. Kim Moody and Mary McGinn, *Unions and Free Trade* (Detroit: Labor Notes, 1992), 1–6.

66. For a defense of fair trade, see George F. DeMartino, *Global Economy, Global Justice* (London: Routledge, 2000), 207–215.

67. Erika de Wet, "Labor Standards in the Globalized Economy: The Inclusion of a Social Clause in the General Agreement of Tariff and Trade/World Trade Organization," *Human Rights Quarterly* 17:3 (1995): 451.

68. Arghiri Emmanuel's *Unequal Exchange* (London: Monthly Review Press, 1972).

69. For a criticism, see John E. Roemer, "Unequal Exchange, Labor Migrations and International Capital Flows: A Theoretical Synthesis," *Marxism, Central Planning, and the Soviet Economy,* ed. Padma Desai (Cambridge, Mass.: The MIT Press, 1983), sections 3–4.

70. Emmanuel, *Unequal Exchange*, pp. 262–270.

71. Michael Walzer, *Spheres of Justice* (New York: Basic Books, 1993), 33–34.

72. Ibid., p. 34.

73. See E. H. Carr, *The Twenty Years' Crisis* (London: Macmillan and Co., Ltd., 1939), 201.

74. Some of these reasons are adumbrated in Michael J. Trebilcock, "The Case for Liberal Immigration Policy," in *Justice in Immigration,* ed. Warren F. Schwartz (Cambridge, Mass.: Harvard University Press, 1995), 234–235. At least a partial defense of the claim that immigration harms the economic interests of native workers can be found in Susan B. Vroman, "Some Caveats on the Welfare Economics of Immigration Law," in *Justice in Immigration*, pp. 212–218.

75. Distribution A is Pareto inferior to B, and B Pareto superior to A, if and only if B makes at least one person better off than A, and makes no one worse off. Since well-being is a moral concern, Pareto superiority indicates not merely superiority from the perspective of efficiency but from the perspective of morality as well.

76. Jean Hampton also argues for this conclusion. See Hampton, "Immigration, Identity, and Justice," in *Justice in Immigration*, pp. 67–93.

77. Walzer, *Spheres of Justice*, pp. 35–42; Rawls, *The Law of Peoples*, p. 39, footnote 48.

78. Kymlicka, *Multi-Cultural Citizenship*, chap. 4, especially pp. 42–44.

79. Rawls, *A Theory of Justice*, pp. 474–480.

80. Arguing from a similar moral premise as mine, Joseph Carens accepts this conclusion. Carens, "Migration and Morality: A Liberal Egalitarian Perspective," in *Free Movement*, eds. Brian Barry and Robert Goodin (College Station: The Pennsylvania State University Press), 39.

81. One possibility, consistent with maintaining state neutrality is Otto Bauer's proposal to permit citizens to elect their national membership and to permit nations to tax their members in order to finance schools (which may be regulated by the state) and other cultural institutions, all of which are distinct from state institutions. See Bauer, *Die Nationalitätenfrage und Die Sozialdemokratie*, in *Werkausgabe*, band 1 (Wien: Europa Verlags—AG Wein, 1975), 401–415.

82. Arthur Ripstein, "Context, Continuity, and Fairness," in *The Morality of Nationalism*, pp. 213–214.

83. Similar conclusions have been reached by Joseph H. Carens in "Aliens and Citizens: The Case for Open Borders," *Review of Politics* 49:2 (spring 1987): 251–273; and Habermas, "Citizenship and National Identity," p. 29. Peter Schuck seems to think (wrongly, as far as I can tell) that this is a concession to illiberal conceptions of community. Shuck, "The Transformation of Immigration Law," *Columbia Law Review* 84:1 (January 1984): 87–88.

84. For a judgment that contradicts this view, at least with respect to institutions of distributive justice, see Carens, "Migration and Morality," p. 42.

85. See Roemer, "Egalitarian Strategies," pp. 73–74.

CHAPTER 4

1. The World Commission on Environment and Development, *Our Common Future* (Oxford: Oxford University Press, 1987), 312.

2. http://www.undp/undp%20world%20poverty.

3. http://www.undp/undp%20poverty%20clock.

4. http://www.undp/undp%20world%20poverty.

5. Donald G. McNeil Jr., "West's Drug Firms Play God in Africa," *Mail and Guardian* (May 26–June 1, 2000): 22. Originally published in *The New York Times*.

6. Ibid.

7. Ibid.

8. "World Health Organization," press release 64 by the WHO (May 31, 1999). See also http://www.who.int./archives/infr-pr–1999/en/pr99–64.html.

9. John Rawls, *The Law of Peoples* (Cambridge, Mass.: Harvard University Press, 1999), 118.

10. Ibid., pp. 117–118.

11. One of the virtues of taking primary goods as the measure of justice, rather than utility, for example, is that it allows for individual responsibility for ends setting. See John Rawls, "Social Unity and Primary Goods," in *Utilitarianism and Beyond*, eds. Amartya Sen and Bernard Williams (Cambridge: Cambridge University Press, 1983), 168.

12. John Rawls, *A Theory of Justice*, rev. ed. (Cambridge, Mass.: Harvard University Press, 1999), 89.

13. Ibid., p. 87.

14. John Rawls, "Reply to Alexander and Musgrave," in *Collected Papers*, ed. Samuel Freeman (Cambridge, Mass.: Harvard University Press, 1999), 253.

15. Brian Barry, "Humanity and Justice in Global Perspective," in *Ethics, Economics, and the Law*, Nomos XXIV, eds. J. Roland Pennock and John W. Chapman (New York: New York University Press, 1982), 233. Similar positions are also taken by Brian R. Opeskin, "The Moral Foundations of Foreign Aid," *World Development* 24:1 (January 1996): 21–44; and Robert E. Goodin, "What Is So Special about Our Fellow Countrymen?" *Ethics* 98:4 (July 1988): 677. Response to this argument can be found in David A. J. Richards, "International Distributive Justice," in *Ethics, Economics, and the Law*, pp. 275–299; and Thomas Pogge, "Rawls and Global Justice," *Canadian Journal of Philosophy* 18:2 (June 1988): 248–249.

16. Pogge, "Rawls and Global Justice," p. 249. Emphasis in original.

17. Terry Nardin, *Law, Morality, and the Relations of States* (Princeton: Princeton University Press, 1983), 14–15.

18. Ibid., p. 10–14.

19. Ibid., p. 17.

20. Ibid., p. 277.

21. Part of the problem here is interpreting Nardin's position. However, the interpretation that takes him as holding that claims to a fair share of the object of distributive justice are claims to substantive rather than procedural goods is consistent with an earlier distinction between "values internal to moral life and the rule of law" as characteristic of practical associations and values "served by cooperation aimed at securing the ends such as wealth, status, power, or the propagation of particular religious or ideological values" as characteristic of purposive associations. Ibid., p. 12.

22. Goodin "What Is So Special About Our Fellow Countrymen?" pp. 663–686.

23. Ibid., p. 682.

24. Henry Shue has convincingly argued for an additional limitation to perspectives such as Goodin's. With respect to global ecological problems such as ozone depletion and climate change, "no state is able to protect its own people against the effects on planetary atmosphere of the choices of other states about whether to use CFC and to use fossil fuels." Shue, "Eroding Sovereignty: The Advance of Principle," in *The Morality of Nationalism*, eds. Robert McKim and Jeff McMahan (Oxford: Oxford University Press, 1997), 353.

25. See Michael Walzer, *Spheres of Justice* (New York: Basic Books, 1983), chap. 3.

26. Michael Walzer, *Thick and Thin* (Notre Dame: University of Notre Dame Press, 1994), chap. 2.

27. Walzer, *Spheres of Justice*, p. 29–30.

28. Ibid., p. 69–74.

29. Ibid., p. 5.

30. Andrew Hurrell makes an important point: "Indeed there is no reason in principle why internalist or conventionalist accounts of justice need to be confined within state borders and used to buttress communitarian positions." See his "Global Inequality and International Institutions," *Metaphilosophy* 32: 1–2 (January 2001): 43.

31. Rawls, *Theory of Justice*, pp. 57–73.

32. Pareto optimality is a measure of efficiency: A distribution is Pareto optimal if and only if no transfers can be made without lessening at least one person's well being.

33. Several other writers have argued that a cosmopolitan original position would yield the difference principle. See Brian Barry, *The Liberal Theory of Justice* (Oxford: Clarendon Press, 1973), 128–133; Barry, *Theories of Justice* (Berkeley: University of California Press, 1989), 189; Charles Beitz, *Political Theory and International Relations* (Princeton: Princeton University Press, 1979), 150–153; R. G. Peffer, *Marxism, Morality and Social Justice* (Princeton: Princeton University Press, 1990), 404–412; and Thomas Pogge, *Realizing Rawls* (Ithaca: Cornell University Press, 1989), chap. 21.

34. Both Joshua Cohen's "Democratic Equality," *Ethics* 99:4 (July 1998): 727–751; and T. M. Scanlon's "Diversity of Objections to Inequality," The Lindley Lecture, University of Kansas, 1996, present arguments for the difference principle that do not rely on the original position.

35. Philip Arestis and Malcolm Sawyer, "How Many Cheers for the Tobin Tax?" *Cambridge Journal of Economics* 21 (1997): 763. On the Tobin tax see James Tobin, "A Proposal for International Monetary Reform," in *Essays in Economics: Theory and Policy* (Cambridge, Mass.: The MIT Press, 1982), 482–494. On the possible uses of the revenue acquired from the Tobin tax, see Inge Kaul and John Langmore, "Potential Uses of the Revenue from a Tobin Tax," in *The Tobin Tax*, eds. Mahbub ul Haq, et al. (Oxford: Oxford University Press, 1996), 255–271. According to Tobin's account, the goal of the tax is less to raise funds for development and more to decrease the instability caused by short-term speculative investments. Whether it would also provide a disincentive for longer-term investment in other countries, particularly the poorer ones, is an important issue.

36. See Thomas Nagel, *Equality and Partiality* (Oxford: Oxford University Press, 1991), chap. 15. A global minimum floor principle is also defended by Henry Shue, *Basic Rights* (Princeton: Princeton University Press, 1980), 128; and R. Bruce Douglass, "International Economic Justice and the Guaranteed Minimum," *The Review of Politics*, 44:1 (January 1982): 3–26.

37. Nagel, *Equality and Partiality*, chap. 15.

38. Ibid.

39. Nagel is aware of this last possibility. See *Equality and Partiality*, p. 50.

40. Shue, *Basic Rights*, p. 128.

41. Stanley Hoffman, *Duties Beyond Borders* (Syracuse, N.Y.: Syracuse University Press, 1981), 155.

42. Rawls, *Theory of Justice*, pp. 54, 386.

43. See Amartya Sen, *Inequality Reexamined* (Oxford: Clarendon Press, 1992), 33; and Sen, "Poor, Relatively Speaking," in *Resources, Values and Development* (Oxford: Basil Blackwell, 1984), 336–337.

44. Sen, "Ethical Issues in Income Distribution," in *Resources, Values and Development*, p. 294.

45. Rawls, "Social Unity and Primary Goods," p. 168, especially footnote 8. For Rawls's account of the four levels of justification see *Theory of Justice*, pp. 171–176.

46. Rawls, *The Law of Peoples*, p. 13, footnote 3.

47. Ibid.

48. John Rawls, "Kantian Constructivism in Moral Theory," *Journal of Philosophy* LXXVII:9 (September 1980): 526–527.

49. Martha C. Nussbaum, "Human Capabilities, Female Human Beings," in *Women, Culture and Development*, eds. Martha Nussbaum and Jonathan Glover (Oxford: Oxford University Press, 1995), 92.

50. Sen, *Inequality Reexamined*, p. 124.

51. Jean Drèze and Amartya Sen, *Hunger and Public Action* (Oxford: Clarendon Press, 1989), 51–52.

52. Ibid., pp. 52–53.

53. Amartya Sen and Bernard Williams, "Introduction: Utilitarianism and Beyond," in *Utilitarianism and Beyond*, p. 20.

54. In his more recent accounts of the capabilities approach, Sen sometimes looks at freedoms as freedoms to meet needs. See *Inequality Reexamined*, p. 109.

55. Ibid., pp. 53–55.

56. See Sen, "Equality of What?" in *The Tanner Lectures on Human Values*, ed. S. M. McMurrin (Salt Lake City: University of Utah Press, 1981), 324–325; and Ronald Dworkin, "What Is Equality? Part 1: Equality of Welfare," *Philosophy and Public Affairs* 10:3 (summer 1981): 228–240.

57. Rawls, "Social Unity and Primary Goods," p. 169.

58. Sen sometimes takes this position; see *Inequality Reexamined*, pp. 108–109.

59. Sen, "Equality of What?" p. 328, and "Poor, Relatively Speaking," p. 334.

60. See Nikolai Bukharin, *Imperialism and World Economy* (London: Merlin Press, 1976); Rudolph Hilferding, *Finance Capital* (London: Routledge and Kegan Paul Ltd., 1981); J. A. Hobson, *Imperialism: A Study* (London: James Nisbet and Co., 1902); and V. I. Lenin, *Imperialism: The Highest Stage of Capitalism*, vol. 19 of *Collected Works* (Moscow: Progress Publishers, 1964). The exception to this account of the etiology of imperialism is Rosa Luxemburg; see *The Accumulation of Capital* (London: Routledge and Kegan Paul Ltd., 1963).

61. The exception to this among Marxists is Karl Kautsky, "Ultra-Imperialism," *New Left Review* 59:1 (January–February, 1970). Hobson also disagreed that war was inevitable; see *Imperialism: A Study*, pp. 94–96.

62. The following texts are a representative survey of the various formulations of this theory: Paul A. Baran, *The Political Economy of Growth* (Harmondsworth, U.K.: Penguin Books Ltd., 1978); Andre Gunder Frank, *Capitalism and Underdevelopment in Latin America* (New York: Monthly Review Press, 1969); and Immanuel Wallerstein, *The Capitalist World-Economy* (Cambridge: Cambridge University Press, 1979).

63. The classic account is Arghiri Emmanuel's *Unequal Exchange* (London: Monthly Review Press, 1972).

64. See Robert Brenner's "The Origins of Capitalist Development: A Critique of Neo-Smithian Marxism," *New Left Review* 104:3 (July–August 1977): 25–92; and Bill Warren's *Imperialism Pioneer of Capitalism* (London: Verso, 1980).

65. John Roemer develops a sophisticated model of imperialism, which takes inequalities as part of its identificatory theory. See Roemer, *Free to Lose* (Cambridge, Mass.: Harvard University Press, 1988), 103–106.

66. One of Emmanuel's solutions for unequal exchange is similar to this remedy; see *Unequal Exchange*, pp. 262–270.

67. Kai Nielsen, "Global Justice, Capitalism and the Third World," in *International Justice and the Third World,* eds. Robin Attfield and Barry Wilkins (London: Routledge, 1992), 32–33.

68. A careful discussion of the claims of Marxist theorists of the relative inefficiency of capitalism can be found in Philippe van Parijs's *Real Freedom for All: What (If Anything) Can Justify Capitalism* (Oxford: Clarendon Press, 1995), 186–233.

69. Some support for this view can be found in Jana Thompson, *Justice and World Order* (London: Routledge, 1992), 78–79.

70. This moral principle might be thought one, which is only sometimes applied. See Barry E. Carter and Phillip R. Trimble, *International Law* (Boston: Little Brown and Co., 1991) 429–433.

71. Samuel C. Wheeler III, "Reparations Reconstructed," *American Philosophical Quarterly* 34:3 (July 1997): 301–318.

72. Jeremy Waldron, "Superseding Historic Injustice," *Ethics* 103:1 (October 1992): 4–28.

73. Since apologies are standardly only owed to those who are harmed by ones' actions, it seems to me that the morality of apologies for colonialism and slavery in previous generations is subject to roughly the same account that I have given of reparations.

74. http://World%20Bank/world%20Debt%20Tables%20Extracts%201996.

75. Barry Wilkins, "Debt and Underdevelopment: The Case for Cancelling Third World Debts," *International Justice and the Third World*, pp. 171–172.

76. United Nations Research Institute for Social Development, *Structural Adjustment in a Changing World*, UNRISD Briefing Paper Series 4 (Geneva: UNRISD, 1994), 12.

77. Ibid., p. 24.

78. Michael Barrat Brown, *Fair Trade* (London: Zed Books, 1993), 41.

79. UNRISD, *Structural Adjustment in a Changing World*, p. 3.

80. Ibid., p. 13.

81. Wilkins, "Debt and Underdevelopment," p. 185.

82. Ibid., p. 20–21.

83. See Amartya Sen, *Development As Freedom* (New York: Alfred A. Knopf, 1999), 216–226; and the World Commission on Environment and Development, *Our Common Future*, p. 103–105.

84. Wilkins, "Debt and Underdevelopment," p. 184. Jeffrey Sachs makes an argument to the same conclusion about the particular case of debt cancellation for Nigeria; see "Everyone Has an Excuse Not to Help Nigeria," *Business Day* (June 22, 2000): 15.

85. Brian Barry, "Statism and Nationalism: A Cosmopolitan Critique," in *Global Justice*, Nomos XLI, ed. Ian Shapiro and Lea Brilmayer (New York: New York University Press, 1999), 28.

86. Garrett Hardin, "Lifeboat Ethics: The Case Against Helping the Poor," in *World Hunger Moral Obligation*, eds. William Aiken and Hugh La Follete (Englewood Cliffs, N.J.: Prentice Hall, 1977), 18. Originally published in *Psychology Today* 8 (1974): 38–43, 123–126.

87. Sen, *Development As Freedom*, pp. 205–209. See also The World Commission on Environment and Development, *Our Common Future*, pp. 128–130.

88. Sen, *Development As Freedom*, pp. 216–226.

89. National Academy of Sciences, *One Earth, One Future: Our Changing Global Environment* (Washington, D.C.: National Academy Press, 1990), 53.

90. Ibid., p. 65.

91. Ibid., p. 68; and The World Commission on Environment and Development, *Our Common Future*, p. 175.

92. National Academy of Sciences, *One Earth, One Future*, p. 69. See also The World Commission on Environment and Development, *Our Common Future*, p. 176.

93. National Academy of Sciences, *One Earth, One Future*, p. 71.

94. Ibid., p. 70; and The World Commission on Environment and Development, *Our Common Future*, p. 176.

95. National Academy of Sciences, *One Earth, One Future*, pp. 78–102.

96. Ibid., p. 89.

97. See also Bernard E. Rollin, "Environmental Ethics and International Justice," in *Problems of International Justice*, ed. Steven Luper-Foy (Boulder: Westview Press, 1988), especially pp. 131–139.

98. National Academy of Sciences, *One Earth, One Future*, p. 117.

99. Ibid., pp. 118–119. See also Ben Jackson, *Poverty and the Planet* (London: Penguin Books, 1990), 16–31.

100. I owe recognition of this problem to Henry Shue, "Global and International Inequality," *International Affairs* 74:3 (July 1999): 520.

101. See Brian Barry, "Humanity and Justice in Global Perspective," pp. 247–250; and "Do Countries Have Moral Obligations? The Case of World Poverty," in *The Tanner Lectures on Human Values*, ed. Sterling M. McMurrin (Salt Lake City: University of Utah Press, 1981), 40–42. Recently Barry has come out strongly against statism. See note 85. So, the view expressed in these pieces may no longer characterize his position.

CHAPTER 5

1. John Stuart Mill, "A Few Words on Non-intervention," in *Dissertations and Discussions*, vol. 3 (Boston: William V. Spencer, 1864), 251.

2. Rawls takes the basic structure to be "the way in which the major social institutions distribute fundamental rights and duties and determine the division of political advantages for social cooperation." Among major social institutions Rawls includes "the political constitution and principal economic and social arrangements." John Rawls, *A Theory of Justice*, rev. ed. (Cambridge, Mass.: Harvard University Press, 1999), 6.

3. Hedley Bull distinguishes internal and external sovereignty. See *The Anarchical Society* (London: Macmillan Press Ltd., 1977), 8.

4. For example, Thomas Pogge takes sovereignty to be a relationship of authority only over other persons. See "Cosmopolitanism and Sovereignty," *Ethics* 103:1 (October 1992): 57.

5. The relationship between countermeasures and intervention is discussed by Fernando R. Tesón, *Humanitarian Intervention: An Inquiry into Law and Morality*, 2d ed. (Irvington-on-Hudson, N.Y.: Transnational Publishers, 1997), 135.

6. My position is close to that of Charles Beitz and owes a great deal to his arguments. But there seem to be three ways in which we differ. The first is that I take sovereignty to be authority over a particular domain. A state may be sovereign in one domain and not another. Beitz does not draw this distinction. The second difference is that I narrow the kinds of comparative domestic injustices that amount to forfeitures of sovereignty to those that are properties of the basic structure. Third, I allow that international injustices may justify intervention. See Charles Beitz, *Political Theory and International Relations* (Princeton: Princeton University Press, 1979), part 2. Serious international injustices, ranging from war to pollution to distributive injustices to harboring international terrorists, may be perpetrated by the domestic policies of states with just basic structures. Henry Shue discusses pollution and sovereignty in "Eroding Sovereignty: The Advance of Principle," in *The Morality of Nationalism*, eds. Robert McKim and Jeff McMahan (Oxford: Oxford University Press, 1997), 340–359. Andrew Kuper's discussion of immigration policy points to the possibility of international distributive injustices created by just basic structures; see "Rawlsian Global Justice: Beyond the Law of Peoples to a Cosmopolitan Law of Person," *Political Theory* 28:5 (October 2000): 644–648. The effects are limited to those of domestic policies because criteria for responding to the unjust effects of foreign policies are a matter of the doctrine of counter-measures.

7. Vattel affirmed the relationship between statism and absolutism as follows: "Every Nation which governs itself, under whatever form, and which does not depend on any other Nation, is a *sovereign State*. Its rights, are, in the natural order, the same as those of every other State. . . . To give a Nation the right to a definite position in this great society, it need only be truly sovereign and independent; it must govern itself by its own authority and its own laws." E. de Vattel, *The Law of Nations of the Principles of Natural Law*, vol. 3, trans. Charles G. Fenwick (New York: Ocean Publications, Inc., 1964), 11. Fernando R. Tesón also recognizes and criticizes the relationship between statism and absolutism in his *A Philosophy of International Law* (Boulder: Westview Press, 1998), 39–71.

8. For various and different examples of the mixed conception of sovereignty, see David Luban, "Just War and Human Rights," in *International Ethics*, eds. Charles Beitz, et al. (Princeton: Princeton University Press, 1985), 195–216; Luban, "The Romance of the Nation State," in *International Ethics*, pp. 238–243; Henry Shue, "Conditional Sovereignty," *Res Publica* 8:1 (1999): 1–7; and Michael Walzer, *Just and Unjust Wars* (New York: Basic Books, 1977), 108.

9. Adam Przeworski, et al., *Sustainable Democracy* (Cambridge: Cambridge University Press, 1995), 4.

10. See Charles Beitz, "Sovereignty and Morality," in *Political Theory Today*, ed. David Held (Stanford: Stanford University Press, 1991), 241.

11. Grotius employs the analogy to property in *De Jure Belli et Pacis* (London: John W. Parker, 1853), book 1, chap. 3, sections 11–12.

12. Friedrich Kratochwil, "Sovereignty As Dominium: Is There a Right of Humanitarian Interventions?" in *Beyond Westphalia? State Sovereignty and International Intervention*, eds. Gene M. Lyons and Michael Mastanduno (Baltimore: The Johns Hopkins University Press, 1995), 26.

13. The analogy with property is also criticized in R. J. Vincent's *Nonintervention and International Order* (Princeton: Princeton University Press, 1974), 338–339.

14. Walzer, *Just and Unjust Wars*, p. 55.

15. Ibid., p. 54.

16. On the relationship between privacy and domestic violence, see Susan Moller Okin, *Justice, Gender, and the Family* (New York: Basic Books, 1989), 128. A comparison of the faults of shielding the family and the state from critiques of justice from the outside can be found in Onora O'Neill, "Justice, Gender and International Boundaries," in *International Justice and the Third World*, eds. Robin Attfield and Barry Wilkins (London: Routledge, 1992), 59–61.

17. F. H. Hinsley, *Sovereignty*, 2d ed. (Cambridge: Cambridge University Press, 1989), 226.

18. "Since the state is mind objectified, it is only as one of its members that the individual himself has objectivity, genuine individuality, and an ethical life." G. W. F. Hegel, *Philosophy of Right*, trans. T. M. Knox (London: Oxford, 1967), 156, paragraph 258. See also Mervyn Frost, *Towards a Normative Theory of International Relations* (Cambridge: Cambridge University Press, 1986), 174–175.

19. Ibid., pp. 162–163.

20. Ibid., p. 183.

21. Ibid., p. 178.

22. Ibid., pp. 162–163.

23. See John Rawls, *The Law of Peoples* (Cambridge, Mass.: Harvard University Press, 1999), 59; and Terry Nardin, *Law, Morality, and the Relations of States* (Princeton: Princeton University Press, 1983), 233.

24. Rawls, *The Law of Peoples*. See also Allen Buchanan's "Recognitional Legitimacy and the State System," *Philosophy and Public Affairs*, 28:1 (winter 1999): especially pp. 52–62.

25. If human rights are understood sufficiently broadly then a conception of sovereignty that requires respect for human rights is a cosmopolitan conception. This appears to be Tesón's position. See *Humanitarian Intervention*, pp. 117–129.

Charles Jones seems to take a position similar to this in his *Global Justice: Defending Cosmopolitanism* (Oxford: Oxford University Press, 1999), 50–84.

26. Vincent makes this mistake in *Nonintervention and International Order*, pp. 345–346.

27. Stanley Hoffman, *Duties Beyond Borders* (Syracuse, N.Y.: Syracuse University Press, 1981), 57.

28. Tesón also makes this point. See *A Philosophy of International Law*, p. 40.

29. The qualification "at least sometimes" indicates that even the cosmopolitan conception of sovereignty can allow that there may be times when the injustice that exists does not merit intervention. The necessary condition of proportionality, which is defended later is meant to proscribe interventions in such cases.

30. Martin Luther King Jr., for example, claims that "the aftermath of non-violence is the creation of the beloved community, while the aftermath of violence is tragic bitterness," in *Stride Toward Freedom* (New York: Harper and Row, 1958), 102.

31. "But the evil [of intervention on behalf of the oppressed] is, that, if they have not sufficient love of liberty to be able to wrest it from merely domestic oppressors, the liberty which is bestowed on them by other hands than their own will have nothing real, nothing permanent." Mill, "A Few Words on Non-intervention," p. 259. "Both for production on a mass scale of this communist consciousness, and for the success of the cause itself, the alteration of men on a mass scale is necessary, an alteration which can only take place in a practical movement, a revolution; this revolution is necessary, therefore, not only because the *ruling* class cannot be overthrown in any other way, but also because the class *overthrowing* it can only in a revolution succeed in ridding itself of all the muck of ages and become fitted to found society anew." Karl Marx, *The German Ideology* in *The Marx-Engels Reader*, 2d ed., ed. Robert C. Tucker (New York: W. W. Norton, 1978), 193. Emphasis in original.

32. In contrast Mill seems guilty of remarkable naiveté when he equates ability to govern with ability to vanquish an oppressor, such as in the following claim: "The only test possessing any real value, of a people's having become fit for popular institutions, is that they, or a sufficient portion of them to prevail in the contest, are willing to brave labour and danger for their liberation." Mill, "A Few Words on Non-intervention," p. 258.

33. Robert H. Jackson, "International Community Beyond the Cold War," in *Beyond Westphalia? State Sovereignty and International Intervention*, p. 76.

34. E. H. Carr insists that "pleas for international solidarity" come from the "dominant nations"; see *The Twenty Years' Crisis* (London: Macmillan and Co., Ltd., 1939), 109.

35. Apparently this was the position of many in the British Labour Party during World War II and was the position taken by Harold Laski in his pamphlet, "Is This an Imperialist War." See S. F. Kissin, *War and the Marxists*, vol. 2 (London: André Deutsch, 1989), 91.

36. See Jackson, "International Community Beyond the Cold War," pp. 59–83; Christopher Clapham, "Sovereignty and the Third World State," *Political Studies* 47 (Special Issue 1999): 522–537; and David Strang, "Contested Sovereignty: The Social Construction of Colonial Imperialism," in *Sovereignty as Social Construct*, eds. Thomas J. Biersteker and Cynthia Weber (Cambridge: Cambridge University

Press, 1996), 22–49. For a qualified exception to the endorsement of absolute non-intervention out of a concern for the conditions of developing countries, see S. C. Nolutshungu, "Non-intervention: 'Ethical Rules of Disregard' and Third-World Conflicts," in *Rights and Duties in North-South Relations,* ed. Moorhead Wright (London: Macmillan, 1986), 131–158.

37. Vincent points out that the principle that American foreign policy was premised on during the Cold War was not the statist conception of sovereignty and its complement nonintervention, but rather a loose bipolar system that permitted intervention to prevent defections to the other block. *Nonintervention and International Order,* pp. 351–353.

38. For an account of the recent history of U.S. imperialist interventions in Latin America see Noam Chomsky's *Turning the Tide* (Boston: South End, 1985), especially chaps. 1–3.

39. R. J. Vincent holds that a consequence of the cosmopolitan account is that "there would be no end of wars of intervention." *Human Rights and International Relations* (Cambridge: Cambridge University Press, 1986), 117.

40. There is a difficult question of application here. Is there just cause for intervention when the basic structure is just, but it is not operational, as when a state may have a just constitution that is ignored? When reasonably just electoral laws and procedures are in place but are ignored, as they were for example prior to the 2000 elections in Zimbabwe, the question of just cause for intervention is particularly vexed.

41. For a somewhat different argument to a similar conclusion, see Buchanan, "Recognitional Legitimacy and the State System," pp. 62–63. As far as I can surmise Tesón's requirement that injustices be systematic is meant to achieve the same purpose. See *Humanitarian Intervention,* p. 123.

42. Aristotle, *Nicomachean Ethics,* trans. H. Rackham (Cambridge, Mass.: Harvard University Press, 1934), 317, at 1137b29–33.

43. A similar point is made by Tesón, *Humanitarian Intervention,* p. 125–126.

44. A good discussion of this can be found in Michael W. Doyle, "The New Interventionism," *Metaphilosophy* 32: 1–2 (January 2001): 212–233.

45. Tesón refers to this criterion as "disinterestedness" in *Humanitarian Intervention,* pp. 121–122. He sees this condition as being fulfilled by certain actions of the intervening party, namely if the intervention lasted no longer than necessary, if the party demanded no advantages, and if the party did not seek domination. All of these are important considerations, but right intent is not needed to ensure them. The requirement of proportionality can do this work more straightforwardly since it judges only actions and not actions as signs of intent.

46. Henry Shue refers to such duties of states as "service duties." See *Basic Rights* (Princeton: Princeton University Press, 1980), 151.

47. See Brian Barry, "Humanity and Justice in Global Perspective," in Nomos XXIV, eds. J. Roland Pennock and John W. Chapman (New York: New York University Press, 1982), 232.

48. Jackson, "International Community Beyond the Cold War," p. 75.

49. A prima facie duty to intervene exists wherever there is an injustice to the basic structure of a state or in the foreign effects of domestic policy. An all-things-considered duty would require that the other justifying conditions also be met. Al-

though not drawing the distinction between prima facie and all-things-considered duties, Henry Shue also argues for the duty to intervene in "Conditional Sovereignty." Elsewhere he limits the duty only to cases where basic rights are violated. See *Basic Rights*, pp. 114ff.

50. Jackson, "International Community Beyond the Cold War," p. 80.

51. Although this is a broad definition of intervention, some define it even more broadly. Tesón maintains that criticism is a form of "soft intervention" in *Humanitarian Intervention*, p. 135. He also holds that intervention is coercive. Hence, he is unable to draw an important distinction between rational argumentation and coercion. Stanley Hoffman asserts that "refusing to intervene . . . is itself a form of intervention" in *Duties Beyond Borders*, p. 34. If this were true, it would be impossible to distinguish intervention from nonintervention.

52. Jackson, "International Community Beyond the Cold War," p. 82.

53. John Mueller and Karl Mueller, "Sanctions of Mass Destruction," *Foreign Affairs* 78:3 (May/June 1999): 49.

54. Ibid., p. 51.

CHAPTER 6

1. Avishai Margalit and Joseph Raz, "National Self-Determination," *Journal of Philosophy* LXXXVII:9 (September 1990): 449.

2. Will Kymlicka, *Multi-Cultural Citizenship: A Liberal Theory of Minority Rights* (Oxford: Oxford University Press, 1995), 6–7.

3. This claim does not require that national groups conceived of themselves as nations prior to the existence of the state. Nations may still be imagined communities in Benedict Anderson's sense and the image of national community a modern phenomenon. See Anderson, *Imagined Communities* (London: Verso, 1993), 6.

4. Kymlicka, *Multi-Cultural Citizenship*, chap. 4, especially pp. 42–44, and *Liberalism, Community, and Culture* (Oxford: Clarendon Press, 1989), 166–167.

5. Kymlicka, *Multi-Cultural Citizenship*, pp. 56–57.

6. Kok-Chor Tan urges that placing value on state neutrality is peculiar to political liberalism and not required of comprehensive liberalism. See his *Toleration, Diversity, and Global Justice* (University Park: The Pennsylvania State University Press, 2000), 64–77. I disagree. As I have argued, state neutrality is a necessary (political) condition of the ability to revise nationally one's conception of the good. This ability is valued by both political and comprehensive liberals.

7. Yael Tamir, *Liberal Nationalism* (Princeton: Princeton University Press, 1993), 72.

8. I am relying upon Allen Buchanan's distinction between individual and group rights. He distinguishes the two according to the object of ascription and the agent of exercise. Individual rights are ascribed to individuals and are exercised by them; group rights are ascribed to groups and are exercised by them. See *Secession* (Boulder: Westview Press, 1991), 74.

9. See Tamir, *Liberal Nationalism*, p. 75; and Joseph Raz, *The Morality of Freedom* (Oxford: Clarendon Press, 1986), 209. See also Margalit and Raz, "National Self-Determination," p. 456.

10. These problems seem to me to also apply to Christopher Wellman's argument that the case for secession depends in large measure on the size of the group wishing to secede. See "A Defense of Secession and Political Self-Determination," *Philosophy and Public Affairs* 24:2 (spring 1995): 162–163.

11. This is often raised as a practical problem for the view that there are group rights. For example, see Fernando R. Tesón, *A Philosophy of International Law* (Boulder: Westview Press, 1999), 136.

12. This model is developed in Otto Bauer, *Die Nationalitätenfrage und die Sozialdemokratie*, in *Otto Bauer Werkausgabe*, band 1 (Wien: Europa Verlags-AG Wien, 1975), especially pp. 401–413.

13. An account of some of these problems is presented by the World Health Organization in Fact Sheet N 153, http://www.who.int/inf-fs/en/fact153.html.

14. For an account of the rights to emigrate and to change citizenship, see Fredrick G. Whelan, "Citizenship and the Right to Leave," *American Political Science Review* 75:3 (September 1981): 636–653.

15. The argument presented here for the moral difference between the rights of immigrant groups and nations does not rely upon Kymlicka's controversial empirical claim that the former unlike the latter are unable to maintain distinct cultural structures. A weakness of the way that I have presented the argument, however, is that the immigrant groups may develop stable cultural structures distinct from those of their homeland. In this case, individuals who wish not to be governed by the state may also have no cultural homeland to which to return. Arguing against the right to secede for such immigrant groups may require invoking either the voluntary nature of immigration as does Kymlicka, *Multi-Cultural Citizenship*, p. 48, or the destabilizing effects of allowing immigrants to secede.

16. These practical considerations militate against extending the right to secede to just any group. Thus, my position differs from others who also argue for a non-remedial constrained right to secede, but one that is not limited to nations. See Daniel Philpott, "In Defense of Self-Determination," *Ethics* 105:2 (January 1995): 352–385; and Wellman, "A Defense of Secession and Political Self-Determination," pp. 142–171.

17. Tesón also makes this point. See *A Philosophy of International Law*, p. 151.

18. Margalit and Raz argue that the right to self-determination requires some sort of supermajority, "National Self-Determination," p. 458. I do not fully address the question of whether simple or supermajority should be required to exercise the right to secede, but it seems to me that, given the protection to minorities under my argument, a simple majority would suffice.

19. The following quotation in the text seems to disprove Hurst Hannum's claim that, for Lenin, support for national self-determination was merely tactical. See *Autonomy, Sovereignty, and Self-Determination* (Philadelphia: University of Philadelphia Press, 1990), 33.

20. V. I. Lenin, "More about Nationalism," in *Collected Works*, vol. 20 (Moscow: Progress Publishers, 1964), 110. Emphasis in original. In the tradition of classical Marxism, Lenin's position is the most permissive. At the other end of the spectrum is Rosa Luxemburg, "The Nation State and the Proletariat," in *The National Question: Selected Writings*, ed. Horace B. Davis (New York: Monthly Review Press, 1976), 168–169. The record of the Bolsheviks under Lenin's lead is far

from consistent on the implementation of the right to secede. For the record, see E. H. Carr's, *The Bolshevik Revolution 1917–1923, A History of Soviet Russia*, vol. 1 (London and Basingstoke, U.K.: Macmillan Press Ltd., 1950), chaps. 10–13.

21. An entirely different criticism of self-determination as a democratic right can be found in David Archard's "Political Philosophy and the Concept of a Nation," *The Journal of Value Inquiry* 29:3 (September 1995): especially pp. 386–387.

22. See Allen Buchanan, "Self-Determination, Secession, and the Rule of Law," in *The Morality of Nationalism*, eds. Robert McKim and Jeff McMahan (New York: Oxford University Press, 1997), 310. Buchanan's requirement of justifying grounds in this paper seems to be motivated primarily by a belief about what is required in order for a proposal on secession to be accepted as international law. Also, my proposed lack of justifying grounds, combined with the constraints of justice, does not fit neatly into Buchanan's distinction between substantive and proceduralist models of a constitutional right to secede. See Buchanan, *Secession*, pp. 132–135.

23. Ernest Gellner, *Nations and Nationalism* (Oxford: Blackwell, 1983), 2. Emphasis in original.

CHAPTER 7

1. St. Augustine, *The City of God*, Books 17–22, trans. Gerald G. Walsh, S. J., and Daniel J. Honan (New York: Fathers of the Church, Inc., 1954), 206.

2. Arthur Schlesinger Jr. is guilty of this when he invokes the "ghastly consequences" of seeing foreign policy in moral terms and calls the Vietnam War a "morality trip." See "National Interests and Moral Absolutes," in *Ethics and World Politics*, ed. Ernest W. Lefever (Baltimore: The Johns Hopkins University Press, 1972), 27, 38.

3. Ibid., p. 24; and George F. Kennan, "Morality and Foreign Policy," *Foreign Affairs* 64:2 (winter 1985/86): 207.

4. I discuss the problems associated with the requirement of actual consensus in greater detail in "Consensus and Cognitivism in Habermas's Discourse Ethics," *South African Journal of Philosophy* 19:2 (June 2000): 65–74.

5. Reinhold Niebuhr, *Moral Man and Immoral Society* (New York: Charles Scribner's Sons, 1932), 48, 88; and E. H. Carr, *The Twenty Years' Crisis* (London: Macmillan and Co., Ltd, 1939), 201.

6. Niebuhr, *Moral Man*, p. 48.

7. Ibid., p. 91.

8. Ibid., p. 88.

9. Kennan, "Morality and Foreign Policy," p. 206. Emphasis in original.

10. Also see Charles Beitz, *Political Theory and International Relations* (Princeton: Princeton University Press, 1979), 24.

11. Hans Morgenthau, *Politics Among Nations*, 5th ed. (New York: Alfred A. Knopf, 1973), 4.

12. Ibid., p. 5.

13. Ibid., pp. 8, 12.

14. Justin Rosenberg notes that this move complicates our understanding of Morgenthau's theory considerably. For it is no longer clear whether he is offering objective laws for how all political agents in fact do act, or for how to understand all action including deviation from ideal laws, or for how they ought to act. See Rosenberg, *The Empire of Civil Society* (London: Verso, 1994), 22–23.

15. Morgenthau, *Politics Among Nations*, p. 8.

16. Ibid., p. 4.

17. Ibid., p. 14.

18. Carr mentions this view in *The Twenty Years' Crisis*, p. 204, as does Raymond Aron in *Peace and War: A Theory of International Relations*, trans. Richard Howard and Annette Baker Fox (Garden City, N.Y.: Doubleday and Co., 1966), 580.

19. See Thomas Hobbes, *Leviathan* (New York: Macmillan Publishing Co., Inc., 1962), especially chaps. 13, 14, and 17; and G. W. F. Hegel, *Philosophy of Right*, trans. T. M. Knox (Oxford: Oxford University Press, 1952), especially paragraphs 321–340.

20. Beitz, *Political Theory and International Relations*, part 1, chaps. 3 and 4.

21. Ibid., pp. 56–58.

22. Jenny Teichman, citing John Yoder, lists as many as ten different kinds of pacifism. See *Pacifism and the Just War* (Oxford: Basil Blackwell, Ltd., 1986), 7–8.

23. There is at least one other possible justification of pacifism, namely, that although the criteria of a just war theory are correct, no war can meet these standards. I do not address this view here since my objective is to investigate challenges to the theory of the just war, not problems of its application.

24. M. K. Gandhi, *Non-Violent Resistance* (New York: Schocken Books, 1951), 3.

25. Elisabeth Burgos-Debray, ed., *I, Rigoberta Menchú*, trans. Ann Wright (London: Verso, 1984), 174. Recently David Stoll has challenged the veracity of some of Menchú's stories about her life, charging that they are rather more like composite sketches of peasant life in Guatemala. See Stoll, *Rigoberta Menchú and the Story of All Poor Guatemalans* (Boulder: Westview Press, 1999). The point that I am trying to make by referring to these passages is simply that acts of torture and intimidation of this kind, regardless of specific details, are unambiguously wrong.

26. Robert L. Holmes, *On War and Morality* (Princeton: Princeton University Press, 1989), 189.

27. Ibid., p. 186.

28. Ibid., p. 187.

29. Elizabeth Anscombe, "War and Murder," in *War and Morality*, ed. Richard A. Wasserstrom (Belmont, Calif.: Wadsworth Publishing Co., Inc., 1970), 45. Jeffrie Murphy equates combatant status with guilt without considering the mental state of the combatant. See Jeffrie G. Murphy, "The Killing of the Innocent," in *Today's Moral Problems*, 3d ed., ed. Richard Wasserstrom (New York: Macmillan Publishing Co., 1985), 331. Originally published in *The Monist*, 57:4 (1973): 527–550.

30. On organic wholes, see G. E. Moore, *Principia Ethica* (Cambridge: Cambridge University Press, 1959), 27ff.

31. Holmes, *On War and Morality*, p. 191.

32. Ibid., p. 211.

33. This line of argument also provides a response to Richard Norman's criticism that war involves killing those who are not responsible. See *Ethics, Killing, and War* (Cambridge: Cambridge University Press, 1995), 172.

34. This position is an example of what Richard Wasserstrom calls the moderate view, derived from the principle that killing innocents is wrong. See Wasserstrom, "On the Morality of War," in *War and Morality*, p. 100.

35. Holmes, *On War and Morality*, p. 210.

36. Ibid., p. 277.

37. Gandhi, *Non-Violent Resistance*, p. 35.

38. Leland M. Goodrich, Edvard Hambro, and Anne Patricia Simmons, *Charter of the United Nations*, 3d ed. (New York: Columbia University Press, 1969), 43.

39. Michael Walzer, *Just and Unjust Wars* (New York: Basic Books, 1977), 54–55.

40. Ellen Meiksins Wood, "Kosovo and the New Imperialism," *Monthly Review* 51:2 (June 1999): 4.

41. *Los Angeles Times*, January 30, 1991, p. A11.

42. See "Why War? Background to the Crisis," *Middle East Report* 20 (November/December 1990): 167.

43. For an account of the threat of indigenous nationalism to U.S. interests in the Middle East and Israel's role as a barrier to it, see Noam Chomsky, *The Fateful Triangle* (Boston: South End Press, 1983), 20–27. Examples of Israeli aggression include the 1956 attack on Egypt and the 1978 and 1982 attacks on Lebanon; see pp. 98–103.

44. Javier Solana, "NATO's Success in Kosovo," *Foreign Affairs* 78:60 (November–December 1999): 114.

45. Michael Mandlebaum, "A Perfect Failure: NATO's War Against Yugoslavia," *Foreign Affairs* 78:5 (September–October 1999): 8.

46. Tariq Ali, "Springtime for NATO," *New Left Review* 234:2 (March/April 1999): 64.

47. Branka Magas, *The Destruction of Yugoslavia* (London: Verso, 1993), 10.

48. Magas gives an account of the strike in *The Destruction of Yugoslavia*, pp. 179–186.

49. "Another Chapter Opens in Kosovo," *The Economist* (October 17–23, 1998): 33; and Solana, "NATO's Success in Kosovo," p. 116.

50. Solana, "NATO's Success in Kosovo," p. 116.

51. "Getting Ready for War," *The Economist* (October 10–16, 1998): 32.

52. "Kosovo on the Brink Again," *The Economist* (January 23–29, 1999): 27.

53. Ibid.

54. Marc Weller, "The Rambouillet Conference on Kosovo," *International Affairs* 75:2 (April 1999): 229. Weller served as legal adviser to the Kosovo delegation at the Rambouillet conference.

55. This point is emphasized by Ali, "Springtime for NATO," p. 68; and Robin Blackburn, "Kosovo: The War of NATO Expansion," *New Left Review* 235 (May/June 1999): 116.

56. See Gilbert Archer, "Is NATO's Onslaught a Just War?" *Monthly Review* 51:2 (June 1999): 17.

57. Blackburn, "Kosovo: The War of NATO Expansion," p. 119.

58. Wood, "Kosovo and the New Imperialism," p. 6.

59. "The West versus Serbia," *The Economist* (March 27–April 2, 1999): 29.

60. Helen Smith, "Dark Secret of Kosovo's War," *Mail and Guardian* (April 20–27, 2000): 14–15.

61. Mandlebaum, "A Perfect Failure: NATO's War Against Yugoslavia," p. 3.

62. For an account of Kosovo a year after the cessation of the war, see David Rohde, "Kosovo Seething," *Foreign Affairs* 79:3 (May/June 2000): 65–79.

63. For an account of Bosnia four years after the cessation of the war, see David Chandler, "The Bosnian Protectorate and the Implications for Kosovo," *New Left Review* 235:3 (May/June 1999): 124–134.

64. Blackburn, "Kosovo: The War of NATO Expansion," p. 107; Ali, "Springtime for NATO," p. 68.

65. Weller, "The Rambouillet Conference on Kosovo," pp. 234, 241.

66. Ibid., pp. 234–235.

67. Christopher Hill, the U.S. ambassador to Macedonia at the time and peace negotiator before and during the Rambouillet conference, apparently agrees that the Serbian rejection of the Rambouillet peace plan was not primarily due to its requirement of a NATO presence. See Tim Judah, "Inside the KLA," *The New York Review of Books* 46:10 (June 10, 1999): 21–22.

CHAPTER 8

1. Imanuel Kant, "The Contest of Faculties," in *Kant's Political Writings*, ed. Hans Reiss, trans. H. B. Nisbet (Cambridge: Cambridge University Press, 1970), 185.

2. One notable exception is Kai Nielsen, "World Government, Security, and Global Justice," in *Problems of International Justice*, ed. Steven Luper-Foy (Boulder: Westview Press, 1988), 263–282.

3. Kant's criticism of a world-state is oft cited: "But in light of the idea of reason, this state [a federal union of states] is still to be preferred to an amalgamation of the separate nations under a single power which has overruled the rest and created a universal monarchy. For the laws progressively lose their impact as the government increases its range, and a soulless despotism, after crushing the germs of goodness, will finally lapse into anarchy." "Perpetual Peace: A Philosophical Sketch," in Kant's Political Writings p.113.

4. For an account of the pacific federation, see ibid., pp. 93–130.

5. Hedley Bull, *The Anarchical Society* (London: The Macmillan Press, Ltd., 1977), 254.

6. There are various contemporary accounts of such a multilayered federation. These do not offer the same institutional solutions, nor are they based upon the same ordering of moral principles. For examples, see Daniele Archibugi, "From the United Nations to Cosmopolitan Democracy," in *Cosmopolitan Democracy*, eds. Daniele Archibugi and David Held (Cambridge: Polity Press, 1995), 121–162; Richard Falk, *This Endangered Planet* (New York: Random House, 1971), especially chap. 7; Falk, *The Promise of World Order* (Brighton, U.K.: Wheatsheaf Books Ltd., 1987), especially chap. 11; Falk, "The World Order Between Inter-State Law and the Law of Hu-

manity: The Role of Civil Society Institutions," *Cosmopolitan Democracy*, pp. 163–179; David Held, "Democracy: From City-States to a Cosmopolitan Order?" in *Prospects for Democracy*, ed. David Held (Stanford: Stanford University Press, 1993), 13–52; Held, "Democracy, the Nation-State, and the Global System," in *Political Theory Today*, ed. David Held (Stanford: Stanford University Press, 1991), 197–235; David Held "Democracy and the New International Order," in *Cosmopolitan Democracy*, pp. 96–120; Mary Kaldor, "European Institutions, Nation-States and Nationalism," in *Cosmopolitan Democracy*, pp. 68–95; and Thomas Pogge, "Cosmopolitanism and Sovereignty," *Ethics* 103:1 (October 1992): 48–75; and Iris Marion Young, *Inclusion and Democracy* (Oxford: Oxford University Press, 2000), 265–271.

7. For more on this, see Andrew Kuper's interesting suggestions in "Rawlsian Global Justice: Beyond the Law of Peoples to a Cosmopolitan Law of Persons," *Political Theory* 28:3 (October 2000): 657–658.

8. The role of transnational actors is increasingly studied in empirical international relations theory. A good survey of the contemporary state of the debate can be found in Thomas Risse-Kappen, ed., *Bringing Transnational Relations Back In* (Cambridge: Cambridge University Press, 1995).

9. James Bohman, "International Regimes and Democratic Governance: Political Equality and Influence in Global Institutions," *International Affairs* 75:3 (July 1999): 499–513.

10. Robert O. Keohane and Joseph S. Nye, "Transgovernmental Relations," in *Perspectives on World Politics*, ed. Michael Smith, et al. (London: Croom Helm Ltd., 1981), 224–225. Institutions may, of course, do more than merely provide for coordinating action and sharing information. I do not mean to be suggesting a theory of international institutions. For an interesting recent attempt at that, see Steven Weber, "Institutions and Change," in *New Thinking in International Relations*, eds. Michael W. Doyle and G. John Ikenberry (Boulder: Westview Press, 1997), 229–265.

11. Bull, *The Anarchical Society*, p. 305.

12. Bull, for example, warns of the growth of private violence. *The Anarchical Society*, p. 268.

13. Michael Doyle, "Kant Liberal Legacies, and Foreign Affairs, Part 1," *Philosophy and Public Affairs* 12:3 (summer 1983): 203–265.

14. John Roemer, *A Future for Socialism* (Cambridge, Mass.: Harvard University Press, 1994), 56.

15. For a defense of the egalitarian virtues of socialism see my "Liberal Values and Socialist Models," *Theoria* 89 (June 1997): 65–77.

16. Reinhold Niebuhr, in his typical manner, made this point well. "The men of power in modern industry would not, of course, capitulate simply because the social philosophy by which they justify their policies had been discredited. When power is robbed of the shining armor of political, moral and philosophical theories, by which it defends itself, it will fight on without armor; but it will be more vulnerable and the strength of its enemies increased." Reinhold Niebuhr, *Moral Man and Immoral Society* (New York: Charles Scribner's Sons, 1932), 33.

17. This point about Marx is made convincingly by Hal Draper, "The Two Souls of Socialism," in *Socialism from Below*, ed. E. Haberkern (Atlantic Highlands, N.J.: Humanities Press, 1992), 2–33.

18. Richard Falk, among others, argues that there is a nascent movement for globalization-from-below in "The World Order Between Inter-State Law and the Law of Humanity: The Role of Civil Society Institutions," p. 171. See also his *Law in an Emerging Global Village* (Ardsley, N.Y.: Transnational Publishers, 1998), 209–224. This point is also stressed by Iris Marion Young in *Inclusion and Democracy*, pp. 271–272.

19. Thomas Pogge, "Moral Progress," in *Problems of International Justice*, p. 301.

20. Richard Devetak and Richard Higgot, "Justice Unbound? Globalization, States and the Transformation of the Social Bond," *International Affairs* 75:3 (July 1999): 493.

21. An interesting historical survey of attempts to build such solidarity can be found in Margaret Levi and David Olson's "The Battle in Seattle," *Politics and Society* 28:3 (September 2000): 309–329. Kim Moody sketches the elements of a program for international social movement unionism in his *Workers in a Lean World* (London: Verso, 1997), 269–292.

22. Immanuel Kant, "The Contest of Faculties," p. 183.

BIBLIOGRAPHY

Ackerman, Bruce. 1994. "Political Liberalisms." *Journal of Philosophy* XCI, no. 7 (July): 364–386.

Akehurst, Michael. 1984. "Humanitarian Intervention." In *Intervention in World Politics*, edited by Hedley Bull. Oxford: Clarendon Press.

Ali, Tariq. 1999. "Springtime for NATO." *New Left Review* 234, no. 2 (March/April): 62–75.

Anderson, Benedict. 1993. *Imagined Communities*. London: Verso.

Anscombe, Elizabeth. 1970. "War and Murder." In *War and Morality*, edited by Richard A. Wasserstrom. Belmont, Calif.: Wadsworth Publishing Co., Inc.

Archard, David. 1995. "Political Philosophy and the Concept of a Nation." *The Journal of Value Inquiry* 29, no. 3 (September): 379–392.

Archer, Gilbert. 1999. "Is NATO's Onslaught a Just War?" *Monthly Review* 51, no. 2 (June): 15–19.

Archibugi, Daniele. 1995. "From the United Nations to Cosmopolitan Democracy." In *Cosmopolitan Democracy*, edited by Daniele Archibugi and David Held. Cambridge: Polity Press.

Arestis, Philip, and Malcolm Sawyer. 1997. "How Many Cheers for the Tobin Tax?" *Cambridge Journal of Economics* 21: 753–768.

Aristotle. 1934. *Nicomachean Ethics*. Translated by H. Rackham. Cambridge, Mass.: Harvard University Press.

Aron, Raymond. 1966. *Peace and War: A Theory of International Relations*. Translated by Richard Howard and Annette Baker Fox. Garden City, N.Y.: Doubleday and Co.

Baran, Paul A. 1978. *The Political Economy of Growth*. Harmondsworth, U.K.: Penguin Books Ltd.

Barry, Brian. 1973. *The Liberal Theory of Justice*. Oxford: Clarendon Press.

———. 1981. "Do Countries Have Moral Obligations? The Case of World Poverty." In *The Tanner Lectures on Human Values*, edited by Sterling M. McMurrin. Salt Lake City: University of Utah Press.

———. 1982. "Humanity and Justice in Global Perspective." In *Ethics, Economics, and the Law, Nomos XXIV*, edited by J. Roland Pennock and John W. Chapman. New York: New York University Press.

———. 1989. *Theories of Justice*. Berkeley: University of California Press.

———. 1999. "Statism and Nationalism: A Cosmopolitan Critique." In *Global Justice,* Nomos XLI, edited by Ian Shapiro and Lea Brilmayer. New York: New York University Press.

Bauer, Otto. 1975. "Die Nationalitätenfrage und die Sozialdemokratie." In *Otto Bauer Werkausgabe,* band 1. Wien: Europa Verlags-AG Wien.

Beitz, Charles. 1979. *Political Theory and International Relations.* Princeton: Princeton University Press.

———. 1983. "Cosmopolitan Ideals and National Sentiment." *The Journal of Philosophy* LXXX, no. 10 (October): 591–600.

———. 1991. "Sovereignty and Morality." In *Political Theory Today,* edited by David Held. Stanford: Stanford University Press.

———. 1999. "Social and Cosmopolitan Liberalism." *International Affairs* 75, no. 3 (July): 531–545.

———. 2000. "Rawls's Law of Peoples." *Ethics* 110, no. 4 (July): 669–696.

Blackburn, Robin. 1999. "Kosovo: The War of NATO Expansion." *New Left Review* 235, no. 3 (May/June): 107–123.

Bohman, James. 1999. "International Regimes and Democratic Governance: Political Equality and Influence in Global Institutions." *International Affairs* 75, no. 3 (July): 499–513.

Brenner, Robert. 1977. "The Origins Of Capitalist Development: A Critique of Neo-Smithian Marxism." *New Left Review* 104, no. 3 (July–August): 25–92.

Brighouse, Harry. 1994. "Is There Any Such Thing As Political Liberalism?" *Pacific Philosophical Quarterly* 75, no. 3–4 (September/December): 318–332.

Brown, Chris. 1992. *International Relations Theory: New Normative Approaches.* New York: Columbia University Press.

Brown, Michael Barrat. 1993. *Fair Trade.* London: Zed Books.

Brownlie, Ian. 1974. "Humanitarian Intervention." In *Law and Civil War in the Modern World,* edited by John Norton Moore. Baltimore: The Johns Hopkins University Press.

———. 1990. *Principles of Public International Law.* 4th ed. Oxford: Clarendon Press.

———. 1992. *Basic Documents on Human Rights.* 3d ed. Oxford: Clarendon Press.

———., ed. 1983. *Basic Documents in International Law.* Oxford: Clarendon Press.

Buchanan, Allen. 1991. *Secession.* Boulder: Westview Press.

———. 1997. "Self-Determination, Secession, and the Rule of Law." In *The Morality of Nationalism,* edited by Robert McKim and Jeff McMahan. New York: Oxford University Press.

———. 1999. "Recognitional Legitimacy and the State System." *Philosophy and Public Affairs* 28, no. 1 (winter): 46–78.

———. 2000. "Rawls's Law of Peoples: Rules for a Vanished Westphalian World." *Ethics* 110, no. 4 (July): 697–721.

Bukharin, Nikolai. 1976. *Imperialism and World Economy.* London: Merlin Press.

Bull, Hedley. 1977. *The Anarchical Society.* London: Macmillan Press Ltd.

Burci, Gian Luca. 1996. "United Nations Peacekeeping Operations in Situations of Internal Conflict." In *The New World Order,* edited by Mortimer Sellars. Oxford: Berg.

Burgos-Debray, Elisabeth, ed. 1984. *I, Rigoberta Menchú*. Translated by Ann Wright. London: Verso.

Caney, Simon. 2001. "Cosmopolitan Justice and Equalizing Opportunities." *Metaphilosophy* 32, nos. 1–2 (January): 113–134.

Carens, Joseph H. 1987. "Aliens and Citizens: The Case for Open Borders." *Review of Politics* 49, no. 2 (spring): 251–273.

_____. 1992. "Migration and Morality: A Liberal Egalitarian Perspective." In *Free Movement*, edited by Brian Barry and Robert Goodin. College Station: The Pennsylvania State University Press.

Carr, E. H. 1939. *The Twenty Years' Crisis*. London: Macmillan and Co., Ltd.

_____. 1950. *The Bolshevik Revolution 1917–1923, A History of Soviet Russia*. Vol. 1. London and Basingstoke, U.K.: Macmillan Press Ltd.

Carter, Barry E., and Phillip R. Trimble. 1991. *International Law*. Boston: Little Brown and Co.

Chandler, David. 1999. "The Bosnian Protectorate and the Implications for Kosovo." *New Left Review* 235, no. 3 (May/June): 124–134.

Chomsky, Noam. 1983. *The Fateful Triangle*. Boston: South End Press.

_____. 1985. *Turning the Tide*. Boston: South End Press.

Clapham, Christopher. 1999. "Sovereignty and the Third World State." *Political Studies* 47 (special issue): 522–537.

Cohen, Joshua. 1998. "Democratic Equality." *Ethics* 99, no. 4 (July): 727–751.

Cohen, Marshall. 1985. "Moral Skepticism and International Relations." In *International Ethics*, edited by Charles Beitz, et al. Princeton: Princeton University Press.

Coleman, Jules L. 1983. "Negative and Positive Postivism." In *Ronald Dworkin and Contemporary Jurisprudence*, edited by Marshall Cohen. Totowa, N.J.: Rowman and Allenheld.

Davidson, Basil. 1980. *The African Slave Trade*. Boston: Little Brown and Co.

DeMartino, George. 2000. *Global Economy, Global Justice*. London: Routledge.

De Vattel, E. 1964. *The Law of Nations of the Principles of Natural Law*. Vol. 3. Translated by Charles G. Fenwick. New York: Ocean Publications, Inc.

Devetak, Richard, and Richard Higgot. 1999. "Justice Unbound? Globalization, States and the Transformation of the Social Bond." *International Affairs* 75, no. 3 (July): 483–498.

De Wet, Erika. 1995. "Labor Standards in the Globalized Economy: The Inclusion of a Social Clause in the General Agreement of Tariff and Trade/World Trade Organization." *Human Rights Quarterly* 17, no. 3: 443–462.

Douglass, R. Bruce. 1982. "International Economic Justice and the Guaranteed Minimum." *The Review of Politics* 44, no. 1 (January): 3–26.

Doyle, Michael. 1983. "Kant Liberal Legacies, and Foreign Affairs, Part 1." *Philosophy and Public Affairs* 12, no. 3 (summer): 203–265.

_____. 2001. "The New Interventionism." *Metaphilosophy* 32, nos. 1–2 (January): 212–235.

Draper, Hal. 1992. "The Two Souls of Socialism." In *Socialism from Below*, edited by E. Haberkern. Atlantic Highlands, N.J.: Humanities Press.

Drèze, Jean, and Amartya Sen. 1989. *Hunger and Public Action*. Oxford: Clarendon Press.

Dworkin, Ronald. 1977. *Taking Rights Seriously*. London: Duckworth.

_____. 1983. "What is Equality? Part 1: Equality of Welfare." *Philosophy and Public Affairs* 10, no. 3 (summer): 228–240.

_____. 1986. *Law's Empire.* Cambridge, Mass.: Harvard University Press.

Eighteenth Assembly of the Heads of State and Government of Organisation of African Unity. 1992. "The African Charter on Human and Peoples' Rights, 1981." In *Basic Documents on Human Rights,* 3d ed., edited by Ian Brownlie. Oxford: Clarendon Press.

Emmanuel, Arghiri. 1972. *Unequal Exchange.* London: Monthly Review Press.

Estlund, David. 1998. "The Insularity of the Reasonable: Why Political Liberalism Must Admit the Truth." *Ethics* 108, no. 2, (January): 252–275.

Falk, Richard. 1971. *This Endangered Planet.* New York: Random House.

_____. 1987. *The Promise of World Order.* Brighton, U.K.: Wheatsheaf Books Ltd.

_____. 1995. "The World Order Between Inter-State Law and the Law of Humanity: The Role of Civil Society Institutions." In *Cosmopolitan Democracy,* edited by Daniele Archibugi and David Held. Cambridge: Polity Press.

_____. 1996. "Revisioning Cosmopolitanism." In *For Love of Country,* edited by Joshua Cohen. Boston: Beacon Press.

_____. 1998. *Law in an Emerging Global Village.* Ardsley, N.Y.: Transnational Publishers, Inc.

Franck, Thomas. 1992. "The Emerging Right to Democratic Governance." *The American Journal of International Law* 86, no. 1 (January): 46–91.

_____. 1999. "Break It, Don't Fake It." *Foreign Affairs* 78, no. 4 (July–August): 116–118.

Frank, Andre Gunder. 1969. *Capitalism and Underdevelopment in Latin America.* New York: Monthly Review Press.

Frost, Mervyn. 1986. *Towards a Normative Theory of International Relations.* Cambridge: Cambridge University Press.

Gandhi, M. K. 1951. *Non-Violent Resistance.* New York: Schocken Books.

Gellner, Ernest. 1983. *Nations and Nationalism.* Oxford: Blackwell.

General Assembly of the United Nations. 1992. "Declaration on the Granting of Independence of Colonial Countries and Peoples, 1960." In *Basic Documents on Human Rights,* 3d ed., edited by Ian Brownlie. Oxford: Clarendon Press.

_____. 1992. "Universal Declaration of Human Rights, 1948." In *Basic Documents on Human Rights,* 3d ed., edited by Ian Brownlie. Oxford: Clarendon Press.

Giddens, Anthony. 1996/97. "Essential Matter," UNRISD News 15 (autumn).

Glennon, Michael. 1999. "Glennon Replies." *Foreign Affairs* 78, no. 4 (July–August): 120–122.

Goodin, Robert E. "What Is So Special About Our Fellow Countrymen?" *Ethics* 98, no. 4 (July 1988): 663–686.

Goodrich, Leland M., Edvard Hambro, and Anne Patricia Simmons. 1969. *Charter of the United Nations.* 3d ed. New York: Columbia University Press.

Grotius, Hugo. 1853. *De Jure Belli et Pacis.* London: John W. Parker.

Habermas, Jürgen. 1992. "Citizenship and National Identity: Some Reflections on the Future of Europe." *Praxis International* 12, no. 1 (April): 1–19.

_____. 1998. *The Inclusion of the Other.* Cambridge, Mass: The MIT Press.

Hampton, Jean. 1993. "The Moral Commitments of Liberalism." In *The Idea of Democracy*, edited by David Copp, Jean Hampton, and John Roemer. Cambridge: Cambridge University Press.

———. 1995. "Immigration, Identity, and Justice." In *Justice in Immigration*, edited by Warren F. Schwartz. Cambridge: University Press.

Hannum, Hurst. 1990. *Autonomy, Sovereignty, and Self-Determination*. Philadelphia: University of Philadelphia Press.

Hardin, Garrett. 1977. "Lifeboat Ethics: The Case Against Helping the Poor" In *World Hunger Moral Obligation*, edited by William Aiken and Hugh La Follete. Englewood Cliffs, N.J.: Prentice Hall.

Hart, H. L. A. 1986. *The Concept of Law*. Oxford: Clarendon Press.

Hegel, G. W. F. 1967. *Philosophy of Right*. Translated by T. M. Knox. London: Oxford.

Held, David. 1991. "Democracy, the Nation-State, and the Global System." In *Political Theory Today*. Stanford: Stanford University Press.

———. 1993. "Democracy: From City-States to a Cosmopolitan Order?" In *Prospects for Democracy*. Stanford: Stanford University Press.

———. 1995. "Democracy and the New International Order." In *Cosmopolitan Democracy*, edited by Daniele Archibugi and David Held. Cambridge: Polity Press.

Hilferding, Rudolph. 1981. *Finance Capital*. London: Routledge and Kegan Paul Ltd.

Hinsley, F. H. 1989. *Sovereignty*. 2d ed. Cambridge: Cambridge University Press.

Hobbes, Thomas. 1962. *Leviathan*. New York: Macmillan Publishing Co., Inc.

Hobsbawm, E. J. 1992. *Nations and Nationalism Since 1780*. Cambridge: Cambridge University Press.

Hobson, J. A. 1902. *Imperialism: A Study*. London: James Nisbet and Co.

Hoffman, Stanley. 1981. *Duties Beyond Borders* Syracuse, N.Y.: Syracuse University Press.

Holmes, Robert L. 1989. *On War and Morality*. Princeton: Princeton University Press.

Honderich, Ted. 1989. *Violence for Equality*. London: Routledge.

Horwich, Paul. 1990. *Truth*. Oxford: Basil Blackwell.

Hume, David. 1983. *An Enquiry Concerning the Principles of Morals*. Edited by J. B. Schneewind. Indianapolis: Hackett Publishing Co., Inc.

Hurka, Thomas. 1997. "The Justification of National Partiality." In *The Morality of Nationalism*, edited by Robert McKim and Jeff McMahan. New York: Oxford University Press.

Hurrell, Andrew. 2001. "Global Inequality and International Institutions." *Metaphilosophy* 32, nos. 1–2 (January): 34–57.

Jackson, Ben. 1990. *Poverty and the Planet*. London: Penguin Books.

Jackson, Robert H. 1995. "International Community Beyond the Cold War." In *Beyond Westphalia? State Sovereignty and International Intervention*, edited by Gene M. Lyons and Michael Mastanduno. Baltimore: The Johns Hopkins University Press.

Jones, Charles. 1999. *Global Justice: Defending Cosmopolitanism*. Oxford: Clarendon Press.

Kaldor, Mary. 1995. "European Institutions, Nation-States and Nationalism." In *Cosmopolitan Democracy*, edited by Daniele Archibugi and David Held. Cambridge: Polity Press.

Kant, Immanuel. 1970. "The Contest of Faculties." In *Kant's Political Writings*, edited by Hans Reiss and translated by H. B. Nisbet. Cambridge: Cambridge University Press.

_____. 1970. "Idea for a Universal History." In *Kant's Political Writings*, edited by Hans Reiss, translated by H. B. Nisbet. Cambridge: Cambridge University Press.

_____. 1970. "Perpetual Peace: A Philosophical Sketch." In *Kant's Political Writings*, edited by Hans Reiss, translated by H. B. Nisbet. Cambridge: Cambridge University Press.

Kaul, Inge, and John Langmore. 1996. "Potential Uses of the Revenue from a Tobin Tax." In *The Tobin Tax*, edited by Mahbub ul Haq, Inge Kaul, and Isabelle Grunberg. Oxford: Oxford University Press.

Kautsky, Karl. 1970. "Ultra-Imperialism." *New Left Review* 59, no. 1 (January–February).

Kennan, George F. 1985/86. "Morality and Foreign Policy." *Foreign Affairs* 64, no. 2 (winter): 203–218.

Keohane, Robert O., and Joseph S. Nye. 1981. "Transgovernmental Relations." In *Perspectives on World Politics*, edited by Michael Smith, Richard Little, and Michael Shackleton. London: Croom Helm Ltd.

King, Martin Luther, Jr. 1958. *Stride Toward Freedom*. New York: Harper and Row.

Kissin, S. F. 1989. *War and the Marxists*. Vol. 2. London: André Deutsch.

Kratochwil, Friedrich. 1995. "Sovereignty As Dominium: Is There a Right of Humanitarian Interventions?" In *Beyond Westphalia? State Sovereignty and International Intervention*, edited by Gene M. Lyons and Michael Mastanduno. Baltimore: The Johns Hopkins University Press.

Kuper, Andrew. 2000. "Rawlsian Global Justice: Beyond the Law of Peoples to a Cosmopolitan Law of Persons." *Political Theory* 28, no. 3 (October): 640–674.

Kymlicka, Will. 1989. *Liberalism, Community, and Culture*. Oxford: Clarendon Press.

_____. 1995. *Multi-Cultural Citizenship: A Liberal Theory of Minority Rights*. Oxford: Oxford University Press.

Lenin, V. I. 1960. "The Economic Content of Narodism." In *Collected Works*, vol. 1. Moscow: Progress Publishers.

_____. 1964. "Imperialism: The Highest Stage of Capitalism." In *Collected Works*, vol. 19. Moscow: Progress Publishers.

_____. 1964. "More About Nationalism." In *Collected Works*, vol. 20. Moscow: Progress Publishers.

_____. 1966. "Re the Monopoly of Foreign Trade." In *Collected Works*, vol. 33. Moscow: Progress Publishers.

Levi, Margaret, and David Olson. 2000. "The Battle in Seattle." *Politics and Society* 28, no. 3 (September): 309–329.

Lichtenberg, Judith. 1981. "National Boundaries and Moral Boundaries." In *Boundaries*, edited by Peter G. Brown and Henry Shue. Totowa, N.J.: Rowman and Littlefield.

Lillich, Richard B. 1974. "Humanitarian Intervention: A Reply to Ian Brownlie and a Plea for Constructive Alternatives." In *Law and Civil War in the Modern World*, edited by John Norton Moore. Baltimore: The Johns Hopkins University Press.

Lillich, Richard B., and Hurst Hannum. 1995. *International Human Rights*. 3d ed. New York: Little, Brown and Company.

Luban, David. 1985. "Just War and Human Rights." In *International Ethics*, edited by Charles Beitz, et al. Princeton: Princeton University Press.

_____. 1985. "The Romance of the Nation State." In *International Ethics*, edited by Charles Beitz, et al. Princeton: Princeton University Press.

Luxemburg, Rosa. 1963. *The Accumulation of Capital*. London: Routledge and Kegan Paul Ltd.

_____. 1976. "The Nation State and the Proletariat." In *The National Question: Selected Writings*, edited by Horace B. Davis. New York: Monthly Review Press.

MacIntyre, Alasdair. 1984. "Is Patriotism a Virtue?" The Lindley Lecture, University of Kansas.

Magas, Branka. 1993. *The Destruction of Yugoslavia*. London: Verso.

Mandlebaum, Michael. 1999. "A Perfect Failure: NATO's War Against Yugoslavia." *Foreign Affairs* 78, no. 5 (September–October): 2–8.

Margalit, Avishai, and Joseph Raz. 1990. "National Self-Determination." *Journal of Philosophy* LXXXVII, no. 9 (September): 439–461.

Marx, Karl. 1977. "Speech on Free Trade." In *Selected Writings*, edited by David McLellan. Oxford: Oxford University Press.

_____. 1978. The German Ideology. In *The Marx-Engels Reader*, 2d ed., edited by Robert C. Tucker. New York: W. W. Norton.

Mill, John Stuart. 1864. "A Few Words on Non-intervention." In *Dissertations and Discussions*, vol. 3. Boston: William V. Spencer.

_____. 1962. "On Liberty in Utilitarianism." In *On Liberty, Essay on Bentham*, edited by Mary Warnock. New York: Meridian.

Miller, David. 1995. *On Nationality*. Oxford: Clarendon Press.

Miller, Richard. 1998. "Cosmopolitan Respect and Patriotic Concern." *Philosophy and Public Affairs* 27, no. 3 (summer): 202–224

Milo, Ronald. 1995. "Contractarian Constructivism." *The Journal of Philosophy* XCII, no. 4 (April): 181–204.

Mirrlees. J. A. 1982. "The Economic Uses of Utilitarianism." In *Utilitarianism and Beyond*, edited by Amartya Sen and Bernard Williams. Cambridge: Cambridge University Press.

Moellendorf, Darrel. 1994. "Marxism, Internationalism, and the Justice of War." *Science and Society* 58, no. 3 (fall): 264–285.

_____. 1996. "Constructing the Law of Peoples." *Pacific Philosophical Quarterly* 77, no. 2 (June): 132–154.

_____. 1996–1997. "Liberalism, Nationalism, and the Right to Secede." *Philosophical Forum* XXVII, nos. 1–2 (fall–winter): 87–99.

_____. 1997. "Liberal Values and Socialist Models." *Theoria* 89 (June): 65–77.

_____. 1998. "Imperialism." In *Encyclopedia of Applied Ethics*, edited by Ruth Chadwick. San Diego: Academic Press.

_____. 2000. "Consensus and Cognitivism in Habermas's Discourse Ethics."
    South African Journal of Philosophy 19, no. 2 (June): 65–74.
Moody, Kim. 1997. *Workers in a Lean World*. London: Verso.
Moody, Kim, and Mary McGinn. 1992. *Unions and Free Trade*. Detroit: Labor
    Notes.
Moore, G. E. 1959. *Principia Ethica*. Cambridge: Cambridge University Press.
Morgenthau, Hans. 1973. *Politics Among Nations*. 5th ed. New York: Alfred A.
    Knopf.
Mueller, John, and Karl Mueller. 1999. "Sanctions of Mass Destruction." *Foreign
    Affairs* 78, no. 3 (May/June): 43–53.
Murphy, Jeffrie G. 1985. "The Killing of the Innocent." In *Today's Moral Problems*,
    3d ed., edited by Richard Wasserstrom. New York: Macmillan Publishing Co.
Nagel, Thomas. 1991. *Equality and Partiality*. Oxford: Oxford University Press.
Nardin, Terry. 1983. *Law, Morality, and the Relations of States*. Princeton: Prince-
    ton University Press.
Nathanson, Stephen. 1989. "In Defense of 'Moderate Patriotism'." *Ethics* 99, no. 3
    (April): 535–552.
National Academy of Sciences. 1990. *One Earth, One Future: Our Changing
    Global Environment*. Washington, D.C.: National Academy Press.
Niebuhr, Reinhold. 1932. *Moral Man and Immoral Society*. New York: Charles
    Scribner's Sons.
Nielsen, Kai. 1988. "World Government, Security, and Global Justice." In *Problems
    of International Justice*, edited by Steven Luper-Foy. Boulder: Westview Press.
_____. 1992. "Global Justice, Capitalism and the Third World." In *International
    Justice and the Third World*, edited by Robin Attfield and Barry Wilkins. Lon-
    don: Routledge.
Nolutshungu, S. C. 1986. "Non-intervention: 'Ethical Rules of Disregard' and
    Third-World Conflicts." In *Rights and Duties in North-South Relations*, edited
    by Moorhead Wright. London: Macmillan.
Norman, Richard. 1995. *Ethics, Killing, and War*. Cambridge: Cambridge Univer-
    sity Press.
Nozick, Robert. 1974. *Anarchy, State and Utopia*. Oxford: Blackwell.
Nussbaum, Martha C. 1995. "Human Capabilities, Female Human Beings." In
    Women, Culture and Development, edited by Martha Nussbaum and Jonathan
    Glover. Oxford: Oxford University Press.
_____. 1996. "Patriotism and Cosmopolitanism." In *For Love of Country*, edited
    by Joshua Cohen. Boston: Beacon Press.
Okin, Susan Moller. 1989. *Justice, Gender, and the Family*. New York: Basic Books.
O'Neill, Onora. 1986. *Faces of Hunger*. London: George Allen and Unwin.
_____. 1992. "Justice, Gender and International Boundaries." In *International Jus-
    tice and the Third World*, edited by Robin Attfield and Barry Wilkins. London:
    Routledge.
_____. 2001. "Agents of Justice." *Metaphilosophy* 32, nos. 1–2 (January):
    180–195.
Opeskin, Brian R. 1996. "The Moral Foundations of Foreign Aid." *World Devel-
    opment* 24, no. 1 (January): 21–44.

Peffer, R. G. 1990. *Marxism, Morality, and Social Justice.* Princeton: Princeton University Press.

Philpott, Daniel. 1995. "In Defense of Self-Determination." *Ethics* 105, no. 2 (January): 352–385.

Pogge, Thomas W. 1988. "Moral Progress." In *Problems of International Justice,* edited by Steven Luper-Foy. Boulder: Westview Press.

———. 1988. "Rawls and Global Justice." *Canadian Journal of Philosophy* 18, no. 2 (June): 227–256.

———. 1989. *Realizing Rawls.* Ithaca: Cornell University Press.

———. 1992. "Cosmopolitanism and Sovereignty." *Ethics* 103, no. 1 (October): 48–75.

———. 1994. "An Egalitarian Law of Peoples." *Philosophy and Public Affairs* 23, no. 3 (summer): 195–224.

———. 2001. "Priorities of Global Justice." *Metaphilosophy* 32, nos. 1–2 (January): 6–24.

Przeworski, Adam, et al. 1995. *Sustainable Democracy.* Cambridge: Cambridge University Press.

Ramsey, Paul. 1971. *War and the Christian Conscience.* Durham, N.C.: Duke University Press.

———. 1983. *The Just War.* Lanham, Md.: University Press of America.

Rawls, John. 1980. "Kantian Constructivism in Moral Theory." *Journal of Philosophy* LXXVII, no. 9 (September): 515–572.

———. 1983. "Social Unity and Primary Goods." In *Utilitarianism and Beyond,* edited by Amartya Sen and Bernard Williams. Cambridge: Cambridge University Press.

———. 1993. "The Law of Peoples." *Critical Inquiry* 20, no. 1 (autumn): 36–68.

———. 1993. *Political Liberalism.* New York: Columbia University Press.

———. 1995. "50 Years after Hiroshima." *Dissent* 42, no. 3 (summer): 323–331.

———. 1995. "Reply to Habermas." *The Journal of Philosophy* XCII, no. 3 (March): 132–180.

———. 1999. *The Law of Peoples.* Cambridge, Mass.: Harvard University Press.

———. 1999. "Reply to Alexander and Musgrave." In *Collected Papers,* edited by Samuel Freeman. Cambridge, Mass.: Harvard University Press.

———. 1999. *A Theory of Justice.* Rev. ed. Cambridge, Mass.: Harvard University Press.

Raz, Joseph. 1986. *The Morality of Freedom.* Oxford: Clarendon Press.

———. 1990. "Facing Diversity: The Case of Epistemic Abstinence." *Philosophy and Public Affairs* 19, no. 1 (winter): 3–46.

Richards, David A. J. "International Distributive Justice." In *Ethics, Economics, and the Law, Nomos* XXIV, edited by J. Roland Pennock and John W. Chapman. New York: New York University Press.

Ripstein, Arthur. 1997. "Context, Continuity, and Fairness." In *The Morality of Nationalism,* edited by Robert McKim and Jeff McMahan. New York: Oxford University Press.

Risse-Kappen, Thomas, ed. 1995. *Bringing Transnational Relations Back In.* Cambridge: Cambridge University Press.

Roemer, John E. 1983. "Unequal Exchange, Labor Migrations and International Capital Flows: A Theoretical Synthesis." In *Marxism, Central Planning, and the Soviet Economy,* edited by Padma Desai. Cambridge, Mass.: The MIT Press.

_____. 1988. *Free to Lose.* Cambridge, Mass.: Harvard University Press.

_____. 1994. *A Future for Socialism.* Cambridge, Mass.: Harvard University Press.

_____. 1999. "Egalitarian Strategies." *Dissent* 46, no. 3 (summer): 64–74.

Rohde, David. 2000. "Kosovo Seething." *Foreign Affairs* 79, no. 3 (May/June): 65–79.

Rollin, Bernard E. 1988. "Environmental Ethics and International Justice." In *Problems of International Justice,* edited by Steven Luper-Foy. Boulder: Westview Press.

Rosenberg, Justin. 1994. *The Empire of Civil Society.* London: Verso.

Sachs, Jeffrey. 2000. "Everyone Has an Excuse Not to Help Nigeria." *Business Day* (June 22): 15.

Satz, Debra. 1999. "Equality of What Among Whom?" In *Global Justice, Nomos* XLI, edited by Ian Shapiro and Lea Brilmayer. New York: New York University Press.

Scanlon, T. M. 1996. "Diversity of Objections to Inequality." The Lindley Lecture, University of Kansas.

Scheffler, Samuel. 1994. "Families, Nations, Strangers." The Lindley Lecture, University of Kansas.

_____. 1997. "Liberalism, Nationalism, and the State." In *The Morality of Nationalism,* edited by Robert McKim and Jeff McMahan. New York: Oxford University Press.

_____. 1999. "The Conflict Between Justice and Responsibility." In *Global Justice, Nomos* XLI, edited by Ian Shapiro and Lea Brilmayer. New York: New York University Press.

Schlesinger Jr., Arthur. 1972. "National Interests and Moral Absolutes." In *Ethics and World Politics,* edited by Ernest W. Lefever. Baltimore: The Johns Hopkins University Press.

Sen, Amartya. 1981. "Equality of What?" In *The Tanner Lectures on Human Values,* edited by S. M. McMurrin. Salt Lake City: University of Utah Press.

_____. 1984. "Ethical Issues in Income Distribution." In *Resources, Values and Development.* Oxford: Basil Blackwell.

_____. 1984. "Poor, Relatively Speaking," In *Resources, Values and Development.* Oxford: Basil Blackwell.

_____. 1992. *Inequality Reexamined.* Oxford: Clarendon Press.

_____. 1999. *Development As Freedom.* New York: Alfred A. Knopf.

Sen, Amartya, and Bernard Williams. 1983. "Introduction: Utilitarianism and Beyond." In *Utilitarianism and Beyond.* Cambridge: Cambridge University Press.

Shuck, Peter H. 1984. "The Transformation of Immigration Law." *Columbia Law Review* 84, no. 1 (January): 1–90.

Shue, Henry. 1980. *Basic Rights.* Princeton: Princeton University Press.

_____. 1983. "The Burdens of Justice." *The Journal of Philosophy* LXXX, no. 10 (October): 600–608.

_____. 1997. "Eroding Sovereignty: The Advance of Principle." In *The Morality of Nationalism,* edited by Robert McKim and Jeff McMahan. Oxford: Oxford University Press.

_____. 1999. "Conditional Sovereignty." *Res Publica* 8, no. 1: 1–7.
_____. 1999. "Global and International Inequality." *International Affairs* 74, no. 3 (July): 515–529.
Sidgwick, Henry. 1919. *Elements of Politics*. 4th ed. London: Macmillan and Co., Ltd.
_____. 1981. *The Methods of Ethics*. Indianapolis: Hackett Publishing Co.
Solana, Javier. 1999. "NATO's Success in Kosovo." *Foreign Affairs* 78, no. 6 (November–December): 114–120.
St. Augustine. 1954. *The City of God*. Books 17–22. Translated by Gerald G. Walsh, S. J., and Daniel J. Honan. New York: Fathers of the Church, Inc.
Stoll, David. 1999. *Rigoberta Menchú and the Story of All Poor Guatemalans*. Boulder: Westview Press.
Strang, David. 1996. "Contested Sovereignty: The Social Construction of Colonial Imperialism." In *Sovereignty as Social Construct,* edited by Thomas J. Biersteker and Cynthia Weber. Cambridge: Cambridge University Press.
Tamir, Yael. 1993. *Liberal Nationalism*. Princeton: Princeton University Press.
Tan, Kok-Chor. 2000. *Toleration, Diversity, and Global Justice*. University Park: The Pennsylvania State University Press.
Teichman, Jenny. 1986. *Pacifism and the Just War*. Oxford: Basil Blackwell, Ltd.
Tesón, Fernando R. 1997. *Humanitarian Intervention: An Inquiry into Law and Morality.* 2d ed. Irvington-on-Hudson, N.Y.: Transnational Publishers, Inc.
_____. 1998. *A Philosophy of International Law*. Boulder: Westview Press.
Thompson, Jana. 1992. *Justice and World Order*. London: Routledge.
Tobin, James. 1982. "A Proposal for International Monetary Reform." In *Essays in Economics: Theory and Policy*. Cambridge, Mass.: The MIT Press.
Trebilcock, Michael J. 1995. "The Case for Liberal Immigration Policy." In *Justice in Immigration,* edited by Warren F. Schwartz. Cambridge, Mass.: Harvard University Press.
United Nations International Children's Fund. "The Progress of the Nations: Statistical Profile." http://www.UNICEF%20/stat/statistical%20profile%20%20Europe.
_____. "The Progress of the Nations: Statistical Profile." http://www.UNICEF%20/stat/statistical%20profile%20%20Sub-sahara.
United Nations Development Program. http://www.undp/undp%20poverty%20clock.
_____. http://www.undp/undp%20world%20poverty.
_____. http://www.undp/undp%20world%20poverty.
United Nations Research Institute for Social Development. 1994. *Structural Adjustment in a Changing World,* UNRISD Briefing Paper Series 4. Geneva: UNRISD.
Van Parijs, Philip. 1992. "Comment: Citizenship Exploitation, Unequal Exchange and the Breakdown of Popular Sovereignty." In *Free Movement,* edited by Brian Barry and Robert Goodin. College Station: The Pennsylvania State University Press.
Van Parijs. Philippe. 1995. *Real Freedom for All: What (If Anything) Can Justify Capitalism*. Oxford: Oxford University Press.
Vincent, R. J. 1974. *Nonintervention and International Order.* Princeton: Princeton University Press.
_____. 1986. *Human Rights and International Relations*. Cambridge: Cambridge University Press.

Vroman, Susan B. 1995. "Some Caveats on the Welfare Economics of Immigration Law." In *Justice in Immigration*, edited by Warren F. Schwartz. Cambridge, Mass.: Harvard University Press.

Waldron, Jeremy. 1992. "Superseding Historic Injustice." *Ethics* 103, no. 1 (October): 4–28.

Wallerstein, Immanuel. 1979. *The Capitalist World-Economy*. Cambridge: Cambridge University Press.

Walzer, Michael. 1977. *Just and Unjust Wars*. New York: Basic Books.

_____. 1983. *Spheres of Justice*. New York: Basic Books.

_____. 1994. *Thick and Thin*. Notre Dame: University of Notre Dame Press.

Warren, Bill. 1980. *Imperialism Pioneer of Capitalism*. London: Verso.

Wasserstrom, Richard. 1970. "On the Morality of War." In *War and Morality*. Belmont, Calif.: Wadsworth Publishing Co., Inc.

Weber, Steven. 1997. "Institutions and Change." In *New Thinking in International Relations*, edited by Michael W. Doyle and G. John Ikenberry. Boulder: Westview Press.

Weller, Marc. 1999. "The Rambouillet Conference on Kosovo." *International Affairs* 75, no. 2 (April): 211–251.

Wellman, Christopher. 1995. "A Defense of Secession and Political Self-Determination." *Philosophy and Public Affairs* 24, no. 2 (spring): 142–171.

Wheeler, Samuel C., III. 1997. "Reparations Reconstructed." *American Philosophical Quarterly* 34, no. 7 (July): 301–318.

Whelan, Fredrick G. 1981. "Citizenship and the Right to Leave." *American Political Science Review* 75, no. 3 (September): 636–653.

Wilkins, Barry. 1992. "Debt and Underdevelopment: The Case for Cancelling Third World Debts." In *International Justice and the Third World*, edited by Robin Attfield and Barry Wilkins. London: Routledge.

Williams, Bernard. 1995. "A Critique of Utilitarianism." In *Utilitarianism For and Against*, edited by J. J. C. Smart and Bernard Williams. Cambridge: Cambridge University Press.

Wood, Ellen Meiksins. 1999. "Kosovo and the New Imperialism." *Monthly Review* 51, no. 2 (June): 1–8.

World Bank. http://www.World%20Bank/world%20Debt%20Tables%20Extracts%201996.

_____. Debt Tables Extracts, http://www.world%20vbank/world%20Debt%20Tables%20Extracts%201996.

The World Commission on Environment and Development. 1987. *Our Common Future*. Oxford: Oxford University Press.

World Health Organization. 1999. Press release 64 by the WHO (May 31). http://www.who.int./archives/infr-pr–1999/en/pr99–64.html.

_____. Fact Sheet N 153. http://www.who.int/inf-fs/en/fact153.html.

Young, Iris Marion. 2000. *Inclusion and Democracy*. Oxford: Oxford University Press.

INDEX